WANDERLUST

Other Books by LAURA BYRNE PAQUET

Non-Fiction:
The Urge to Splurge: A Social History of Shopping (2003)
Secret Ottawa (2000)
Write Better, Right Now, as co-author (1997)

Fiction:
The Incomparable Cassandra (2004)
An Honorable Match (2004)
A Rakish Spy (2004)
Lord Hawksmoor Takes Flight (2004)
Trusting Lady Lucy (2003)
Mr. McAllister Sets His Cap (2003)
Miss Scott Meets Her Match (2002)
Lord Langdon's Tutor (2000)

Wanderlust

LAURA BYRNE PAQUET   a social history of travel

Dear Amy + Michel,
Thanks so much for
coming to the launch – and
for putting up with all
my moaning while I was
writing this!

Laura

GOOSE LANE

Cover images: "Directions?" © Shoutforhumanity, Dreamstime (top); Pura Ulun Danu, Bali, Indonesia, Brand X Pictures (bottom). Cover and interior page design by Julie Scriver. Printed in Canada. 10 9 8 7 6 5 4 3 2 1

Library and Archives Canada Cataloguing in Publication

Paquet, Laura Byrne, 1965- Wanderlust: a social history of travel / Laura Byrne Paquet.

Includes bibliographical references and index. ISBN 978-0-86492-445-2 (pbk.)

1. Travel — Social aspects. 2. Travel — History. I. Title.

G156.P36 2007   306.4'819   C2007-900469-5

Goose Lane Editions acknowledges the financial support of the Canada Council for the Arts, the Government of Canada through the Book Publishing Industry Development Program (BPIDP), and the New Brunswick Department of Wellness, Culture and Sport for its publishing activities.

Goose Lane Editions Suite 330, 500 Beaverbrook Court Fredericton, New Brunswick CANADA E3B 5X4 www.gooselane.com

Contents

7   Acknowledgments

9   Why Leave Home?

15   Pilgrim's Progress

33   The Grand Tour: Where Modern Leisure
      Travel Began

39   Putting on the Ritz: Hotels and Other Homes
      Away from Home

69   Going Down to the Sea in Ships

97   All Aboard: Our Enduring Love Affair with Trains

123   On the Road

153   Flight Patterns: A Century of Air Travel

187   To Your Health: Spas and Other Cures

199   If You Build It, They Will Come: Resorts and
      Theme Parks

215   The Well-Packed Bag: Don't Forget Your...

245   The Business of Travel

271   The Future of Travel

279   Endnotes

283   Bibliography

289   Index

Acknowledgments

I'd like to thank some wonderful people without whom this book would never have been published: my agent Robert Lecker, who never stopped believing that the proposal would sell; Laurel Boone of Goose Lane Editions, who took a brave leap of faith in signing a new-to-her author; all the staff at Goose Lane Editions, who skilfully shepherded me through the publication process with ceaseless good cheer and understanding; editor Barry Norris, who tightened up my windy sentences and checked multitudinous facts with an eagle eye; my family and friends, who lent me books, sent me encouraging e-mails, put up with my grizzling and just generally kept me going; and, especially, my ever-patient husband Paul, who revised the drafts multiple times, brought me endless mini Kit Kats and never once suggested that we both would have been better off if I'd just taken up a career in something simple, like nuclear physics.

Laura Byrne Paquet
Ottawa, Ontario
January 2007

Why Leave Home?

*If a man take no thought about what is distant, he
will find sorrow near at home.*
— *Confucius*

At first glance, travel — especially leisure travel — seems like one
of the most incomprehensible and ridiculous activities we humans
undertake.

Here in the West at the dawn of the twenty-first century, many of
us slave at jobs to pay mortgages on houses that we decorate with
infinite care. We weave patterns of cozy habit, where we feel safe
among old friends and familiar streets. We put all sorts of effort into
creating lives that suit us to a T. And then, many of us can't wait
to escape this meticulously crafted, eminently comfortable environment, to hurl ourselves onto cramped airplanes that will take us to
impersonal airports where we'll get into cabs with drivers whose
language we do not speak, who will take us through streets whose
names mean nothing to us, to a hotel room that may be lovely but
may just as easily overlook a Dumpster that will emptied each morning at 3:52 AM.

We will spend the next days or weeks giving undue thought to the
foods we will eat and the clothes we will wear and the things we will
do, when at home all those decisions would be simple.

We will worry about purse snatchers, dysentery, late flights, lost
passports, altitude sickness, dodgy Internet connections and deep
vein thrombosis, when at home none of these things would ever
cross our minds.

At the end of the trip, once we've checked out of the hotel and gone back to the anonymous airport and eaten more mysterious airline food and waited forty-five minutes for our bags to turn up at the carousel and fought our way through insane traffic, we finally put the key in the front door, walk in and sigh, "It's good to be home."

So *why* do we ever leave in the first place?

For the same reasons travellers have been hitting the road since we first hauled ourselves upright onto two feet. To find things to eat. To do business. To relax. To seek truth. To test ourselves. To learn. To escape. To come back.

Many of the epics that form our cultural foundations are stories of people moving from place to place in pursuit of some higher goal, whether it's Rama trying to rescue his wife Sita from a far-off island in the Ramayana, Jason and the Argonauts sailing off in search of the Golden Fleece or Moses leading the Israelites out of Egypt and into the Promised Land.

Stories of travel as transformation pop up in culture high and low across the centuries. A tentmaker named Saul was on the road to Damascus sometime around AD 36 when a flash of bright light and the voice of Jesus inspired his conversion to Christianity. The Qur'an describes a miraculous one-night journey by Muhammad from Mecca to Jerusalem and heaven that would shape the future of Islam. The medieval knights of King Arthur's Round Table met their fiercest tests after setting out from Camelot on the quest for the Holy Grail. The knights' deluded literary descendant, Don Quixote, journeyed from exuberant madness to melancholy sanity via an eventful trip across the Spanish plains in Miguel de Cervantes' 1605 novel. Seven decades later, an everyman named Christian made an allegorical pilgrimage from the City of Destruction to the Celestial City in John Bunyan's *Pilgrim's Progress*, while in 1749 a decidedly earthier English hero wended his debauched way across the countryside in Henry Fielding's *Tom Jones*. Mark Twain picked up the thread of travel as transformation when he put Huck Finn and Jim in a boat and set them off along the Mississippi River in 1884. Ernest Hemingway inspired the Lost Generation, restless after the upheaval of the First World War, to discover themselves in France and Spain with *The Sun Also Rises*. In the wake of the Second World War, Jack Kerouac would similarly encourage the Beat Generation to discover their own country in *On the Road*.

Influential as these books have been, the influence of movies has surpassed the cultural clout of books over the past half-century or so. But even here, the power of travel as a metaphor for personal growth and adventure — and escape — is unabated.

It's no coincidence that the first of the seven Bob Hope–Bing Crosby *Road* movies, *The Road to Singapore*, came out in 1940, just as the world was leaving the Depression behind and catapulting into the Second World War. Even as the foreign newsreels were showing the dark, dangerous side of foreign locales, Bing, Bob, and Dorothy Lamour were cavorting through silly, sunshine-filled capers in deserts and on tropical islands.

Each movie had a very similar, lightweight plot. Bing and Bob, playing wisecracking conmen, would get into a spot of trouble — Bing selling Bob to a slave trader, for example — and then lie, cajole, and trick their way out of it. No one believed for a moment that anyone was in real danger, which was a consoling thought in a world gone up in flames. The movies also slaked audiences' thirst for travel to exotic lands, which there was little way to satisfy until the war was over.

When the war finally did end, the *Road* movies continued (the last, *Road to Hong Kong*, came out in 1962). By that point, jet airplanes were just beginning to bring exotic locales like the Far East within the realm of possibility for middle-class travellers. By the 1970s, many people didn't need to live their dreams of foreign travel vicariously via celluloid. More and more of them were heading abroad in the real world.

But that didn't mean the road movie was dead — far from it. Just like travel itself, it can expand to encompass just about every type of human story. In many cases, the actual destination is secondary.

There's the romantic road movie, which has a long lineage stretching from *It Happened One Night* (1934) to *The Sure Thing* (1985) and far beyond. There's the "trap estranged family members in a vehicle to work out their differences" film, which encompasses everything from 1988's *Rain Man* (hotshot yuppie comes to terms with his autistic brother) to 2005's *Transamerica* (man in the middle of a sex-change operation gets acquainted with the son he never knew). Some road movies remove people from their dull lives to make them accidental outlaws, like the feminist classic *Thelma & Louise* (1991). Sometimes the whole purpose of the trip is a crime or killing spree, as in *Thieves Like Us* (1940), *Bonnie and Clyde* (1967), *Badlands* (1973) and *Drugstore Cowboy* (1989).

Once you start trying to list and classify road movies, it's hard to stop. There are movies about criminals on the lam (*The Blues Brothers*; *O Brother, Where Art Thou?*; *Raising Arizona*). There are films centred on an event, such as Spike Lee's *Get on the Bus* (1996), where the characters are off to the Million Man March in Washington, and the Canadian flick *South of Wawa* (1991), where a Dan Hill concert is the somewhat less exalted destination.

And on it goes, from *The Grapes of Wrath* and *Easy Rider* to *About Schmidt* and *The Motorcycle Diaries*. In the movies, at least, the promise of excitement, self-knowledge, and success is never further away than the nearest interstate.

WHAT ROAD WILL THIS BOOK TAKE?

Even though mass-market leisure travel is a relatively modern invention, there have always been travellers. And most of them have endured discomforts that make our modern complaints about cramped airline seats seem laughable. Sea travellers in the ancient world used to tie small pieces of gold around their necks so that, if the ship went down, anyone finding their body would (theoretically) use the gold to fund a decent burial. Medieval tourists spent five bumpy days on horseback to travel the one hundred and ninety-three kilometres (one hundred and twenty miles) from Naples to Rome. Eighteenth-century bon vivant James Boswell had to be carried over the Alps on a litter on his way to Italy, as roads there were non-existent. And the first two people who successfully drove a car across Canada, in 1912, needed fifty-two days for the task.

And yet, we continue to travel.

The litany of travellers' woes that began this chapter actually encapsulates the elements that make most trips worth the effort. It's thrilling to see a strange city flash by our cab windows, since its unfamiliarity forces us to really *look* at the world instead of simply sleep-driving through it on our way to work. Unusual foods, unfamiliar languages, unknown hotel rooms: all of them hold the possibility of discovery and adventure. Travelling tosses us out of our comfort zone, and we crave that once in a while.

When we hop in that car or board that plane, we're aching for something that casts our normal routine into vivid relief, shakes us out of our complacency, gives our lives colour and texture and spice and context. That longing, that ache, that anticipation — that's wanderlust.

Wanderlust prompted ancient traders to cross dusty deserts and enticed Grand Tourists to see the ruins of Rome. It led the *nouveau riche* to summer in the Catskills and winter on the Riviera, in increasingly opulent hotels. It lent its allure to what James Stewart's character in the classic Christmas movie *It's a Wonderful Life* called "the three most exciting sounds in the world...anchor chains, plane motors, and train whistles." It drew health seekers and working class families to chilly seashores. It spurred entrepreneurs to write guidebooks, invent travellers' cheques, and build a fairy-tale castle in Anaheim, California. And depending whose arguments you believe, wanderlust has fostered international understanding, despoiled the environment, and raised the fortunes of nations.

Why do we travel? I'd argue we travel because we can't help ourselves. For most of us, leisure travel offers at least the promise of some form of salvation: from boredom, from routine, from insularity, from ignorance. It may be as simple as sunny salvation from the purgatory of a dark Canadian winter. But for many of history's earliest travellers, one particular type of trip — the pilgrimage — offered a much more literal form of salvation. And that's where I'll begin.

Pilgrim's Progress

A vacation is easy to embark upon; everything has been laid out for us to have a predictable, comfortable, and reassuring holiday. But a pilgrimage is different; we are actually beckoning to the darkness in our lives. The fear is real.
— *Phil Cousineau,* The Art of Pilgrimage

"Pilgrimage" can encompass just about any kind of journey to a site that holds a special resonance for the traveller: a childhood home, the setting of a famous book, Graceland, the National Baseball Hall of Fame. However, most of the earliest human pilgrimages fit the classical definition of the word: a trip to a religious site with the aim of improving the traveller's spiritual sinew.

In fact, religious travel was the first real tourism, in the sense of travel for completely "non-essential" reasons. A soldier or merchant might justifiably cross hundreds or thousands of kilometres to further the interests of a king or to buy fabrics and spices.

But that's not tourism. That's business. For anyone else to court danger and discomfort by wandering far from home — a radical act until quite recently in human history — there had to be a compelling reason. In the centuries when faith was more central to life than it is today, the desire for inspiration or redemption could propel travellers far from family, friends and familiarity.

Think of it this way. Remember how hard it was to get Bilbo or Frodo to leave the Shire in *The Lord of the Rings*? It took the spectre of the all-encompassing conquest of good by evil to get those furry-footed little guys moving, and even then, they grumbled continuously.

Pilgrimage has a long history across a wide range of cultures. In

the West today, many people think of Chaucer's pilgrims making their
way to Canterbury, or perhaps the Crusaders fighting their bloody
way to Jerusalem. But Christians still make pilgrimages today. In
Canada, for instance, pilgrims make their way to Ste-Anne-de-Beaupré
near Quebec City, and literally crawl up the steps of St. Joseph's
Oratory in Montreal. A wall in the oratory's basilica is covered with
the crutches of those who claim to have been cured of their disability
on reaching the top.

Nor are pilgrimages a uniquely Christian phenomenon. The
impulse has also driven ancient Egyptians to visit Sekket's shrine at
Bubastis; Buddhists to walk a circuit around eighty-eight shrines on
the Japanese island of Shikoku; Muslims to travel to Saudi Arabia
and circle the holy Kabaa in Mecca; and the indigenous peoples of
South America to worship the sun at Cuzco in Peru. Today, twenty
million Hindus make pilgrimages to one or more of India's eighteen
hundred holy sites annually, and Jews trade fond wishes for "next
year in Jerusalem."

HELLO, APOLLO? IT'S ME, MARCA

In ancient times, a network of shrines throughout the Mediterranean
basin attracted pilgrims: Delos, island birthplace of Diana and Apollo;
Crete, birthplace of Zeus; the temple of Artemis at Ephesus; and *ne
plus ultra*, the Oracle at Delphi.

It is easy to see why Delphi was deemed a sacred place. A natural
amphitheatre high on the slopes of Mount Parnassus in Greece, it
commands a staggeringly beautiful view of undulating valleys in every
direction. In the distance, the sea sparkles. Originally, the shrine
honoured the earth goddess Gaia, and priestesses called the Sybils
provided cryptic prophesies to truth seekers. A notorious python
guarded the site, but it was no match for Apollo, who is said to have
slain the snake and set up his own prophesy shop on the mountain.
He dispensed with the Sybils and spoke through a single priestess.

After Apollo took over, the timeworn procedures for the arriving
pilgrim remained. The first stop was a sacred place partway down the
mountain, where the traveller would sacrifice a goat or sheep. Luckily

for the blood-smeared pilgrim, the next step was a ritual bath in a nearby spring. Then began the long climb up the mountain, which was not for the weak — the last stretch was little more than a steep, rocky path.

Likely, however, most thought the destination well worth the climb. At the top, a seventy-foot-high statue of Apollo surveyed a glittering array: gold bracelets and bronze figurines, jewelled breastplates and exotic idols, carried from Egypt and Britain, Asia Minor and India, and places even more distant and foreign, all to appease Apollo and cajole his priestess, the Pythia, into answering the pilgrim's most burning questions. Inside the temple itself, murals told tales of heroic conquests and godly doings.

In the early days, the Greeks had consulted the Oracle on matters of state; in later years, the questions were more along the lines of those posed to a modern-day fortune teller. A surviving fragment of papyrus from the site reveals that visitors wanted to know whether they would receive a windfall, repair a poor relationship with their child, get divorced or die soon, among other things.

Pilgrims submitted their questions to the priestess on a lead tablet. After chewing on laurel leaves, the priestess would enter a crevice in the mountain, there to inhale a mysterious frosty gas emanating from it. Whether due to the gas, the laurel leaves or, as the ancients believed, divine inspiration, the priestess would go into a frenzied trance. Climbing onto a special tripod, she would deliver her pronouncement. In the days of the Sybils, resident poets transformed these pronouncements into elegant Greek hexameter, but by the Roman era the pilgrims received them unadorned.

Even at that, the Oracle liked to offer vague predictions that could be retrofitted, if not changed entirely, when things went badly. Croesus, king of Lydia, visited the Oracle in 550 BC. He wanted to invade the Persian Empire, but picking on Persia back then was a bit like challenging Wayne Gretzky to a few rounds of shinny. So Croesus sacrificed 300 head of cattle to Apollo, melted down 117 bricks of gold and silver and, for good measure, tossed in a quarter-ton gold bowl. The Oracle mulled it over and concluded, "Croesus will destroy a great empire."

Hearing the great news, Croesus invaded Persia. Unfortunately, the Persians ended up kicking his butt all the way back to Lydia, which they conquered. Then, for good measure, they also captured Croesus. A little upset, he was allowed back to Delphi in chains, to ask for a bit of customer satisfaction. The Oracle mulled it over and responded that, just as it had foretold, Croesus had destroyed a great empire — his own.

That was a close call. Needless to say, it wasn't long before pilgrims couldn't pose their questions directly to the Pythia anymore — who, by the time Apollo was running things, was working only six days a year anyway. Instead, an army of freelance soothsayers and fortune tellers swarmed the mountain, happy to provide their own take on the pilgrim's question for a small fee. No magic gases, no gilded tripod, but at least a bit of hope to sustain the traveller on his long journey home.

ONWARD, CHRISTIAN PILGRIMS

Some of history's most peripatetic pilgrims have been Christians. For them, pilgrimage was less about answering their questions than it was about reaffirming their faith, which they often did by tallying up their encounters with the mummified remains of saints that were spread over most of Europe and Asia Minor.

In all cultures, the desire seems to arise to see the places where an honoured person lived, worked, and died (for a modern equivalent, witness all those trips to Graceland). For early Christians, however, pilgrimages were inspired by the uniquely Christian notion that very holy people, in their dying moments, could purify sinners. That notion expanded, it seems, until Christians came to believe that even a saint's remains could retain that magical privilege, when venerated properly, to release the pilgrim from punishments for even the worst sins. With the threat of eternal damnation hanging over their heads, many pilgrims had a pretty strong motivation to hit the road. And one of the places they headed was the Holy Land.

Christians have been making pilgrimages to the Holy Land since at least the fourth century, encouraged in this endeavour by church fathers such as St. Jerome, who translated the Bible into Latin around the year 400. As far as celebrity endorsement goes, it doesn't get any more elevated than Jerome. But the journey was so hazardous that even Jerome began to wonder whether he had created a bit of a monster. "Do not think that something is lacking in your faith because you have not seen Jerusalem," he warned would-be pilgrims, hoping to keep the pilgrimage craze from getting out of hand. "The palace of heaven is just as accessible from Britain as from Jerusalem."

The fall of the Western Roman Empire brought most long-distance travel to a halt for a few centuries, and the number of Christians in the eastern Mediterranean wasn't bolstered by many new arrivals. Then, as Europe began to recover from the Dark Ages, western Christians sought to visit the Holy Land again. But the problem with the Holy Land was that it had become holy not just to Jews and Christians, but also to followers of a new religion, Islam, who had built their own mosques in Jerusalem and its environs.

At first, Muslims in the Holy Land were relatively accepting of Christian pilgrims. Then, in 1065, a caravan of some twelve thousand pilgrims under the leadership of Gunther, Bishop of Bamberg, was attacked after it left Caesarea Palaestina, a city about two days' journey northwest of Jerusalem. An unknown number of pilgrims was killed. Eventually, news of this attack filtered back to Europe and people started agitating for measures to protect the safety of Christian pilgrims to the Holy Land.

In November 1095, Pope Urban II gave a speech at Clermont, France, calling for the pilgrimage to end all pilgrimages: a military expedition to free Jerusalem from the Seljuk Turks. About one hundred thousand people answered his call, although only about fourteen thousand of them would eventually make it to Jerusalem. Even so, Urban's speech kicked off two bloody centuries of warfare that included five major Crusades and a flurry of smaller ones. The Crusades were a combustible combination of pilgrimage and violence: many Christians believed they would earn redemption from sin on the journey, even if they killed a lot of non-believers in the process.

THE PILGRIM'S ROMAN HOLIDAY

Of course, not everyone wanted to go, or could go, to the Holy Land. Fortunately, there was a somewhat more accessible destination, one that offered almost as many spiritual opportunities and that was replete with relics and other holy objects that competed for pilgrims' attention: Rome.

As soon as it was safe for Christians to visit the city without fear of being tossed to the lions, pilgrims began visiting the tombs of the Apostles. In the late fourth century, St. John Chrysostom expressed regret that his duties as the Patriarch of Constantinople made it impossible for him to see the Roman sites associated with his hero, St. Paul: "If I were freed from my labours and my body were in sound health I would eagerly make a pilgrimage merely to see the chains that had held him captive and the prison where he lay."

By the Middle Ages, the number of holy objects housed in Rome had ballooned. Among the purported attractions was the table at which the disciples ate the Last Supper, surprisingly fresh scales and crumbs from the loaves and fishes that fed the multitudes, some of Jesus's swaddling clothes and hay from the innkeeper's stable in Bethlehem. Pilgrims not sufficiently impressed by these artefacts could make a side trip to Venice, whose attractions included one of St. Paul's ears, three of the rocks used to stone St. Stephen, a water vessel from Cana and a twelve-pound object purported to be one of Goliath's teeth.

WE'RE OFF ON THE ROAD TO SANTIAGO

In AD 44, St. James the Greater was martyred in Palestine. According to tradition — although not supported by historical evidence — St. James had once made an evangelical journey to Spain, and in the years after his death, believers carried his body back there. Roman persecution of Christians, however, led to the burial site's being abandoned and forgotten. Centuries later, in 813, a hermit was reputedly guided to the burial site by a star and heavenly music.

The timing could not have been better for the Catholic Church, which was trying to maintain a Christian presence in the area as Islam reached the Iberian peninsula. The Church made James Spain's patron saint and built the first church over the relics in 829. According to some accounts, the Church even hired storytellers to spread the news of the saint's miraculous local deeds, such as his appearance before a group of Christian soldiers, which had helped them prevail on the battlefield.

Within a century, significant numbers of pilgrims had begun making their way to Santiago de Compostela to pay homage to the saint, ask for favours and leave donations. In 1122, Pope Calixtus II announced a "plenary indulgence": pilgrims who travelled to Santiago during a Jubilee year — when the saint's day (July 25) fell on a Sunday — would have their sins forgiven and gain additional blessings. (According to modern Catholic thought, pilgrims who make a Jubilee year pilgrimage on foot, by bicycle or on horseback can earn the same indulgence as their medieval forebears.)

This declaration spurred a bit of a tourist boom along the four main pilgrimage routes, which stretched across France and the Pyrenees into northern Spain, where they eventually converged on one main trail from Puente la Reina (south of Pamplona) to Santiago de Compostela. Not long after the pope's decision came the publication, probably by a group of French monks, of the *Codex Calixtinus*, the route's first guidebook. By 1200, the Camino de Santiago had become the busiest pilgrimage route in Europe, drawing half a million pilgrims a year.

Despite its popularity, the trip to Santiago was far from an easy trek; the section from the Pyrenees village of Roncesvalles to Santiago alone stretches 745 kilometres (463 miles). To avoid a long hike, many English pilgrims travelled most of the way to Santiago by sea, but that wasn't a much more pleasant journey. Captains would pack as many as a hundred passengers into rickety, smelly ships for the voyage. One anonymous pilgrim left behind a rhyming tale of his experience that paints an unpleasant picture. As soon as the coast of England disappeared below the horizon, he related, passengers' "hertes begyn to fayle."[1] Soon, many fell seasick, only to have the crew laugh at them for their weakness. Some of the few not hanging

over the side or retching into bowls tried to read, but even that backfired, since the ship's rocking of the ship led quickly to headaches.

Pilgrims who arrived at the famous cathedral in Santiago performed
a closely prescribed set of rituals, which evolved over the centuries. In
the early days, pilgrims went directly to the saint's tomb, then to Mass.
As time went on, however, church officials realized that donations were
more generous if the travellers attended a night-long vigil, confessed
their sins and took Holy Communion before seeing the tomb.

PLANNING THE PERFECT PILGRIMAGE

How did a Christian pilgrim prepare for a holy journey?

The earliest pilgrimages often were so difficult that the wise pilgrim was accompanied by soldiers. Indeed, by the end of the first
millennium, the hardships of the journey alone were deemed to have
some of the purifying properties of the penance assigned to a be-
liever by his priest. A late-tenth-century canon enacted by England's
King Edgar read: "It is a deep penitence that a layman lay aside his
weapons and travel far barefoot and nowhere pass a second night
and fast and watch much and pray fervently, by day and by night
and willingly undergo fatigue and be so squalid that iron come not
on hair or on nail."

As time went on, laws and routes became more formal. Hospices
sprang up along major pilgrimage roads, and civil and religious authorities tried to frame the scope of pilgrimages. For instance, rules
for the canons of Hereford Cathedral specified that a canon could
take three weeks in any given year to visit an English pilgrimage
site and could make only one pilgrimage beyond England in their
lifetime. Canons who chose to travel aboard were allowed sixteen
weeks to visit Rome or Santiago and a full year if their destination
was the Holy Land.

By the high point of pilgrimages in the Middle Ages, the journey
had become slightly less terrifying. The Church had even established
a list of "top sites" to which a pilgrimage was considered appropriate
penance for particularly heinous crimes: the tomb of the Apostles in
Rome, Santiago, St. Thomas Becket's shrine at Canterbury and the

relics of the three kings at Cologne. (Ironically, this list appears in a set of records related to the Inquisition, whose inquisitors history would later deem to have been among the most heinous medieval sinners of all.)

Having decided to make the journey, the pilgrim would ensure all his affairs were in order, in case he failed to return. A crucial step was to ask the local priest for his blessing and a letter attesting to the pilgrim's sincerity, which could be handy if someone along the route grew suspicious of the stranger passing through.

Since literacy wasn't widespread, the pilgrim would take the extra precaution of putting together the widely recognized "pilgrim" ensemble: an early form of backpack called an *escarcela*, a wallet called a *scrip* that was worn around the neck or on a belt, a drinking gourd, a broad-brimmed hat and a walking stick called a *bordon*. (*Bordons* got a bit of a bad reputation after the bishop of Chichester forbade them from his cathedral in 1478. It seems some pilgrims, impatient to see the remains of St. Richard on his feast day, had used their *bordons* to bash the heads of those ahead of them in the vast crowd.)

The pilgrims' parish church would send them off on their journey with a special Mass. Parishioners would sing psalms celebrating courage, and the priest would bless the pilgrims' travelling equipment with the following words:

> We humbly call upon Thee that Thou wouldst be pleased to bless these scrips (or this scrip) and these staves (or this staff) that whosoever for the love of Thy name shall desire to wear the same at his side or hang it at his neck or to bear it in his hands and so on his pilgrimage to seek the aid of the Saints with the accompaniment of humble prayer, being protected by the guardianship of Thy Right Hand may be found meet to attain unto the joys of the everlasting vision through Thee, O Saviour of the World, Who livest and reignest in the unity of the Holy Spirit, God for ever and ever.

With these words, the pilgrims would begin their journey.

IT TAKES A VILLAGE TO RAISE A PILGRIM

If the pilgrim was a member of an industrial guild, his fellow members would often be required by guild law to support the journey. According to the rules of the Guild of the Resurrection at Lincoln, written sometime after 1374, "If any brother or sister wishes to make pilgrimage to Rome, St. James of Galicia [Santiago] or the Holy Land, he shall forewarn the gild; and all the bretheren and sisteren shall go with him to the city gate, and each shall give him a halfpenny at least."[2]

One guild required its members to greet the returning pilgrim outside the gates and walk with him to the monastery, if he had informed them in advance that he was on his way home. Another asked its members to pay the pilgrim's dues in his absence.

Such rules were formal expressions of a longstanding pilgrimage tradition. People with neither the time, the money nor the inclination to set out on such a trip still could share in some of the benefits of the challenge — namely, forgiveness of sins and a better shot at Heaven — by supporting the pilgrim's journey. Even kings found the notion appealing: Edward III gave one of his servants the substantial sum of one pound, six shillings and eightpence to support him on a pilgrimage to the Holy Land. People with a lot on their conscience could even hedge their bets after death: when he died in 1361, the Earl of Hereford and Essex left behind a will that offered money to people who would undertake pilgrimages in his name. Such a culture of generosity was a godsend to many a pilgrim, to whom pious folks along the route would often also provide free or inexpensive food and shelter.

I can't help but wonder if some of the people living along the busiest pilgrim routes ever tired of meeting this ceaseless obligation. But modern practice shows that the power of reflected piety is strong: by tradition, Buddhist monks in several Asian countries meet their basic survival needs through the generosity of the people whose spiritual needs they sustain. It's not a bad deal, really. Help the monk in this life, and he will help you with your existence on a higher plane.

In addition to the support of the charitable, the pilgrim on the major routes could make use of the many hostels and inns that had sprung up for the comfort of travellers. Sometimes, as in the case of a thirteen-bed inn run by a Coventry guild, these were operated by secular organizations. More often, they were the responsibility of religious orders such as the Knights Hospitaller. Secondary shrines, too, emerged along the routes, to sustain the religious fervour of pilgrims and attract their donations.

EACH FOR HIS OWN REASONS

Many pilgrims were indeed pious, heading toward a famous holy site for noble reasons: to cure an illness (their own or someone else's), to atone for sins, to thank God or a saint for bringing them safely through storm, shipwreck or financial debacle. But not all pilgrims had pure motives. Some had been sentenced to make the trip as an alternative to prison. Others were fulfilling the wishes of more devout relatives, as a condition of receiving an inheritance.

Politically minded pilgrims occasionally visited the tombs of recently deceased rebels, such as the fourteenth-century earl of Lancaster, as a relatively safe way to make a point — it wouldn't do for the monarch to jail or hurt a bunch of holy pilgrims, no matter how much their purported pilgrimage stuck in his craw.

And stick it did. In 1323, Edward II wrote an exasperated letter to the bishop of London to berate him for allowing supporters of the late Lancaster to cluster around a supposedly miraculous picture of the earl: "Silly visitors, without any authorization from the Roman Church, venerate and worship this image as a holy thing, and affirm that it there works miracles: this is a disgrace for the whole Church, a shame for us and for you, a manifest danger for the souls of the aforesaid people, and a dangerous example to others."[3]

If creating a holy cult served a purpose for rulers and clerics, as it had at Santiago, that was one thing. But people willy-nilly inventing their own relics was something else altogether.

One English monastery's attempt to market itself as a pilgrimage destination backfired spectacularly. Early in the fourteenth century, Abbot Hugh of Leven commissioned a new crucifix for his Yorkshire monastery's chapel. The resulting piece, with its unclothed image of Jesus, was widely renowned for both its beauty and its miraculous properties. So the abbot allowed both men and "honest women" to enter the monastery to see the crucifix. The resulting onslaught of female tourists was apparently not sufficiently holy. "In them devotion is cool," complained the abbot, who perhaps had not realized that a sculpture of a naked man might not be the best way to draw pious women. Even worse, from the abbot's point of view, the female pilgrims were cheap: the monastery spent more money accommodating them than the women contributed to the institution's coffers.

More than a few pilgrims simply had seized the one socially acceptable opportunity available to them to escape the daily grind. Still others went on pilgrimage mainly to make a little money from their fellow pilgrims, either by selling necessities to them or by begging. Such false pilgrims were widely reviled, but a *testimoniales* could help a pilgrim prove his heart was true. Only the most daring profiteer, it was believed, would lie to a priest about his intentions for the journey.

As time went on, kings and other authorities grew increasingly suspicious that "pilgrims" were using the faked excuse of a holy journey as a quick way to slip away from a brutal master and find one they liked better. Such manoeuvres, it was feared, would fill the countryside with uppity peasants getting ideas above their station. So in 1388, Richard II decreed that all pilgrims had to have an official travel permit, without which they would be arrested.

PAY YOUR RESPECTS,
BUT DON'T FORGET THE SOUVENIRS

Arrival at the pilgrimage destination was cause for great rejoicing — in most cases. Pilgrims who had not properly prepared themselves to meet the local rules could be in for a nasty surprise. Vain women got a particularly public comeuppance at Rocamadour, a French shrine dedicated to the Virgin Mary. As one medieval author recalled, the shrine was festooned with hanks of women's hair "that had be[en] wasshe in wyne, and in other thinges for to make the here of colour otherwise thanne God made it."[4]

Such wanton women had to agree to have the offending locks lopped off before they could enter the sanctuary. And in case they had second thoughts, a story was circulated about one particularly beautiful woman who had been blinded because she had led a wicked life. She made a pilgrimage to Rocamadour and prayed to the Virgin to restore her sight. The prayer worked, but the pilgrim was still not allowed to enter the sanctuary until the priest had cut off her hair. When the now-bald pilgrim cried out to the Virgin in dismay, her hair was restored — but her sight was once again taken away.

For those pilgrims who weren't blinded on arrival, the viewing of a saint's relics was the high point of the journey for many an exhausted pilgrim. On his knees, amazed that he had actually managed to reach one of the world's most famous sights, the traveller would pay homage to the remains. Surrounded by crowds of other pilgrims, each lost in private contemplation, the pilgrim would silently ask the saint for assistance with his most pressing worries.

With that duty done, the pilgrim would likely purchase some souvenir of his journey — often, a lead or pewter medallion unique to the site, such as the scallop shell associated with Santiago or an image of the Virgin Mary from Rocamadour — which he would later embed on a mantel or lintel back home. Finally, with what was likely a mixture of jubilation, sadness and relief, the pilgrim would take his leave and begin the long walk home.

Back home, the former pilgrim would relive the journey for years, spinning tales of foreign landscapes, strange languages and holy treasures for the vast majority of villagers who would never leave their birthplace. It appears some pilgrims became the medieval equivalents of modern tourists whose five-hour home movies bore their acquaintances senseless. William Thorpe, a reformist priest, complained that "if these men and women be a month out in their pilgrimage, many of them shall be, a half-year after, great janglers, tale-tellers, and liars."[5]

SO A KNIGHT AND A MILLER WALK INTO A TAVERN...

Thanks to Geoffrey Chaucer, one of the best chronicled of all medieval pilgrimages was the trek from London to Canterbury to visit the shrine of St. Thomas Becket, the "meddlesome priest" of whom Henry II was so anxious to be rid. Pilgrimages to this site began soon after Becket's brutal murder on December 29, 1170, and increased after Becket was quickly canonized in 1173.

One early pilgrim was none other than Henry II himself. More than a little unnerved by the wave of revulsion that had swept across Europe in the wake of Becket's murder in a sacred cathedral, Henry felt the need to do penance. Providing extra incentive was the pope's threat to excommunicate the king if he didn't make a pilgrimage to Canterbury. On July 12, 1174, the king walked barefoot through the streets of Canterbury. Dizzy from several days of fasting on bread and water, itching from the haircloth and wool in which he was clothed, Henry prostrated himself on the cathedral floor and kissed the place where Becket had been martyred. Next on the agenda was a public flogging by a group of clerics. Finally, Henry carried out an all-night vigil on the cold stone floor in front of the saint's tomb.

Not to be outdone, King Louis VII of France, Henry's great rival, showed up five years later. His son had recently fallen ill, and the French king had seen visions of St. Thomas Becket — one promising the prince's recovery if the king went to Canterbury, and another warning of disaster if he did not go. Such was the power of faith in those days that Louis risked antagonizing the volatile Henry by setting foot on English soil. Luckily, Henry was still feeling a bit guilty about the whole Becket affair and deemed that a pilgrimage to Canterbury superseded even grave political rivalries. He himself met the hated French king at Dover and accompanied him to Canterbury.

The Canterbury pilgrimage became something of a tradition for monarchs: Richard the Lion-Heart, John, Edward I and various continental monarchs came to pay their respects at the cathedral. The popularity of the pilgrimage surged in 1220 when the saint's feast day was moved from the wintry anniversary of his death to the more travel-friendly date of July 7.

By the time Chaucer began writing *The Canterbury Tales* in 1387, the pilgrimage had become so popular that it had attracted the disdain of people like the Lollards, reformers inspired by Oxford theologian John Wyclif who wanted to reduce hierarchy and corruption in the Church. Lollards and others complained that the pilgrimage had degenerated from a pious journey to a good excuse to see a bit of the world and enjoy the company of new friends. In 1407, Thomas Arundel, archbishop of Canterbury — who had a vested interest in maintaining the tourist traffic pouring into his city — interrogated William Thorpe, the Lollard priest whose jibe at tale-telling pilgrims we've already read about. Thorpe admitted he was no fan of pilgrims who ventured forth "to seek and visit the bones or images... of this saint and of that." Rather, he argued, poorly prepared pilgrims had an unfortunate habit of running out of supplies en route, then stealing what they needed from the locals.

Like good religious reformers throughout history, Thorpe also complained that some pilgrims just seemed to be having too much fun:

> They will ordain beforehand to have with them both men and women that can well sing wanton songs; and some other pilgrims will have with them bagpipes: so that every town they come through, what with the noise of their singing, and with the sound of their piping, and with the jangling of their Canterbury bells, and with the barking out of dogs after them, they make more noise than if the king came there away, with all his clarions and many other minstrels.[6]

Certainly, the scenes conjured up in Chaucer's tales have more in common with a village fair than Sunday Mass. The jolly company of thirty pilgrims, who meet by chance at the Tabard Inn in Southwark on the night of their departure for Canterbury, includes a knight, a housewife, various clerics, a farmer, a doctor, a miller, a cook, a squire and the innkeeper himself, who is so taken with their company that he decides to join them.

ONE HAPPY PILGRIM

Christians were far from the only people who went on pilgrimages in the Middle Ages, and they weren't the only ones to enjoy themselves thoroughly while doing so, either. In 1324, from his perch atop the Mali Empire, Mansa Musa decided to go on *hajj*, the Muslim religious commitment to visit Mecca. Along the way, the African king stopped in Cairo, and dropped so much wealth that it took the city twelve years to recover from the resulting inflation. Arab historian al-Umari says that Musa was so profligate on his journey that he had to take out a loan to pay for the trip home.

The next morning they set out in fine form. They draw lots to see who will tell the first tale. The honour falls to the knight, who begins his story "with right a merry cheer." The jovial, often ribald tone continues as the pilgrims make their way along the road, occasionally accompanied by the miller's bagpipe. If Chaucer had lived to complete his ambitious project, it seems likely the pilgrims would have continued singing, arguing and generally enjoying themselves all the way to the shrine and back.

Despite criticisms that Canterbury pilgrimages had become frivolous, they continued for more than a century after Chaucer's death in 1400. Even Henry VIII made one. Belatedly, however, Henry realized that Becket was something of a soul mate to his own troublesome cleric, Thomas More, whose criticisms of the monarch had led to a similarly untimely end. Disliking the parallels, Henry ensured that all traces of Becket's shrine were obliterated during the Dissolution of the Monasteries. Adding insult to injury, in his new role as head of the Church of England, he even had Becket "un-canonized." To make sure his subjects got the message, Henry ordered that all pictures of

Becket throughout the kingdom "be plucked down...to the intent his grace's loving subjects shall be no longer blindly led and abused to commit idolatry." Anyone who ignored the edict could be packed off to jail. More than three centuries of Canterbury pilgrimages thus came to an abrupt halt.

ARE PILGRIMAGES DEAD?

Although pilgrimages are closely linked to the Middle Ages in the popular imagination, they are still very much a going concern. Believe what you will about saintly "apparitions," their drawing power is staggering.

Countless major shrines are devoted to the Virgin Mary: the shrine in Walsingham, England, became one of the major medieval pilgrimage sites after an apparition in 1061; numerous Mary sightings have been reported in Clearwater, Florida, since 1996; and Knock, location of an 1879 apparition, is now home to one of the busiest regional airports in Ireland. Interestingly, Marian sightings have spread geographically as Christianity itself gained ground in various parts of the world. Since 1900, appearances have been reported in China, Egypt, Japan and Ghana.

One of the most popular of all the Marian pilgrimage sites is Lourdes, a town of 17,000 in the French Pyrenees. In February 1858, a fourteen-year-old girl named Bernadette Soubirous claimed to see an apparition of the Virgin Mary in a cave. Soon, miracles were attributed to the site, in particular to the water found in the grotto where Bernadette had had her vision. By 1860, pilgrims had already begun flocking to the site. A statue of the Virgin was built in 1864, soon to be followed by a chapel and, still later, a basilica. By 1904, the site had attracted nearly four hundred thousand pilgrims, including sixty-three cardinals, and the local train station was handling more than a million visitors annually. By 2006, some two hundred million people — more than three times the population of France — had visited the shrine, many in search of miraculous cures. The Catholic Church has officially recognized sixty-seven miracles associated with the site.

WILL PILGRIMAGES ENDURE?

The popularity of Lourdes and other sites indicates that the classical pilgrimage is far from dead, despite the fact that Westerners live in an increasingly secular world. And if you expand the definition of "pilgrimage" to include trips to non-religious sites, I suspect such trips have a long and busy future ahead of them.

While no non-religious "pilgrimage" site, to my knowledge, can make a claim to official miracles, many of the modern trips people take to places associated with a celebrity, a historical event or even a corporate brand have significant similarities to classical pilgrimages. People may not want to be saved in a sacred sense, but they do want to see the places that their peers consider larger than life. Canadians head to Louisbourg or the Plains of Abraham to get a sense of the landscapes that shaped our history. Amateur astronauts visit the John F. Kennedy Space Center in Florida to watch a space shuttle launch. Celebrity watchers drive along well-mapped routes past movie stars' homes in Beverly Hills and Bel-Air, while New Agers travel thousands of kilometres to immerse themselves in the special vibes they believe exist at England's Stonehenge or Australia's Uluru.

The idea of touching or seeing greatness — however greatness is defined — underpins the secular pilgrimage as much as the sacred, as the folks who run James Joyce walking tours in Dublin or "Sex and the City" bus trips through Manhattan could attest. And like the pilgrims who brought back "signes" as tangible proof to themselves and others of the transformative journey, today's travellers come home with digital photos or commemorative key chains marking their visit to the Hockey Hall of Fame, Antietam or the Tower of London. Not all pilgrimages in this odd modern era are traditional ones, but who's to say that a six-year-old heading toward the Cinderella Castle at Walt Disney World feels any less wonder and awe than the pilgrim who finally espied the cathedral at Compostela?

The Grand Tour
WHERE MODERN LEISURE TRAVEL BEGAN

*As for Pictures and Statues, I have really seen so
many that I remember nothing. In a very large
mixed company, one seldom contracts a lasting
acquaintance.*
— *British tourist in Rome, 1772*

If English biographer James Boswell had come of age in the 1960s
instead of the 1760s, he might have headed to San Francisco during
the Summer of Love or run off to India to sit at the feet of the
Maharishi Mahesh Yogi. The destination probably wouldn't have
mattered, as long as it gave him ample opportunity to indulge in
several deadly sins and simultaneously annoy his father, the staid
Lord Auchinleck.

As it was, Boswell craved the one practical escape route open to
young men of his situation and class: a trip to the Continent. Initially,
Auchinleck wasn't keen on the idea. After much badgering, he finally
agreed to let Boswell go to Holland for a year to further his legal
studies.

To Boswell, this sounded like a bit of a snore, but deciding that
a trip to Holland was better than nothing, he headed off to the
Continent and duly put in a year of law study. When he was done, he
again approached his father for permission to see Paris and Rome. His
father deemed Italy too "intoxicating" for a young man and thought
most of France not worth the bother, but he eventually capitulated.
After all, a notion among the aristocracy was the notion that trips to
view famous artworks and classical ruins helped build character, and

Auchinleck strongly suspected that young Boswell could do with a bit more character.

Assuring his father that he would be a responsible young tourist, Boswell bounded off to Europe in 1764. And, to be fair, he did check out most of the usual "educational" sights; in fact, he claimed to be so overwhelmed by the ancient ruins in Rome that he spontaneously started speaking Latin.

To his father's despair, however, Boswell brought that same gusto to all his other adventures in Europe. He hung out with Voltaire in Paris, rubbed elbows with a Corsican guerrilla leader, carted a small dog named Jachone over the Alps, drank copious quantities of Montepulciano in Siena, caught a venereal disease from both a Roman prostitute and a Venetian opera dancer and returned home with the mistress of his friend Jean-Jacques Rousseau in tow. In short, he made the "Grand Tour" worthy of the adjective.

WHAT WAS THE GRAND TOUR?

Historians debate the exact dates of the Grand Tour. Certainly, touring the Continent for pleasure and edification came into vogue among aristocratic Britons in the late sixteenth century. For about a century, however, few people could afford such a tour — or had the intestinal fortitude to bear the physical hardships it required.

The first true Grand Tourist may have been Thomas Coryat, who in 1608 left Odcombe, Somerset, and walked all the way to Venice, apparently to show up the uncultured Prince of Wales. The resulting account, called *Coryat's Crudities*, described Coryat's gastronomic adventures on his 3,175-kilometre march through Europe. Sadly, the prince had the last laugh by having a panel of his buddies edit the work, twisting Coryat's accounts of his own brilliance and sophistication into self-parody. Undaunted, Coryat then walked 5,310 kilometres to India, but expired shortly after reaching Ajmer in Rajasthan. Today, he is probably best remembered for popularizing the use of the table fork in Britain — and for planting the idea in aristocratic British minds that travel could help one become a well-rounded individual.

By the early eighteenth century, significant numbers of tourists were following in each other's footsteps along a route that quickly became standard: London to Dover to Calais and on to Paris, where one could brush up on the finer points of dancing, fencing and riding. From there, it was off to see the Renaissance masterpieces of Florence (with possible side trips to Geneva and Venice), the ruined antiquities of Rome and the musical treasures of Naples, where the lucky traveller would bask for a few months in the sunshine while his compatriots shivered through a damp English winter.

In a trend that fed on itself, increasing tourism to these popular cities led to improving conditions for travellers. As the years went on, it became easier to find short-term accommodation, English-speaking guides and other amenities. As a result, the contrast between these popular spots and less-touristed parts of Europe, such as Spain and the Balkans, became greater by the year. Grand Tourists, by and large, stuck to the tried and true.

In 1749, the year Thomas Nugent published the first edition of *Grand Tour*, his popular multi-volume guidebook, the custom was in its heyday. But that would end in 1789, when first the French Revolution and then the Napoleonic Wars made travel on the Continent tricky for British aristocrats. After the Battle of Waterloo, in 1815, the Grand Tour experienced a modest revival, but the arrival of passenger railways in the 1830s would spell the end of the age when leisure travel was largely limited to a cultured elite.

Although women, older men, members of the merchant and professional classes and continental Europeans all participated in the Grand Tour to some extent, the phenomenon was primarily associated with aristocratic young Britons recently graduated from university. These men were a bit of a societal liability: they had money, status and prospects, but not a lot to *do*. Many were simply waiting around to take over the family estate, which in the interim was running perfectly well without them. Those from high-ranking families were strongly discouraged from adopting a profession or, heavens, going into trade. The military and the church were the only respectable ways to earn a living. If the prospect of commanding a regiment in some wild forest or preaching sermons to pews of drowsy parishioners didn't appeal — and in many cases, it clearly didn't — such young men often drifted into a life of conspicuous dissipation: gambling, drinking, chasing women and generally embarrassing the family. As Edward Carteret remarked in 1728 of his grandson-in-law, the newly installed Lord Dysart,

> The misfortune is, that young men who want experience; and have not the happiness to be under the influence of somebody, who should have an authority over them, they are guided by their own humours and make themselves appear in the world to great disadvantage, and commit many follies, which they may possibly live long enough to repent of, but can never retrieve.[7]

Lofty families eventually came to realize that the Grand Tour offered the perfect outlet for their exuberant, incorrigible youth. On the surface, it was an efficient way to turn young Cecil or Basil into a well-rounded young man: he would see the paintings of Leonardo and Lorrain, tread in the steps of Cicero and Virgil and polish his French in Paris and his aesthetic sensibilities in Florence. And if he was going to get into trouble anyway, he might as well do it far from the wagging tongues of London.

LIKE SPRING BREAK...WITH CHAPERONES

It was taken for granted that young men couldn't be allowed simply to roam the Continent unsupervised. The purpose of the trip was to broaden the mind, so it stood to reason that the traveller needed an older, wiser tutor to instruct him in the fine points of art, architecture, music, history and science. Fortunately, there was no shortage of impoverished scholars who appreciated the opportunity to accompany a twenty-year-old on one of these all-expenses-paid trips across the Continent.

Intellectual Grand Tourists — or those simply looking to impress their parents back home — could also hire guides on site in major cities who would provide in-depth knowledge of a particular place or concept: Boswell took a week-long course in Rome on arts and antiquities, offered by a British expatriate.

Nevertheless, if the idea was to open the young mind, many such minds remained resolutely closed. In a 1678 book, a French Grand Tourist named Jean Gailhard judged the people he encountered thusly: "French courteous. Spanish lordly. Italian amorous. German clownish."[8]

Closed-minded or not, the aristocratic young traveller did have certain privileges. In these early days of travel, there were few museums: aside from pieces in churches, most artworks were housed in private collections. Fortunately for the art-loving Grand Tourist, many wealthy collectors were happy to open their homes to visitors — of the right social class. As Grand Tourist Philip Thicknesse remarked in the 1770s, "[T]he appearance of a gentleman, and particularly a stranger, is a ticket to go any where."[9] The French royal family was happy to let the upper crust into Versailles to view the palace's treasures, and even rented swords to those who showed up without one.

By the end of the eighteenth century, however, locals in popular destinations began to realize what a gold mine their "tourist attractions" — often buildings, artworks and landscapes they'd barely given a thought to — could be. On a 1788 visit to Naples, Welsh writer Hester Lynch Piozzi — better known to her readers as Mrs. Thrale — spotted a mountain in the distance spewing lava and fire, and asked a Franciscan friar if that was the famous Vesuvius. The cleric's response sounds surprisingly modern in its cynicism: "Yes, . . . that's our mountain, which throws up money for us, by calling foreigners to see the extraordinary effects of so surprising a phaenomenon."[10]

With those words, the friar raised a warning flag: to paraphrase Yeats, the rough beast of mass-market travel was slouching towards the Western world to be born.

Putting on the Ritz
HOTELS AND OTHER HOMES AWAY FROM HOME

*The great advantage of a hotel is that it is a refuge
from home life.*

— *George Bernard Shaw*

When I first heard about the Berghotel Obersteinberg, more than a
thousand metres above the Swiss village of Lauterbrunnen, I eagerly
joined a group that would hike to the isolated inn. The brochures
described it as a "candle hotel," cut off from the noise and clamour
of the modern inn. How charming, I thought — something out of
Heidi.

Indeed, the rustic inn wouldn't have looked out of place on Alm-
Uncle's mountain, and the candles certainly gave the dining room a
lovely glow. But when you've just spent all day hiking up a narrow
mountain path in early fall, the charm of a hotel with no electric
light, heat or hot running water quickly wears thin.

As I shivered in my bunk late that night, still wearing my wind-
breaker and gloves, I thought about the traveller's eternal quest to
find the perfect accommodation — a place magically free of loud
neighbours, temperamental air conditioning systems, insect residents
or quirky plumbing. I tried to remember why I hadn't chosen the tour
based in a posh hotel in Geneva. It's almost impossible to pick wisely
from a distance every time. Even the Bates Motel probably looked
pretty in the brochure.

I also tried to ignore the call of nature, as answering it would require a trip outside to the small shed housing the WC. Finally, I could
ignore my bladder no longer. I threw off the covers, clambered down

the ladder, crept through the dorm and tugged on my hiking boots. Candle hotel, my foot — this was Girl Guide camp gone bad.

I yanked open the door and stumbled outside. To my astonishment, I didn't need my flashlight. I looked up to see a three-quarter moon and a blanket of stars lighting my way. The only sounds were the faint rumble of the Schmadribach waterfall and some jingling cowbells. No greenish street lamps, no hum of traffic, no whiff of asphalt — just utter peace. All thoughts of that posh place in Geneva fled my enchanted mind.

With hotels, as with any real estate, it's all about location, location, location. And it always has been.

IN THE BEGINNING...

One of the oldest surviving remnants of a hotel is the hostel near the palace of Knossos on the island of Crete. Dating back to about 1500 BC, in its heyday the inn featured a common room painted with birds and flowers, an enclosed pool where travellers could wash their dusty feet and bathtubs for a more thorough cleansing.

But inns existed long before this hostel on Crete. A Sumerian hymn written sometime around 2100 BC mentions public houses built in Mesopotamia for the comfort of travellers, and historians estimate that such public houses existed from about 2500 BC onwards. These buildings were, however, primarily bars where travellers could pick up women; it appears their rooms often served the same function as those in a modern charge-by-the-hour motel. As one account from sometime before 1500 BC makes clear, Mesopotamian inns were hardly candidates for the *Good Housekeeping* seal of approval: "If a man urinates in the tavern in the presence of his wife, he will not prosper," the writer advises. "He should sprinkle his urine to the right and the left of the door jambs of the tavern and he will prosper."[11]

Slightly more advanced accommodation appeared in ancient Greece, where travellers who didn't know anyone in town could spend the night in a *pandokeion* ("place for receiving all"). By about 400 BC, most major Greek towns, ports and roads were well supplied with these rustic inns. Some of the largest were built near major tourist attractions: a two-storey inn stood near the temple of Hera at Plataea in Boeotia, and a spacious hostel with an imposing arcade was built at the Olympic games site in the fourth century BC. In the same century, a particularly well-equipped *pandokeion* in Corinth, a major trading centre, included a row of thirty-one taverns on the first floor (each with a well where wine and food could be kept cold) and a corridor of two-room suites on the second floor.

Little information has come down to us about urban inns in ancient Greece, but rural ones were generally laid out around a large enclosed courtyard. After a long day on the hot road, a traveller would have few creature comforts to enjoy: an often-windowless room, perhaps already home to a few other travellers, with a hard, bare pallet for a bed and a dank commode for a toilet. If he hadn't brought bedding, he used his cloak as a blanket. And if he hadn't brought food, he was at the mercy of the local markets or the avaricious landlady, as few inns included room and board. Even baths were outside the inn's purview — to wash off the day's dust, the traveller had to hike to the nearest public bath.

FRIENDS, ROMANS, COUNTRYMEN, LEND ME YOUR VILLA FOR THE WEEKEND

Not surprisingly, most ancient travellers planning to stay awhile in one place often bought or rented private homes. In the Roman Empire, the country villa became the mark of a successful man, much like a home in the Hamptons is a status symbol for the modern-day titans of Wall Street, Broadway and Madison Avenue. It was usually luxuriously appointed, complete with murals, indoor plumbing and mosaic-decorated floors warmed by an under-floor heating system called a *hypocaust*.

People whose villa was more than a day's travel from their main residence would also buy small shelters where they could rest along the way. This network of real estate could be quite extensive, as many Romans owned more than one villa — one or more on the coast for spring, a few more in the mountains to take advantage of cool summer breezes. Cicero, for instance, owned at least six villas along with their associated way stations, and he was not a particularly rich man.

Even with the plethora of villas, there was still a thriving market for temporary accommodation throughout the Empire. Government officials could usually find a room at one of the many outposts of the *cursus publicus* (postal system), which also sheltered couriers and their mounts.

Along the major travel routes, such as the Appian Way and the passes through the Alps, so many different types of accommodation arose that Latin developed a number of words to distinguish them, including *mutatio* (a small hostel consisting of just a kitchen, central room and bedroom), *taberna* (a modest tavern or inn) and *mansio* (a larger structure with stables, blacksmithing facilities, multiple bedrooms and niceties such as central heating). Some words denoted the relative "class" of the establishment; a *hospitium* ("place of hospitality") would be fairly tame, but in a *caupona* you might find yourself keeping company with rowdy slaves and sailors.

In any case, hotels, with their constant influx of strangers coming and going, weren't necessarily the safest places in town. Under Roman law, innkeepers were among the few people you could sue for a theft on their premises (in most other cases, you had to get restitution directly from the thief).

Whatever their name, inns often prompted the growth of a town — European place names such as Saverne, in Alsace, can be traced back to the Latin *taberna*. Inns in the country were relatively prominent, but even in the city they were easy to spot. They clustered near the gates of major towns, and at each a lamp was kept burning night and day over the door (along with a sign promoting the inn's bar) to distinguish one from the next. Usually, a plaque near the door extolled the hotel's virtues over the competition. In Lyons, an innkeeper named Septumanus posted a sign that boasted: "Here Mercury promises you wealth, Apollo health, and Septumanus room and board."

On arriving at the inn, the traveller would follow a servant (laden with the guest's baggage) to a small bedroom equipped with a bed, a mattress full of bedbugs and a candle. Graffiti left behind by previous guests was often the only form of decoration. As in Greece, travellers were often required to bunk down in dorms with strangers and to use a public bath to get clean. On the bright side, most Roman inns had a decided advantage over their Greek predecessors: a latrine — no doubt more than one traveller had cause to bless the advanced state of Roman plumbing.

AN OASIS OF COMFORT

To the weary traders who trekked across the vast plains of Anatolia, leading camels laden with goods, few sights were more welcome than the high, arched entrance of a *caravanserai*.

These fortified stopping places, also known as *khans* or *hans*, were crucial lynchpins in the history of trade. Traders needed safe places to sleep, where their animals and goods would be protected from bandits. The caravanserais — found throughout North Africa, Asia Minor and the Middle East beginning in the early eighth century — were the answer.

These wayside shelters reached a high point during the twelfth and thirteenth centuries in Anatolia (modern Turkey), when the Seljuk dynasty went on a caravanserai-building binge. The Seljuk Turks were far from the first to realize the importance of securing the safety of travelling merchants. The Babylonians, Assyrians and Persians had all passed special laws to protect traders. But having concluded that safe havens were crucial to the development of trade — and that Anatolia imported far more than it exported — the Seljuks made a point of rolling out the welcome mat for traders. Whether they were bringing sugar from Egypt, tin from Afghanistan, pepper from India or glass from Iraq, Anatolia was open for business. In fact, the Seljuk rulers took the Islamic injunction to welcome wayfarers very seriously indeed: travellers were welcome to spend up to three days at each caravanserai at no cost. These free, relatively safe accommodations gave traders at least some confidence that they might make it back home with body, goods and profits intact.

Early evening was a chaotic time at a caravanserai. As dusk crept over the landscape, dusty trains of men and beasts would make their way to the compound's gate. If the gatekeeper recognized them, or if they could present some sort of recommendation letter or other *bona fides*, the heavy iron door would slowly swing open and allow them to pass through the decorated archway into the clamour of the courtyard.

Inside, merchants and labourers would be unloading goods onto raised platforms above the livestock's sleeping quarters. Every camel, horse, mule and donkey would be divested of its burden, then grouped by caravan and led away for food and water. Wainwrights, blacksmiths and cobblers would be on hand to fix broken axles, re-shoe horses or patch worn sandals. Stalls sold everything a traveller might want or need, and tax collectors and customs officers made certain that the ruling monarch and local functionaries received their share of the traders' profits. (Then, as now, there was no such thing as a truly free lunch.)

Pragmatic travellers would head first to the stone water fountain to slake their thirst; more spiritual men might consult an imam. Large caravanserais often had their own mosques, while others simply encouraged the faithful to pray on the roof. Then, as darkness fell, travellers would gather around communal tandir ovens in the courtyard (similar to the clay tandoor ovens used in modern Indian restaurants to make naan) to devour warm unleavened bread and cook simple stews. As the night wore on, those not too tired from the day's journey would trade gossip, spin stories and, perhaps, enjoy a performance by a troupe of dancers (some of whom provided services besides dancing to the lonely traders).

Finally, after a visit to the latrine and one last check of the horses, travellers would unroll the bedding they had brought with them and settle down to sleep before the glowing embers of a fire, secure in the knowledge that guards were keeping watch, arrows poised at window slits overlooking the surrounding countryside.

A few mornings later, once they'd finished the required paperwork and done all the trading they wished to do with their fellow travellers, these traders — from Genoa and Athens, Baghdad and Damascus — would roll up their sleeping rugs, load their goods back onto their camels and horses, whistle for their dogs and head back out onto the dusty plain. As the iron door clanged shut behind them, they surely prayed for an uneventful journey that would take them, after a slow trek of fifteen or twenty kilometres, to next safe haven.

THE EVOLUTION OF ENGLISH HOSPITALITY

In England, special-purpose inns were much slower to develop, as trade routes were short and settlements much closer together than they were in the Middle East, Africa and Asia. Monarchs and their entourages were among the few to travel long distances in the British Isles until the Middle Ages. And when the king journeyed, the usual approach to accommodation was to drop in on the local lord and ask for a bed for the night. The earl of Such-and-Such knew the political value of making His Royal Highness feel welcome, even though the cost of feeding and sheltering a large party of soldiers, courtiers and tradesmen could take a severe bite out of milord's fortune. If the option of lodging with the local aristocracy was not available, the marshal and chamberlain rode ahead of the monarch's party, marked the best homes with chalk and informed the residents they were about to have some exalted company.

This sort of accommodation, understandably, was not open to most travellers. But people of all ranks could prevail upon the hospitality of monasteries and convents. Some monastic orders, such as the Knights Hospitaller, were founded in large part to shelter wayfarers and dedicated much of their wealth to this purpose.

At times, however, it was difficult for some monasteries to carry the costs of such hospitality, particularly when high-living lords came to stay for weeks at a time. In 1338, for example, the prior of Clerkenwell noted "much expenditure which cannot be given in detail, caused by the hospitality offered to strangers, members of the royal family, and to other grandees of the realm who stay at Clerkenwell and remain there at the cost of the house."

After some abbots complained, Edward I forbade anyone but the very poor to ask for accommodation at a monastery, while travellers were only to lodge at such institutions only when expressly invited. Such edicts were frequently ignored, however, and the monks themselves had to tread a fine line. Since providing hospitality was one of their reasons for being, refusing to do so would breed resentment of their special privileges.

As the feudal system waned and people of all ranks grew somewhat less tied to the place they were born, the roads the Romans had left behind saw greater use for trade and posting inns sprang up where travellers and their horses could rest for the night.

Unlike the contemporaneous caravanserais, some of which could house up to two hundred travellers a night, most English inns of the Middle Ages were small and cramped. Many were simply large houses in which rooms were available for rent. But as time went on, some inns grew into substantial buildings. In a popular configuration, galleried buildings surrounded an inner courtyard where plays and other entertainments could be presented.

Henry VIII's dissolution of the monasteries between 1536 and 1540 destroyed the formal link between Christianity and the provision of hospitality to travellers in England. But even when innkeepers rather than religious orders offered the service, it was still seen as a religious duty. A seventeenth-century broadside listing the house rules of one inn noted, "Our Saviour in the Gospel commends the use of Innes (Luke 10.3-4.) and brought to an Inne the Christ himself by his owne presence did sanctifie the use of Innes by eating his passover there. (Mat. 26.18.)"

While some of these early inns, particularly those that saw a lot of royal custom, could be well equipped, many offered comforts barely a step above the hazards of the road. Most guests who cared about hygiene brought their own linens, which they spread on straw pallets laid on dirty, rush-strewn floors. Fleas, rats and drafts were standard amenities.

Like the Seljuk rulers in Turkey, English monarchs came to realize that it was in the kingdom's best interest to ensure that travellers had a place to stay for the night. James I passed a law requiring all innkeepers and alehouse-keepers to reserve at least one spare bed for strangers. The law was more honoured in the breach than in the observance, as many travellers told stories of spending the night in an abandoned barn or under a hedgerow.

By the 1600s, however, inns had gained a position of some prominence in England. In small towns in particular, they began to serve local civic functions. The justice of the peace might hear cases in the large dining room during the day and at other times the same chamber might come in useful for military recruiters. The inns also came to have an increasingly large physical presence. The famous wooden sign of the "White Hart" in Suffolk — more of a gate, really — stretched across the entire road and was carved with scenes from mythology, such as the story of Actaeon and Diana.

In these inns, guests were treated more as houseguests than as customers. The innkeepers were known generally as the *host* and *hostess*, and sat down to dinner with the guests if the travellers didn't prefer to take their meals in their rooms. After dinner, the innkeeper would often arrange for entertainment, perhaps an amateur musical performance or a cockfight. It all sounds rather cheerful, and likely was on many occasions. But a man who considers that he is doing you a favour by sheltering you in his home, rather than providing a service, is as apt to be cranky as kind. Unlike modern hoteliers — many of whom pride themselves on providing polite service to every sort of customer — seventeenth-century innkeepers felt no particular compunction to be obsequious.

Just one example of poor service comes from John Taylor, an English sailor, tavernkeeper and poet. He was an enthusiastic traveller, yet occasionally he found himself among the legions who complained about the unpleasant nature of some English country inns. In 1649, during a trip to Land's End, he stayed at an inn in the town of Nether Stowey in Somerset. It was a visit that would put modern complaints about dripping taps and noisy televisions to shame:

> Mine host was very sufficiently drunk, the house most delicately decked with exquisite artificial and natural sluttery, the room besprinkled and strewed with the excrements of pigs and children: the walls and ceilings were adorned and hanged with rare spider's tapestry, or cobweb lawn: the smoke so palpable and perspicuous,

that I could scarce see anything else, and I could scarce
see that, it so blinded me with weeping.[12]

To add insult to injury, the innkeeper refused to feed Taylor either
dinner or breakfast.

As mobility increased and cities grew, more people began to travel
for more varied reasons. Coaching inns gave travellers a place along
the highway to sleep and rest their horses. Except in large cities,
however, when English travellers reached their destination, they
would generally stay with family or friends in a private home.

In the eighteenth century, though, this began to change as demand
rose for long-term accommodation in county and resort towns. If a
group or family wished to stay somewhere for several weeks, they
sought a higher level of service than the quick meals and simple entertainment of a roadside inn. By the late 1700s, entrepreneurs were
constructing larger, purpose-built hotels complete with private sitting
rooms and multiple dining rooms, as well as "assembly rooms" for
social functions. These assembly rooms, whether located in a hotel
or in a stand-alone building, provided an important venue where
visitors could mix with locals. It is in just such an assembly room
that Elizabeth Bennet first meets the haughty Mr. Darcy in *Pride and
Prejudice*.

ADVENTURES ON THE CONTINENT

Once the Grand Tour kicked into high gear, English tourists encountered all sorts of unfamiliar sleeping arrangements, to their great
dismay. During a trip through Germany in the 1730s, Sacheverell
Stevens was unnerved by a one-room inn in Westphalia, where he
found that necessity made for some strange bedfellows:

[N]ext the fire place were several little places, like cloaths
presses, or closets with folding doors, in each place was a
bed, to which you ascend by a little step ladder; you are
obliged to undress before the landlord and landlady, who
see each passenger to his respective bed, and then shut

the folding doors; but I begged to have mine left open, for fear of being smothered; at about ten yards from me, on one side of the room, there were several cows in their stalls, and on the other hogs in little pens; I never had so disagreeable a lodging.[13]

Three decades later, his compatriot Walter Stanhope had complaints about his accommodation during a sojourn in France. While conceding that the French beat the English hands down in matters of cuisine, he contended that the English were far ahead in terms of hygiene:

I hardly remember one place where some of us did not sleep in the same room in which we supped; — for it was generally furnished with two or three beds, and those beds almost as generally occupied with troops of bugs, and whole armies of fleas. The nightly excursions, and attacks of those hopping, and creeping gentry were a great annoyance to all the company except myself, who happily have not the honour of being to their taste.[14]

Yet another three decades later, while travelling in Scandinavia in the late 1790s, author Mary Wollstonecraft became highly dissatisfied with what sounds like a feather bed combined with a duvet:

The beds too were particularly disagreeable to me. It seemed to me that I was sinking into a grave when I entered them; for, immersed in down placed in a sort of box, I expected to be suffocated before morning. The sleeping between two down beds, they do so even in summer, must be very unwholesome during any season; and I cannot conceive how the people can bear it, especially as the summers are very warm.[15]

To avoid this sort of comfort — or, more likely, to avoid being forced to sleep on the carriage floor if no inn were available — savvy travellers soon learned to come prepared when travelling in places off the beaten path. On a 1762 trip from Constantinople to Krakow, British diplomat Sir James Porter carted along an entire set of furniture, though when Lady Craven headed from Moscow to the Crimea in 1786, she made do with just a travelling bed.

ACCOMMODATION ON A GRAND SCALE

The invention and refinement of the steam engine in the late eighteenth and early nineteenth centuries changed travel, and thus the hotel business, in several major ways. First, the rise of manufacturing created a new middle class, most of whom didn't have the connections to wangle a weekend's stay with Cousin Percy at an aristocratic country estate. If Mr. Upstart Jones, owner of a woollen mill or china factory, wanted to holiday in the country, he'd have to rent his own rooms — and he'd want rooms suitable to his new, wealthy station. Second, steam trains made this newly wealthy middle class much more mobile. Places once reachable only via a long, uncomfortable carriage ride on bumpy roads soon became popular holiday destinations. Moreover, the new factories were able to mass-produce everything from napkin rings to armoires, making it suddenly more affordable for an entrepreneur to equip a large venue to a consistent, comfortable standard.

The stage was set for the emergence of the "grand hotel." One of the things that made a hotel "grand" was sheer size. And for the birth of the big hotel, we need to move across the Atlantic to that larger-than-life country, the United States.

Europe's trends had also taken hold there, with one crucial difference: the United States was a nation of immigrants. In America, there were no centuries-old grand country manors to inherit, buy or invite oneself to. The truly rich built elaborate new mansions, but for increasing numbers of the only moderately rich at the turn of the nineteenth century, the logical alternative was to move the whole family, lock, stock and barrel, into a hotel.

One of the earliest large hotels in the US was Boston's Exchange Coffee House, a seven-storey landmark built between 1806 and

1809 that featured 200 guest rooms, a grand ballroom and a seventy-foot-long dining hall. It burned down in 1818, but other ambitious establishments would soon follow in its stead.

The amenities of such early "grand" hotels were certainly basic by later standards. Families planning to spend more than a day or two in a hotel needed regular meals. In US hotels, it was customary for guests to stay on the "American plan," which included not only a room but also three to five meals a day, which guests would pay for whether they ate them or not. The richly attired guests would troop into a communal dining room, where huge platters of food would be placed on long tables all at once, to be shared by the assembled guests, much like an overgrown family dinner.

In 1842, during a tour of North America, Charles Dickens described what it was like to partake in one of these meals at the Tremont House, a 170-room hotel in Boston that had opened twelve years earlier:

> A public table is laid in a very handsome hall for break-fast, and for dinner, and for supper. The party sitting down together for these meals will vary in number from one to two hundred: sometimes more. The advent of each of these epochs in the day is proclaimed by an awful gong, which shakes the very window-frames as it reverberates through the house, and horribly disturbs nervous foreigners.[16]

It sounds more like a university dorm than a modern five-star hotel. And communal dining tables were not the only things that distinguished the mid-century American grand hotel from its later counterpart.

First, few but the most exclusive hotels accepted advance reservations — not surprisingly, in those pre-telephone days. The wise traveller would do research before leaving home, asking friends for recommendations or consulting a hotel guidebook. Others would press porters, conductors and fellow travellers for leads. Procrastinators would have to do their research on arrival, or rely

on tips from hotel "runners" who touted their establishment's virtues
in train stations or on waterfront piers.

But even after finding a hotel that seemed suitable, the weary
traveller still might not find a room available, and his only option
would be to keep moving from hotel to hotel until discovering one
with a spare bed. And a spare bed didn't necessarily mean a spare
room. Until the end of the 1800s, crowded American hotels routinely
expected their patrons to share a dorm, a room — even a bed — with
a stranger of the same sex. That room might not even be particularly
private — one exhausted visitor to Chicago in 1854 found himself
relegated, with three other guests, to a parlour that was also home
to mounds of luggage and a large piano.

As for privacy, except in the long-stay apartments in many of
these hotels, private toilets and bathing facilities were unheard of.
Boston's Tremont House, with eight toilets and eight bathrooms, was
the height of luxury when it opened in 1830; four years later, New
York's 309-room Astor House won raves for having seventeen tubs in
the basement and at least one toilet on every floor. In even the most
elegant establishments, guests paid an extra fee to bathe.

Men and women might well mix in the dining rooms and ballrooms of these new grand hotels, but in many other aspects they were
kept apart as rigorously as the adherents of a conservative religion. By
mid-century, couples arriving at an American grand hotel separated
at the front entrance. Men would stroll through the grand portal and
into the lobby, where they would book and pay for the room. Their
wives, meanwhile, would head for a separate entrance, often at the
side of the building, that led to the upstairs ladies' parlour — after
all, no respectable lady would be seen in such a public place as a hotel
lobby, lest she be thought a woman of ill repute.

After unpacking and freshening up in their (shared) bedroom, the
couple would once again go their separate ways — she to a fussily
decorated parlour, where she could read, sew or receive callers; he
to the dark-panelled bar, reading room or billiard room.

THE HOTEL SPACE RACE

By the late 1800s, American hotels had grown to gargantuan size. The Palace Hotel in San Francisco, which opened in 1875, had 755 rooms and cost $4 million to build (it burned down during the 1906 earthquake). The Grand Union hotel in Saratoga Springs, New York, had 824 rooms by the late 1870s, while its chief competitor, the United States Hotel, boasted almost a thousand. In the days before electric light and elevators, catering to such numbers of guests must have required a Herculean effort. The corridors of the Grand Union alone stretched more than three kilometres (two miles).

In 1897, Manhattan's Waldorf-Astoria opened, one of the first hotels to offer more than a thousand rooms. Its famous ball memorably associated the new hotel in the public mind with Manhattan Gilded Age society. The party's hosts, Mr. and Mrs. Bradley Martin of Troy, New York, spent $369,200 on the glittering dinner for hundreds of guests attired as though they were courtiers at Versailles — in the midst of a devastating depression, when one in eight Americans made less than $400 a year.

As the nineteenth century progressed, so did grand hotels' amenities. By mid-century, dorms had largely fallen from favour, with private rooms — complete with lockable doors and water jugs for washing — taking their place. Sprung mattresses became widely available in the 1870s.

Whether in terms of sheer size or luxury or, in most cases, a combination of both, hotels had decisively moved far from their roots as home-like spaces where the innkeeper sat down to dinner with his guests. As American high society grew increasingly sophisticated, wealthy guests became increasingly reluctant to be herded like cattle into a huge dining hall at the sound of a huge gong. Eventually, "family-style" dining collapsed under the weight of numbers and the increasing desire of guests to be pampered and made to feel special. No longer did many guests want a "home away from home." More and more, they wanted a place to stay that had very little in common with the homely, domestic comforts they'd left behind.

A MENU OF OPTIONS

The Leland family, which ran New York's Metropolitan Hotel in
the 1850s, started a trend by allowing guests to eat at smaller tables
at different times, to choose their dishes from a menu and to eat at
least some of their meals somewhere other than at the hotel. All of
these innovations would eventually become known as the "European
plan," and by the 1890s they were the norm at most of the leading
American city hotels. Not only did they make life more convenient
for the guests; they also made the hotels more profitable. No longer
did hoteliers have to hire huge numbers of waiters to serve hundreds
of guests at once. And no longer did the dining room exist solely to
serve hotel guests. In effect, this decision meant that many hotels ran
two separate, complementary businesses: renting rooms to travellers,
and serving meals to both visitors and locals. The locals could keep
the business in business during slow tourism times.

Not all hotel guests were immediately comfortable with the extra
degree of choice. Rather than simply eating what was placed on the
table, as they would at home, they found themselves in an alien
situation where they needed to make discerning choices. For many,
reading a French-strewn menu was as intimidating as perusing a thick
wine list can be today, but at least one headwaiter cautioned his staff
not to attempt to help the frazzled guest: "[A] waiter is more apt to
give offense than to receive thanks should he attempt to enlighten
him."

But people soon learned the intricacies of deciphering a menu,
and not a moment too soon. Hotel cuisine — and hotels in general
— were about to take another great leap forward. For that story, it's
time to head back to Europe.

HAIL, CÉSAR

At first glance, César Ritz seems an unlikely candidate to develop a signature luxury hotel culture. Born in 1850, the thirteenth child of the mayor of a small Swiss village, he was fired from his first job as an apprentice waiter at a Swiss hotel because his employer was convinced he'd never make it in the hospitality business.

Undaunted, Ritz made his way to Paris. After drifting through a series of restaurant jobs, he became an assistant waiter at the Restaurant Voisin in the Faubourg Saint-Honoré, then popular with politicians, authors and royalty. At later hotel and restaurant posts in Vienna, Nice, Switzerland and elsewhere he honed his talent for serving the rich and famous. In particular, he made a point of remembering each VIP's likes and dislikes. He also developed an uncanny knack for solving problems quickly: when a large group arrived unexpectedly for lunch at the Rigi-Kulm hotel in Switzerland, on a cold day when the central heating had given up the ghost, Ritz quickly developed a menu of hot dishes (including flaming crepes), evicted a few potted palms from their containers to create improvised braziers and wrapped fire-heated bricks in flannel to be used as footstools. By all accounts, the guests were delighted, and no one remarked on the frosty hotel interior.

In the 1870s, Ritz first crossed paths with an up-and-coming chef named Auguste Escoffier when they were both working in hotels in Monte Carlo. They soon realized they shared several traits: obsessions with service, simplicity and hygiene, coupled with rampant perfectionism. Together, the pair would revolutionize the grand hotel industry. Ritz would manage (and later own) superlative hotels, while Escoffier would create flavourful, pared-down dishes that appealed to refined diners who had grown weary of the heavy, sauce-laden food popularized half a century earlier by French chef Marie-Antoine Carême.

Ritz eventually became the first celebrity hotelier. Peripatetic glitterati such as Queen Victoria's dissolute son, the Prince of Wales, would follow him like sheep to whatever establishment he deigned to grace with his presence. When Richard D'Oyly Carte built the Savoy

Hotel in London in 1889, he expected that it would attract all the right people. When it didn't, D'Oyly Carte knew he needed the Ritz touch to rescue his investment.

The main problem with D'Oyly Carte's hotel was that it had been built and was being run by people with little experience in the hotel business. They didn't realize that gilded ceilings and luxurious linens alone would not attract and retain the loyalty of the famous. What the privileged classes really wanted, along with material luxury, was deference and cosseting. They wanted the manager to know their name, to inquire about their children and to make sure that their favourite waiter served them at dinner and that their favourite sherry was available in the hotel bar. In short, they wanted to feel like honoured guests, rather than walking pocketbooks. This experience was exactly what Ritz, with his encyclopedic knowledge of the rich and powerful, was uniquely able to provide.

Realizing this, D'Oyly Carte begged and cajoled and wheedled Ritz to manage his failing London hotel. Ritz was reluctant. Not only did he already have profitable positions in several European hotels, but he also knew that the English had been very slow to come around to the idea of dining in public. Since fine restaurants were key to the success of so many Ritz properties, he worried that taking an appointment at the Savoy would lead to the first major disaster of his golden career. D'Oyly Carte eventually made him a financial offer he could not refuse, however, and Ritz came to London to lend his sheen to the Savoy.

To persuade Londoners that it was socially acceptable to eat in public, Ritz began by promoting the idea of after-theatre meals. The novelty of this concept drew the curious and the avant-garde, and the rest of London's high society soon followed. For D'Oyly Carte, the scheme had the added benefit of promoting the nearby Savoy Theatre, which D'Oyly Carte also happened to own, having built it as a staging ground for Gilbert and Sullivan operettas.

The Savoy Hotel, incidentally, has two other oddball claims to fame. One is that Escoffier allegedly invented melba toast there, after accidentally delivering extra-thin toasted bread to Australian opera singer Dame Nellie Melba. The other peculiarity is that the forecourt,

known as Savoy Court on maps, is said to be the only place in the
United Kingdom where vehicles are required to drive on the right.
Two explanations have been floated for this anomaly. One traces it
to the days when hackney carriage drivers would reach out of the
driver's door window to open the rear passenger door — which was
hinged at the back of the vehicle — without having to get out of the
cab themselves. The other theory, much less interesting, is that traffic
flows this way so that drivers lining up to let off patrons at the Savoy
Theatre won't block the hotel entrance.

As for Ritz, he also played a role in developing London's Carlton
Hotel, which opened in stages in the 1890s. In particular, he encouraged the architects and interior decorators to keep the needs of
female patrons uppermost in their minds. Gone were the days when
women were shuffled off to some upstairs parlour to avoid being seen
in hotels; by the end of the nineteenth century, society's leading ladies
had begun to treat grand hotels as something of a stage upon which
they could legitimately act and preen. One of Ritz's strokes of genius
at the Carlton was to insist, at significant expense, that the architects
create a sunken level in the hotel's Palm Court. The resulting design
required a set of grand, shallow stairs from the French doors at the
entrance, giving London's upper-class beauties the perfect place to
make a grand entrance or exit. In a further inspired move, Ritz incorporated a private balcony overlooking this display for the use of
the Prince of Wales, never a man to miss an opportunity to admire
beautiful women.

Ritz would eventually go on to build and run his own eponymous
hotels, beginning with the Hotel Ritz in Paris. When it opened in
1898, it gained instant fame for the then-rare luxury of a private
toilet and bathroom for every suite — further evidence of Ritz's
promotion of good hygiene, which also led him to paint walls instead
of paper them, and to hang light, white curtains instead of dusty,
brocaded drapes in his hotels' windows.

Ritz was known throughout the hotel industry as a tireless per-
fectionist who rarely took a day off. While it made him the leading
hotelier of his day, it may also have been his undoing. As Ritz was
feverishly planning an elaborate celebration to mark the coronation

of the Prince of Wales as Edward VII in June 1902, the prince fell ill
with peritonitis two days before the ceremony and the festivities had
to be postponed. The shock — coupled, according to some biograph-
ers, with the early effects of syphilis — sent Ritz spiralling into a
nervous breakdown from which he never recovered. By that point,
however, he had established the idea of creating a hotel that was at
least as much of a draw as the place in which it was located.

ALL THIS AND GRETA GARBO, TOO

In the darkest years of the Great Depression, a movie proved that interest in the rarefied world of fine hotels remained high, even though
few people could actually afford to stay in one. The film was MGM's
Grand Hotel, based on a German-language novel by former hotel
chambermaid Vicki Baum. The movie won the Academy Award for
Best Picture of 1932. The entire movie takes place within the confines
of the luxurious Art Deco Grand Hotel in Berlin, where someone has
apparently forgotten to tell the fur-stole-wearing socialites strolling
through the marble lobby that the economy has crashed.

The movie ingeniously brings together a range of disparate characters: Greta Garbo's burnt-out ballerina Madame Grusinskaya, whose
weary plea, "I just want to be alone," would haunt Garbo for the
rest of her life; John Barrymore's rakish thief, Baron von Geigern;
Joan Crawford's sexy stenographer, Miss Flaemmchen; Lewis Stone's
cynical physician, Dr. Otternschlag; Wallace Beery's obnoxious factory owner, Mr. Preysing; and Preysing's mousy bookkeeper, Otto
Kringelein, played by Lionel Barrymore.

It is Kringelein, more than any other character, who serves as the
voice of the vast majority of the audience that made this movie a
huge hit. The tweedy bookkeeper is dying of some unnamed disease,
and as his last fling he is blowing all his savings on a stay at the
fabled Grand Hotel. From the moment he arrives, he is touchingly
amazed by everything from the light switches and velvet upholstery
in his room to the attached private bath. "I can have a bath anytime
that I like," he breathes in wonder. He orders champagne and caviar
with abandon, multiplies his savings in a profitable card game and

even makes friends with the stylish baron, who gives him a bit of a makeover and introduces him to the sexy stenographer.

Cash and a grand hotel are all Kringelein needs to transcend class and circumstance. When his hated boss, Preysing, tries to shoo him away in the hotel bar, Kringelein declares, "I am not taking orders from you here... I'm my own master for the first time in my life." After a night of drinking, dancing and gambling, he tells Miss Flaemmchen, "For the first time in my life, I've tasted life."

Such a declaration of independence was heady stuff for people hemmed in by the grimness of Depression life. In the Grand Hotel, well-dressed employees bow to guests and rush to fulfill their every wish. Elegant couples in evening wear, unfettered by Prohibition, knock back martinis in the hotel bar. There are sexually loaded conversations in the mezzanine, a thief sneaking through open windows, a ballerina swanning through the lobby trailed by bellboys loaded down with enormous bouquets. Intrigue, drama and excitement are everywhere. And in the end, the rich industrialist, Preysing, gets his comeuppance, while Kringelein gets one of the girls.

Through it all, the hotel itself is portrayed as a magical place where anything could happen, where people who otherwise might never have met collide with fascinating force. Most intriguingly, the drama plays out eternally. As the doctor puts it: "What do you do in the Grand Hotel? Eat, sleep, loaf around, flirt a little, dance a little. A hundred doors leading to one hall. No one knows anything about the person next to them. And when you leave, someone occupies your room. Occupies your bed. That's the end."

Indeed, as the movie ends, the main characters we've followed for the last two hours have all checked out. As the last few drift away, a bubbly pair of honeymooners arrives to check in — the insinuation being that another set of adventures is about to begin. When the doctor delivers his dyspeptic final lines — "Grand Hotel. Always the same. People come. People go. Nothing ever happens" — the audience chuckles knowingly at the irony. On the surface, the hotel might look bland. But we know the drama that seethes just beneath the marble surfaces.

AROUND THE WORLD IN A THOUSAND HOTELS

As travellers fanned out across the globe, hotels sprang up in other countries to cater to their needs. In Asia, some of the most energetic hotel developers were the Sarkies brothers, Armenian immigrants who created a string of hotels in locations as diverse as Penang and Rangoon. Arguably their most famous and romantic hotel was the storied Raffles in Singapore, which they bought in 1887 and named for the city's founder, British merchant trader Sir Stamford Raffles.

Raffles Hotel has long had a mystique concocted from a heady mix of Eastern exoticism and Western tradition. British authors, in particular, made it their home away from home for months at a time — drawn in part, perhaps, by the Singapore Sling, invented by an enterprising Raffles bartender. Noël Coward was a frequent guest, and Somerset Maugham wrote short stories under a frangipani tree in the front yard. Until well into the 1970s, only men were employed to clean the rooms; every time the management attempted to replace the "old boys" with women, long-time hotel guests complained vociferously.

Despite the fact that it was owned in its heyday by an Armenian family and run for many years by a series of German and Italian general managers, Raffles has always had the unassailable air of a stalwart outpost of the British Empire. Before the territory fell to invading Japanese forces in 1942, fleeing British colonists gathered in the lobby sing a few brave rounds of "There'll Always Be An England."

HOTELS FOR THE MASSES

By the early decades of the twentieth century, the days of the quirky individual hotel and small, family-run chain were waning. In the United States, particularly, nationwide businesses that could provide a standard, reliable level of service were on the rise. Just as a multitude of small automobile manufacturers would coalesce into the Big Three, brand-name hotel chains emerged whose owners would embark on a relentless campaign of buying and building hotels. Conrad Hilton launched his worldwide chain with the purchase of the Mobley hotel in Cisco, Texas, in 1919. Western Hotels (now Westin) started with a chain of properties in the Pacific Northwest in 1929. And seven motel owners set up a referral system in 1939 that would evolve into Choice Hotels.

Some of these chains catered to a distinctly upscale clientele — Cary Grant once phoned Conrad Hilton personally to complain when half of an English muffin he ordered for breakfast at the Beverly Hilton did not arrive. But other entrepreneurs began to realize that hotel travel was not just for the rich.

Until the 1950s, however, the middle- and working-class traveller didn't have a great deal of choice in accommodation outside the major cities. Many camped; others stayed with friends. Some tried their luck with the new motor hotels or "motels," and although some of these were perfectly safe and acceptable, many others weren't exactly the sorts of places one would take the family for a wholesome holiday. As early as the 1940s, then-FBI director J. Edgar Hoover was denouncing them as "camps of crime." Enter a Memphis real estate developer named Kemmons Wilson.

During a 1951 family vacation to Washington, DC, Wilson was shocked by the lack of modestly priced accommodation suitable for family travellers. In particular, he was particularly annoyed that he should have to pay extra for children who were staying in the same room as their parents.

Wilson was far from the only dad to take to the open road to explore the country with his children. The growth of the US interstate highway network and booming post-war prosperity were opening new vistas for millions. But he was one of the first to see the potential market. The following year, he opened his first Holiday Inn (the name was inspired by a Bing Crosby movie) on the outskirts of Memphis. Accommodations were priced per room rather than per person, starting at $6 a night, and amenities such as free parking and ice machines were standard. Within seven years, Wilson had a hundred properties, and by 1975 there were more than seventeen hundred Holiday Inns around the world.

From the beginning, Wilson had no ambition to run a grand hotel where maitre d's in tuxedos fawned over rich and titled guests. He once told his more elegant competitors: "You can cater to rich people, and I'll take the rest. The good Lord made more of them."

FROM HOSTELS TO HIPSTERS

As travel became more available to the masses, the hotel market fragmented in ways that César Ritz and even Kemmons Wilson could hardly have imagined.

As early as 1909, a German schoolteacher named Richard Schirrmann noticed that large numbers of young people had begun to travel. When a group of students he was supervising took temporary shelter in an empty school building during a storm, he realized that many such buildings were empty for part of the year, and that they could be put to use as inexpensive accommodation. By the 1930s, hundreds of youth hostels were open in Germany alone, and the idea had spread to other countries. Today, budget travellers of all ages who don't mind sleeping in dorms or sharing cooking facilities — who, indeed, go out of their way to do so in order to meet other travellers — can choose from thousands of hostels worldwide, including a refurbished nineteenth-century jail in Ottawa that claims to be the site of Canada's last public hanging, a tree house hostel in the American Deep South and a castle in Scotland.

Oddball accommodations are not limited to the hostel market. Novelty-seeking guests can stay on a former icebreaking ship in Kingston, Ontario, a converted caboose in Silverton, Colorado, or a yurt in Kyrgyzstan in Central Asia. At least two entrepreneurs are building extensive underwater hotels, including the $500 million, 220-suite Hydropolis Hotel in the emirate of Dubai (which, interestingly, is also home to the sail-shaped Burj al-Arab Hotel, where rates start at US$1,000 a night).

Guests who don't mind a bit of a chill in their room can check out the Ice Hotel in Jukkasjarvi, Sweden, and snuggle into sleeping bags on beds made of snow and ice, covered with reindeer skins. Each winter, ten thousand tons of river ice and thirty thousand tons of snow are used to build this meltable hotel, complete with sauna and chapel. If Lapland is a little far for your tastes, there is now a Hôtel de Glâce in Duchesnay, west of Quebec City. Choosing offbeat hotels comes with its own risks, however; a friend of mine who stayed in an ice hotel woke up one morning to find a lock of her long hair frozen to the wall.

Some sub-genres of hotel have had the good fortune to reflect an emerging *Zeitgeist* at just the right time. In 1945, a tuned-in business-man named Rudolf von Hoevenberg realized that a wedding boom was imminent, as GIs returned from the Second World War deter-mined to quickly marry the girls they had left behind. He opened the Farm on the Hill, a rustic retreat in Pennsylvania's Poconos Mountains that he billed as the area's first "honeymoon hotel." Starry-eyed couples soon followed. When Interstates 80 and 81 cut through the area in the 1950s and 1960s, tourist traffic boomed. But the area really took off as a romantic destination in 1963, when the owners of the Cove Haven Resort in Lakeville introduced a startling innovation: heart-shaped tubs. *Life* magazine did a story, the phones rang off the hook, and the Poconos would be associated for decades afterwards with red plush bedspreads and champagne-dazzled newlyweds.

These days, home renovation is all the rage, with décor shows crowding the TV dial and "shelter" magazines capturing advertisers' attention (four new national décor magazines hit the stands in the US in 2004 alone). That may be part of the reason for the recent glut of boutique hotels in trendy world capitals.

The definition of a "boutique" hotel seems to depend on whom you ask. Is it one where guests can buy versions of everything from the soaps to the beds? Or does "boutique" simply mean a hotel is trendy, cool, hip and small (and, usually, expensive)? Despite every hotelier's claim that boutique means "unique," by 2005 a fairly stan-dard boutique aesthetic had emerged, heavy on earth tones, natural materials, low lighting and self-consciously arty design elements, such as one green apple placed on each hall table, lit by its own spotlight. Once the chain hotels got in on the act — Westin launched its "W" boutique hotel brand in 1998 — the days of the hipper-than-thou boutique hotel seemed numbered.

THE LANGUAGE OF HOTELS

 *Inn* is one of the oldest English words for temporary accommodation. It appears sometime before the year 1000, rooted in an Old English word for *house*. Interestingly, however, there was no word for the person who ran such an establishment until about 1550, when the term *innkeeper* emerged.

As English inns began to evolve beyond their humble coaching roots, a new name was needed to describe these increasingly grand buildings that were much more than a private home or a few rooms over a publican's bar. For generations, the English aristocracy had had the habit of using French words for anything they wished to give a touch of class. Around 1635, the French word *hôtel* (from the Old French word *hostel*) entered the language, although by some accounts it didn't come into widespread use for more than a century. *Hostel*, in fact, had crossed into Middle English by the early thirteenth century, and can trace its roots back to the Latin *hospitale*, or guest room. By the end of that century, the person operating such an establishment had also gained a name, *hosteller*.

The link to Latin also explains a chain of related English words. *Hospital*, while now used exclusively for an institution that cares for the sick, came into English around the same time as *hosteller*, although the crusading Knights of St. John of Jerusalem had been known by an English/Latin moniker, the Knights Hospitallers, since about 1100. (The close link between the two concepts can also be seen in a French word for hospital, *hôtel-Dieu*, or "mansion of God.")

As with *innkeeper*, several centuries passed before a specific word emerged for someone who ran a hotel. *Hotelkeeper* came into vogue in the United States around 1820. When, inevitably, a sense emerged that hotels were elegant establishments requiring equally elegant French terminology, around 1900 the word *hotelier* crossed from French to English.

HOTELS AS THEATRE

The one thing boutique hotel designers realize — and many managers of both chain motels and large luxury properties seem periodically to forget — is that a large part of a hotel's appeal is its sense of theatre. César Ritz, with the dramatic entrance steps to the sunken Palm Court at the Carlton Hotel, understood this emotion implicitly. One British architect put it this way, in a 2004 article in the magazine of the European Hotel Managers Association:

> Lobby design is vital; lobbies set the stage. Hotel design — whatever segment of the market you're in — is like theatre design; there's an element of fantasy involved. Receptions and lobbies are the first act of the drama. They're your entry into what you hope will be a world of luxury and comfort, and they should also provide an indication of the nature of the hotel and establish its theme.[17]

If you've ever had the chance to see the access corridors and kitchens of a major hotel, you'll instantly see the similarities to the backstage area of a theatre. In the lobby, all may be thick carpet and quiet-voiced clerks. But in the fluorescent-lit service areas hidden behind panelled doors, harried waiters and cleaners shout instructions at each other as they push laden, clacking carts along concrete floors.

In a successful hotel, though, the "sense of theatre" goes far beyond matters of rich drapes and vaulted ceilings. It underpins the management of the entire operation. Ritz knew the value of creating the illusion that each customer was a treasured, beloved guest. And the annals of hotel history are filled with stories of employees who have been able to conjure similar magic. As Mackenzie Porter, a former employee of the Fairmont Chateau Laurier Hotel in Ottawa, once recalled:

> In Room Service, Mrs. Mabel Egan was in charge. She was said to have a fabulous memory for voices. Once she

had spoken on the phone to a guest, she would always remember that voice and be able to put a name to it. One regular guest moved to Japan on business and was away for ten years. When he returned and called Room Service, Mrs. Egan called him by name, saying, "Your usual order, sir?"[18]

Most modern hotels are too large, their staffs too transient, to pull off this feat from memory alone. But at today's Chateau Laurier — and many other big hotels — guests can join a free loyalty club and fill out a detailed survey of their likes and dislikes. Those will be recorded in a chain-wide database, so that habitués of the Chateau Laurier who travel to the Rockies and check into the Chateau Lake Louise will enter a room already equipped with their preferred type of hypoallergenic pillow. The guests know this magic is wrought by computers. But, deep down, they're impressed and feel nurtured.

Managers of historic hotels have a particular advantage in creating a sense of theatre, as they can use the property's storied history to dramatic effect. Roberto Pregarz, the manager of Raffles in Singapore from 1967 to 1989, was one of many masters of this art. To inspire a journalist who wanted a new angle on Somerset Maugham's long association with the hotel, Pregarz booked her into Maugham's suite and then rigged up a hidden tape recorder. At 1:30 in the morning, a low, disembodied voice sounding like Maugham's filled the room, scaring the journalist half to death but inspiring a story about the hotel's "ghost." In another instance, when a murder mystery novel set in the hotel was published, Pregarz and his staff buried a fake treasure chest of "loot" below the marble floor of the billiard room, only to unearth it with a flourish during the book launch.

The billiard room was also the site of Pregarz's most complicated and potentially dangerous publicity stunt. The last tiger to be shot in Singapore had been killed under the hotel's raised billiard room in 1912. To celebrate the Year of the Tiger (and, not coincidentally, the hotel's centennial) in 1986, Pregarz convinced a travelling circus to lend him a tiger, which he used to stage an elaborate photo op on the Raffles billiard table.

The publicity stunt may have seemed needlessly elaborate, but Pregarz understood the unspoken maxim that Ritz had laid down almost a century before: in coming to a grand hotel, a guest doesn't want to feel "at home." Most want more than a clean bed and a hot meal. They want an escape from the mundane and the everyday — one of the main reasons people endure the inconvenience and expense of travel.

Going Down to the Sea in Ships

*Travel by sea nearly approximates the bliss of
babyhood. They feed you, rock you gently to
sleep and when you wake up, they take care
of you and feed you again.*

— *Geoffrey Bocca*

"Oh no, there's Mr. Sweaty," I murmured to my husband Paul as we
sat baking on deck chairs near the pool on the Carnival cruise ship
Paradise, floating somewhere in the Caribbean. "Don't look."

I'm not proud that we had nicknamed the other passenger Mr.
Sweaty. But after he had danced up a storm in the ship's disco a
few nights previously, then wandered over to our table, picked up
our cocktail napkins and started wiping the perspiration from his
underarms before realizing with obvious distress that he didn't know
us, we couldn't help ourselves.

Consequently, for the rest of the trip, we spent a good deal of
time avoiding making eye contact with him to spare us all the mutual
embarrassment. He seemed equally eager to avoid us. But even on a
ship with a capacity of 2,052 passengers, we couldn't avoid bumping
into each other.

In that way and in many others, a week aboard a modern cruise
ship resembles a week in a small town — albeit with its own casino,
Vegas-style theatre and spa, of course. Out of a disparate group of
passengers, a floating society quickly emerges. And when the allure
of the bellyflop contest and the art auction begins to pale (as it will),
there's nothing more amusing than observing your fellow passengers
and imagining their life stories. In the absence of real small-town

gossip, it's only human to invent some. Ports and shops are all well and good, but people watching is a large part of the entertainment on any modern cruise ship.

The diversity of people is fascinating, from the squad of sleek teenage girls, who bond within five minutes of setting foot on the ship with their parents, to the middle-aged couple dressed in matching outfits and playing out some sort of Freudian angst I don't even want to think about, to the exquisitely coiffed woman whose handbag, shoes and fingernails coordinate perfectly with her sarong.

Think of the popular culture related to passenger liners, and the image comes up time and again of a community afloat where people develop instant relationships. Deborah Kerr and Cary Grant fell in love crossing the Atlantic in *An Affair to Remember* in 1957. Two decades later, a bewildering number of sexy single people set sail on TV's *The Love Boat* and found romance in under an hour. Two decades after that, Leonardo di Caprio and Kate Winslet voyaged to a doomed romance in *Titanic*. The idea of a community of strangers coming together to survive disaster also shows up time and again, in films such as the original version of *The Poseidon Adventure* (with its disparate cast of characters, from a minister to a swimming champion) and its 2006 remake (where the cast is younger, sexier and less diverse, but the idea of instant community remains).

As well as providing instant community, cruise ships today strive to provide as many of the amenities of an actual urban area as they can recreate afloat: gourmet restaurants, glittering nightclubs, boutiques, spas, cultural attractions and more. The *Queen Mary 2*, in fact, markets itself as a "City at Sea."

But life on the waves didn't always have such a romantic, friendly image. Until the evolution of air travel, anyone who wanted to cross an ocean had to do so by ship. Few people undertook such a voyage lightly. Before the middle of the nineteenth century, sea travel was a nightmare of long voyages, stale air, rancid food, seasickness, quarantine, storms and shipwrecks.

ROMANS SET SAIL

In the Mediterranean basin during the days of the Greek and Roman empires, sailing was generally a much more efficient way to get from place to place than travelling by road. Instead of spending a month on horseback between Rome and Spain, for instance, a merchant — or an army — could make the trip in about a week by ship, if the captain sailed there directly and the winds were favourable.

The seas were somewhat safer than the roads, too, because the mighty Roman Empire was able to keep the sea lanes of the Mediterranean relatively free of brigands — something it was never quite able to manage on land. And yet, many traders and armies still took to the roads, because not even Caesar could control the weather. (That may be one reason the image of Jesus calming the rough waters of the Sea of Galilee held such resonance for early Christians.)

One might think that because the Mediterranean doesn't freeze, classical Greeks, Romans and Egyptians blithely plied it all year round. But until the mariner's compass — invented in China in the fourth century — came to Europe around 1200, ancient mariners were largely "portbound" from November through February, for the simple reason that they usually couldn't figure out where they were going.

From spring until early fall, the weather was often clear enough for sailors to use the sun and stars as navigational aids. But once the late fall clouds began rolling in, they would be sailing blind, aside from the nominal guidance they could get from taking soundings of the sea's depth to ascertain how close they might be to shore. Only war, some other calamity or significant economic advantage — such as the large bonuses the Emperor Claudius offered to grain ship owners willing to risk late fall sailings from Egypt in order to relieve food shortages in Rome — could impel most sailors to leave safe harbour in the cooler months of the year.

When the weather was fair, all sorts of vessels could be found on the Mediterranean, from small coasting ships that stayed close to shore as they shuttled across short distances, to huge vessels that brought enormous cargoes of grain from Egypt to Rome. The latter were so famous that when one was blown off course about AD 150 into Piraeus, the port of Athens, it attracted a crowd of sightseers. The historian Lucian described the ship in glowing terms that sound eerily like the words used to hype modern ships such as the *Titanic* and the *Queen Mary*:

> What a size the ship was! 180 feet in length, the ship's carpenter told me, the beam more than a quarter of that, and 44 feet from the deck to the lowest point in the hold. And the height of the mast, and what a yard it carried, and what a forestay held it up!...The crew was like an army. They told me she carried enough grain to feed every mouth in Athens for a year.[19]

These grain ships were a marvel of Roman engineering, but they were not specifically designed to carry passengers. That innovation in travel would have to wait another seventeen hundred years, for the development of the packet ship in the nineteenth century. Before that date, all ocean-going ships were cargo ships; any passengers who managed to squeeze aboard were usually welcome but always incidental.

As a result, few conveniences existed for the intrepid sea traveller. Even finding the right ship was a complicated affair. Travellers had to wander the waterfront of the nearest harbour, asking sailors and passers-by which ships in port were headed in which direction. Unless they were travelling between two major cities, such as Rome and Alexandria, or making a short run between adjacent ports, they were unlikely to find a ship sailing exactly where they wanted to go on their first attempt. Instead, they'd take their chances and board a vessel heading in roughly the right direction, get off where it landed and start the whole process over again.

Ostia, Rome's port city, was one of the few places in the Roman Empire where any effort was made to create a more efficient system. There, shippers serving various seaports maintained offices clustered around a central piazza, so travellers could make their inquiries efficiently rather than relying on waterfront gossip.

As if the process of finding a ship didn't make sea travel complicated enough, there were no set sailing schedules. Even if the weather
was good, any one of a host of bad omens — a sailor's nightmare, a
crow in the rigging, a sneeze as someone boarded the vessel — could
delay a ship's departure if a superstitious captain decided to wait
for more favourable signs from the gods. To make sure they literally
didn't miss the boat, travellers had to bunk down close to the port
and keep one ear cocked to hear the heralds who walked throughout
the port area shouting out news of ships' imminent departures — the
ancient equivalent of modern air passengers straining to hear garbled
flight announcements over crackling airport public address systems.

Once passengers had actually walked up the gangplank, life didn't
get much easier. Very important passengers might wangle a tiny, bare
cabin in which to shelter from the weather. Everyone else slept on
deck. If they were organized, they'd have brought makeshift tents;
otherwise, they slept in the open air. To ensure at least minimum
comfort, wise passengers also brought their own food, wine, pots
and pans, linens, mattresses and servants.

Passengers could also be pressed into service in times of emergency. The Bible (Acts 27) describes how, when St. Paul was travelling
as a prisoner from Palestine to Rome, his ship hit a storm in mid-
November. He and the rest of the travellers helped the crew dump
the ship's tackle and load of grain. Eventually, however, the vessel ran
aground in a Maltese harbour. As the ship broke apart, the unlucky
passengers grabbed bits of wreckage and floated or swam to shore.
None drowned, but they had to stay on Malta for three months, until
they could catch another ship when Mediterranean shipping restarted
in the middle of February.

NOT EXACTLY CLEOPATRA'S BARGE

Ships on the Mediterranean weren't the only vessels ancient travellers used. Around 37 BC, the poet Horace boarded a mule-drawn
canal barge for an overnight trip through the Pontine Marshes east
of Rome. He hoped it would save him a day of road travel on his
way from Rome to Brindisi, but the cure may have been worse than

the disease. It took an hour to cram the three hundred travellers aboard and collect their fares. Then the unfortunate passengers were alternately tortured by mosquitoes (they were travelling through a swamp, after all), chirping frogs and a drunken passenger and the boatmen singing songs about their girlfriends. When the sentimental passenger finally passed out, the boatman unhitched the mule and followed suit. "By now it's dawn, and we notice that the boat is standing still," Horace relates. "A hothead jumps up, flails away at sailor and mule on flanks and head with a willow branch, and finally, about 10 AM, we dock."[20]

CHARTING A COURSE FOR THE EDGE OF THE WORLD

With the collapse of the Roman Empire, European trade, travel and commerce in the Mediterranean basin fell largely moribund for more than five centuries as the continent entered the Dark Ages. That's not to say no one ever travelled by sea — Arabs crossed the Mediterranean to invade Spain in the eighth century, for instance, and Viking sailors made frequent raids on coastal towns across western Europe between about 800 and 1000. But open water was largely the province of marauders and soldiers.

Into the Middle Ages and the Renaissance, as Western ingenuity revived on so many fronts, the oceans were still widely regarded as dangerous. Few, other than explorers, missionaries, merchants and other people with compelling reasons ventured onto them. "Here be dragons" supposedly delineated unsafe waters on medieval maps, although the Latin phrase, *Hic sunt dracones*, appears only on the 1511 Lenox Globe — and some historians believe "dracones" refers to a Sumatran tribe rather than a fire-breathing serpent.

Eventually, however, the hearty, the greedy and the adventurous opened up such rich channels of trade that more and more people began to venture abroad by sea — particularly colonial administrators and settlers heading to the Americas, India, Australia and elsewhere.

GRAND TOURISTS TAKE TO THE WATERS

Rich eighteenth-century Britons were among the modern world's first leisure travellers. Many were young men participating in the Grand Tour, while others were older men and women with enough time and wealth to spend an extended time away from England. Not a few were people who had compelling reasons beyond simple sightseeing — debt, an out-of-wedlock pregnancy, a duel gone bad — for going on "holiday" for a few months or years.

The vast majority headed to the Continent, but the notoriously tricky crossing of the English Channel likely gave more than a few of them second thoughts about the wisdom of the entire venture. At a minimum, the trip took three hours, but most travellers budgeted for six at the very least. Today, when people traverse the Channel quickly by ferry or zip through the Chunnel from London to Paris in less than three hours by train, it's hard to comprehend the frustrations early tourists faced as they attempted to make this short crossing.

Winds — too strong or too weak — were one of the main obstacles. Passengers could be forced to hang around port cities for days when conditions were too calm to sail. And excessively windy conditions frequently blew ships off course, playing havoc with tourists' plans. In 1730, Charles Thompson got on board in Dover, fully expecting to land in Calais. Due to strong east winds, he eventually disembarked in Dieppe, a hundred kilometres from his intended destination.

Rainstorms or high winds often prevented large ships from docking safely. Getting passengers ashore meant lowering them into rowboats — a dangerous process that often led to bumps, bruises and broken limbs. The local sailors at the rowboat oars charged whatever extortionate price they thought travellers might pay to get away from the rough seas and onto dry land. Even then, no one could guarantee that the rowboats would land at the ship's intended destination. In 1764, for instance, Lady Mary Coke boarded a rowboat off Calais and ended up over six kilometres (four miles) from town. Once ashore, the soaked and weary passengers, surrounded by mountains of baggage, would have to find their own way back to town, relying on the good graces of passing coach drivers.

Not surprisingly, once they arrived on the Continent, eighteenth-century travellers rarely ventured forth again by ship if they could help it. Shipboard conditions abroad were often as miserable as those in the Channel. For a 1739 voyage between Marseilles and Genoa, for instance, a British tourist named Sacheverell Stevens brought aboard enough food — cold tongue, ham, bread, wine and more — to stand him in good stead if the ship was blown off course. He was indeed caught in a storm, and became so seasick he couldn't eat his carefully prepared provisions or join the other passengers in bailing out the ship with their hats.

Visitors to southern France and the Low Countries were among the few who benefited from relatively pleasant water travel, as river and canal boats could be welcome alternatives to bumpy carriages for short trips. Many travellers heading through France to Italy took the two-day boat trip along the Saône River from Chalon-sur-Saône to Lyons, where pretty views of cow pastures and mountains relieved the tedium of the journey. Since there were no sleeping or dining facilities on board, the boat stopped frequently so that travellers could avail themselves of riverside inns.

All was not perfect on these voyages, however. The first Earl St. Vincent, who made this trip in November 1772, generally enjoyed it but warned other travellers that the boatmen would do little to protect them from the attention of local touts.

> [Passengers on these boats] have the bad habit of reward-ing their coachmen and boatmen before they arrive at their place of destination whereby the passengers are entirely neglected and left a prey to a crowd of canaille under the name of porters, many of them sharpers and all imposters — which we had full demonstration of on our arrival at Lyons — the boat being constantly filled with these people, who but for the friendly interposition of a French gentleman, would have fleeced us handsomely.[21]

THE SHIP OF FOOLS

In the medieval allegory of the Ship of Fools, a town packs up its "mentally challenged" aboard a ship, then lets it drift away in the general direction of some other town, which presumably is either stuck with the passengers itself or has to add its own "fools" to the crew and keep it moving. Thus, any situation where people seem to be headed together toward disaster, neither knowing nor caring where they are going, is a metaphorical Ship of Fools.

For many Christians, the Ship of Fools is a perfect description of a hedonistic society that pursues its vices. This was certainly the interpretation that Hieronymus Bosch painted in *Ship of Fools*, dated to the 1490s, in which the dissolute fools gather around a table, wasting their lives with gluttony, cards and the vague hint of promiscuity.

Katherine Ann Porter adapted the Ship of Fools for her only long novel, published under that name in 1962. In it, Porter explores the frailty of both human nature and human civilization as her characters travel aboard ship from Mexico to Nazi Germany.

Since then, the Ship of Fools has been a steady inspiration for pop songs by everybody from the Doors and Robert Plant to the Grateful Dead and World Party. Oh, and the Unabomber wrote a play called *Ship of Fools*, too.

Rock stars, terrorists...it seems the Ship of Fools has room for everybody.

French riverboats could also be rustic, to say the least. In 1777, an English traveller reported that the flat-bottomed mail boats that also ferried tourists through the castle-studded landscape between Lyons and Avignon were sold as firewood at the end of each voyage. And instead of a tent, he was forced to use his carriage for shelter: "My cabriolet served me for a cabin: The wheels being taken off were laid flat at the bottom of the boat, and the body of the carriage being set upon them, was thus kept above the bilge water, which came in so plentifully as to require frequent bailing."

By most accounts, canal travel in the Low Countries around the same time was a much more comfortable experience. There, horse-drawn barges often offered hot meals on board, enclosed compartments for wealthy passengers and fast, inexpensive, regularly scheduled service. In a 1754 letter, Irish author Oliver Goldsmith describes life aboard a typical Dutch canal ship: "[I]n these you are sure to meet people of all nations. Here the Dutch slumber and the French chatter and the English play cards, any man who likes company may have them to his taste." It sounds suspiciously like shipboard life on the Carnival *Paradise*, 250 years in the future.

KNOWING WHEN YOUR SHIP WILL COME IN

Although scheduled river and canal boat service existed in a few limited areas in the eighteenth century, scheduled ocean voyages would not emerge until the early nineteenth century. The main obstacle was the unreliability of wind-powered transport. Boats pulled by horses or propelled by river currents were relatively predictable; a sailing ship crossing the Atlantic could be becalmed for weeks, slowed by storms or blown off course.

Things started to change on the cold, snowy morning of January 5, 1818, when eight paying passengers boarded the *James Monroe* on the South Street wharf in lower Manhattan. For months, the owners of the Black Ball Line had been advertising that their fast, comfortable ships would soon offer something unprecedented among ocean-going ships: regular, predictable, scheduled service between designated ports.

Today, when the hub-and-spoke airline system causes passengers to grit their teeth when forced to endure even a one-hour layover en route, it's hard to imagine the frustration of early nineteenth-century travellers on the North Atlantic run. Shipping line owners refused to let their vessels leave port until they were loaded with as much cargo and as many people as they could hold and until the weather was as favourable as possible. Paying passengers might be forced to stay in a nearby hotel for weeks until the captain gave the nod to set sail. Once at sea, British travellers, in particular, faced more frustrations as their ships often stopped at either Bermuda or Halifax along the way to unload and take on additional passengers and cargo. The eastbound trip to Liverpool could take weeks, but on the slower western run, back to the US east coast, the passage often required two or three months.

Despite the bitterness of America's struggle for independence less than fifty years earlier and the recently ended War of 1812, links with Britain were the young country's lifeblood. Merchants striving to make their fortunes wanted quicker service between the two. Families eager to be reunited wanted a predictable reunion day. So when the Black Ball Line promised that a packet ship (so named because they also carried mail) would leave New York's South Street wharf regularly on the first and the sixteenth of each month, passengers were delighted yet skeptical. What did these Quaker ship owners know that their competitors didn't?

It wasn't so much what they knew as what they were willing to try. Unlike some of their competitors, who used huge, slow ships nicknamed "kettle-bottoms" to move two tons of merchandise across the ocean on each voyage, the Black Ball Line made speed rather than tonnage its competitive advantage. You might pay more to travel on a Black Ball ship, but you would reach your destination in a timelier, more predictable fashion. For the growing class of rich merchants and entrepreneurs, it was a reasonable bargain.

When the *James Monroe* sailed right on time that January day in 1818, despite the wind and snow that many predicted would have Captain James Watkinson re-thinking his bosses' schedule, New Yorkers took note. The ships of the Black Ball Line became the Concordes of their day: sleek, fast transit for passengers with money.

Not that the facilities aboard the *James Monroe* were particularly elegant. First-class passengers would be invited to dine with the captain, but repaired at night to small, spartan quarters. As they took the air on deck, their noses would be assaulted by the barnyard odours wafting on the salty breeze from the foredeck, where cows, chickens, sheep and other livestock were kept to supply fresh milk and meat to passengers during the long voyage. Pigs and goats roamed freely, serving as janitors of sorts by munching on garbage.

At least the first-class passengers had access to the deck, where they could walk and take the air. Steerage passengers had no such perks. After boarding, they climbed down ladders into the space between the decks, where they would spend the next weeks or months crammed into narrow berths. If families were lucky, they travelled together, and if women were lucky, they had a bit of privacy, but little was guaranteed. Fresh air came through ventilators and hatches, but the hatches were shut during storms, leaving steerage passengers to cope with their seasickness — and worse — in dark, airless gloom.

But conditions were similar on every packet ship, and Black Ball passengers had to endure them for shorter periods than did passengers on other lines. In its early days of scheduled service, the line ferried travellers between New York and Liverpool in an average of twenty-three days; the return trip (with its less favourable winds) took an average of forty. The company's owners goaded captains into maintaining such speeds with an early form of incentive bonus: any captain who made the run to Liverpool in less than twenty-two days or the return trip in less than thirty-five received a new coat — and a dress for his wife.

It didn't take long for other shipping companies to see the wisdom of Black Ball's approach and launch competing scheduled sailings helmed by equally daredevil skippers. Within a decade, ships evolved to become both faster and more luxurious. In 1823, Black Ball launched the *Canada*, which soon set a record with a fifteen-day, eight-hour sailing to Liverpool. As well as speed, passengers on the *Canada* enjoyed such perks as a dining salon kitted out with mahogany tables.

Speed and onboard amenities were not the only factors that bolstered the popularity of certain ships and lines. In a gossipy small city like New York — in 1820, it had a population of just 152,000 — word got around quickly that certain captains were more personable than others. As a *New York Times* writer looking back on the era in 1891 noted:

> The fastest ship and the most popular Captain secured the largest passenger list. Full cabins were always assured on certain vessels, while other ships commanded by men equally worthy in every particular, but perhaps a little less affable and a little more "salt" had to be content with second place.[22]

But even as the packet ships' captains were competing fiercely for the growing transatlantic passenger trade, a new technology was rapidly evolving that would soon have them taking down their sails forever.

FULL STEAM AHEAD

On August 17, 1807, more than a decade before the *James Monroe* set off on its first scheduled run to Liverpool, another vessel left New York City on a momentous voyage. The *North River Boat*, later known as the *Clermont*, pulled away from the Christopher Street dock that day on its way to Albany, 233 kilometres (145 miles) upriver from Manhattan. Like the more ghoulish spectators at auto races, crowds gathered at the dock in expectation that inventor Robert Fulton's unusual craft would explode. No such mishap took place, however, and the ship arrived safely in Albany the following morning, having maintained a then-startling average speed of 7.2 kilometres (4.5 miles) an hour. It was the world's first workable steamboat.

Fulton immediately tried to capitalize on the publicity by selling tickets for the return trip at $7 a pop — an extravagant rate, more than double what passengers were used to paying to make the same trip by sailing sloop. He managed to sell just two fares. Undaunted, the following month he launched scheduled service to Albany from Manhattan's Cortlandt Street dock. To attract the elite New Yorkers whose approval could mean the difference between success and bankruptcy for this premium service, Fulton spruced up the ship with mahogany-fitted overnight cabins, a deck awning (like those that sheltered river barge passengers in the Low Countries) and a bar. Nothing draws the rich like the promise of luxury, and by 1812 Fulton was running six steamboats. He had also commissioned the *New Orleans*, a larger steamboat, to ply the Mississippi River.

Transferring steam technology to seaworthy vessels, however, would take several more decades of ingenuity. And the honour of developing the first ocean-going steamship would go, not to an American, but to a British genius with the delightful name of Isambard Kingdom Brunel.

Brunel was the chief engineer of the Great Western Railway when he saw the potential of steam-powered transatlantic shipping. He commissioned a wooden ship called, naturally enough, the *Great Western*, powered by a combination of sail and a steam-driven paddlewheel. The ship made the first steam-assisted crossing of the Atlantic in April 1838, taking just fifteen days to reach New York and fourteen days to travel back to Bristol. Unlike later transatlantic shipping magnates, who would come to realize that small numbers of first-class passengers provided cachet but huge volumes of third-class passengers paid the bills, Brunel did not offer steerage tickets on the *Great Western*. Passengers paid a flat rate of thirty guineas for a cabin berth and fifty guineas for a private stateroom, including all meals and wine, while children under thirteen travelled at half price.

For their money, passengers enjoyed a ship with all the modern conveniences of the day, including a grand saloon decorated with Watteau-style murals and supported by Gothic Revival arches. Each cabin had an innovative bell rope to summon the steward — before the *Great Western*, even the most aristocratic passengers had to head into the corridor and bellow for help when they desired the services of their personal assistant. But such amenities came at a price. The steward's fee of £1 10s was additional to the standard ticket, foreshadowing the myriad gratuities cruise ship passengers would find themselves paying to stewards, maître d's and maids more than a century later.

The speedy *Great Western* was a hit, so Brunel quickly commissioned an even bigger ship, the iron-hulled *Great Britain*. Instead of a paddlewheel, the steamship was powered by a screw propeller. She set out on her maiden voyage to New York on July 26, 1845, completing the journey in just fourteen days.

The *Great Britain* was even more luxurious than the *Great Western*, but "luxury" in the puritanical mid-Victorian period meant something a bit different than it does today. Far from whiling away their days being pampered in onboard spas and risking their hard-earned gold in the ship casino, passengers on the *Great Britain* — like those on its competitors — were expected to adhere to well-publicized rules of behaviour. A surviving set of rules from 1849 shows that all passengers were required to get up at seven in the morning unless they had a special dispensation from the ship's surgeon. Passengers then rolled up their beds and swept out their compartments, while a rotating team of five male passengers swept the decks. "Breakfast not to commence till this is done," the rules warned sternly. The sweeping team would also be responsible for cleaning the ladders and sweeping out the dining and hospital rooms over the course of the day. Finally, passengers were expected to be in bed by ten in the evening, pretty much negating any hope of a midnight chocolate buffet.

FLOATING IN THE LAP OF LUXURY

In the course of cutthroat competition for passengers throughout the second half of the nineteenth century, however, ship owners soon realized that the rich and famous had little interest in sweeping their own rooms. Instead, moneyed travellers wanted to spend their weeks at sea in the equivalent of the grand hotels that were beginning to emerge on both sides of the Atlantic. These establishments accustomed travellers to the idea that their days abroad should be spent swaddled in a rich mixture of velvet, satin, marble and potted palms, with their every need anticipated and fulfilled.

Accordingly, transatlantic steamship companies raced to be the first to provide the latest comforts: better food, bigger staterooms, more elegant public areas, even hot running water and electric light. In the early 1870s, the new White Star liner *Oceanic* aggressively boasted of its dining room, which stretched across the full width of the ship and had fireplaces with marble mantels, and of the fact that its first-class staterooms were further from the noisy propeller than top-price quarters on its competitors' ships. In 1884, the *America* became the first transatlantic liner with an overhead glass dome that brought welcome sunlight into its dining room. Later that decade, the *City of New York* and *City of Paris* introduced a small number of suites, where wealthy passengers could relax in their own private sitting room adjacent to their stateroom.

Despite their interest in the finer things in life, passengers were still keenly aware of the dangers ocean travel presented, and shipping companies went to great lengths to reassure them of the safety of their vessels. So it was only a matter of time before one line would announce the construction of a ship that was both opulent and "practically unsinkable."

THE WORLD'S MOST INFAMOUS LINER

An à la carte restaurant managed as a concession by a famous European chef. An indoor pool. A gym with all the latest fitness equipment. A smoking room stocked with the finest cigars. Over the past few years, cruise line PR agents have touted amenities such as these as the newest perks to hit the industry. But, like so many modern tourism purveyors, their memories are short and selective. More than ninety years ago, the world's most infamous passenger liner had all this and more.

When the *Titanic* set sail on its maiden voyage from Southampton to New York on April 10, 1912, its passengers — particularly the 325 people travelling in first class — enjoyed amenities comparable to those of any land-based hotel. There were Turkish baths and massage rooms, shuffleboard courts and a squash court, a library (where passengers could read the ship's newspaper, the *Atlantic Daily Bulletin*) and a photography darkroom. In the evening, gentlemen played cards in the smoking room while their wives took tea in the reading and writing room. Like Type A workaholics frantically e-mailing their offices from extortionately priced Internet cafés at sea today, the *Titanic*'s elite passengers could keep in touch with the rest of the world via Marconigram: the ship's radio operator would transmit their message via Morse code to a land-based telegraph operator, who would create a telegram for delivery by courier.

In 1912, as now, food was an important aspect of any sea voyage. Unlike on today's largely egalitarian cruise ships, however, on the *Titanic* what you ate depended on what class you were travelling in. The 706 third-class passengers, whose one-way fares started at roughly $36.25, ate simple fare such as vegetable soup, boiled potatoes, roast pork and oranges. The 285 second-class passengers, whose fares began at $66, could choose from slightly fancier fare, including spaghetti au gratin and tapioca pudding.

But the chefs pulled out all the stops for the first-class passengers, whose fares ranged from $125 (about one-fifth of the average annual wage in the United States at the time) to $4,500 (almost eight times the price of a Model T). On the last night the *Titanic* was afloat, these high-paying passengers — who included luminaries such as John Jacob Astor and Benjamin Guggenheim — enjoyed roasted squab on cress or filet mignon garnished with foie gras, artichoke hearts and truffle, followed by peaches in chartreuse jelly for dessert.

The fate of the *Titanic* hardly needs retelling; for our purposes, the doomed vessel's significance is its place on the continuum of transatlantic passenger ships stretching from the swift (for their day) packets to the stately, modern-day *Queen Mary 2*.

Around the time the *Titanic* entered the fiercely competitive transatlantic travel business, ship owners had been compelled to decide whether to compete on the basis of speed or comfort. The *Titanic* had not been designed to match the speed records attained a few years earlier by its main competitors, Cunard's *Mauretania* and *Lusitania*. Instead, the ship had been aimed squarely at people who truly believed the clichéd travel slogan that getting there was half the fun. Half a century before jet planes superseded transatlantic liners, people had already begun to associate the sea voyage from North America to Europe with images of leisure and luxury, rather than efficiency. Even though most of the passengers entertained themselves with singalongs in the third-class lounge rather than dancing to the strains of the ship's orchestra in the first-class dining room, the popular imagination cast ships like the *Titanic* as places where one's every wish was fulfilled.

GLAMOUR BETWEEN THE WARS

Three years after the *Titanic* sank, the *Lusitania* was torpedoed by a German U-boat off Ireland, with the loss of 1,195 lives. For American travellers, citizens of a country not yet engaged in the First World War, the waters of the North Atlantic were no longer the carefree playground they had been a few years before. Transatlantic leisure travel sputtered to a virtual halt until hostilities ended. Besides, ocean liners were increasingly being pressed into service as troopships.

Once the war was over, however, the golden age of the transatlantic ocean liner began. Former ocean liners were released from their wartime service and former battleships were converted into passenger vessels. Shipping companies in the victorious Allied countries also purchased liners that had been captured or seized from the losing side, such as the unfinished German liner *Bismarck,* which became White Star's *Majestic.* As historian Paul Fussell once succinctly put it, "After every war ship travel is notably cheap for the victors."

Passenger ships sailed from many ports in Canada and along the Eastern seaboard, but the iconic locus of the North American industry was hyperkinetic Manhattan. Here, the old and new worlds came together, and people began great careers or sailed home in disgrace. A sixteen-year-old English acrobat named Archie Leach attracted no attention when he first stepped off a ship there in 1920; less than two decades later, as debonair Cary Grant, he would draw mobs of photographers and fans to the same piers anytime he travelled to or returned from Europe.

Unlike modern airports, hidden away in cities' distant suburbs, ocean liners came into the heart of the cities they served — in New York, the sleek ships docked on the Hudson River not far from Broadway. "In New York, in the twenties and thirties, you were always conscious of the liners that you saw from your office and apartment windows," novelist Alec Waugh once recalled.

One of the most celebrated vessels was the French Line's *Île de France*, which made its first voyage from Le Havre to New York in 1927. Its list of amenities shows how the range of amusements and facilities on board these floating hotels had continued to expand in the years since the *Titanic* captured the world's attention. In addition to a gothic-style chapel, the *Île de France*'s 1,586 passengers could also enjoy a shooting gallery, a carousel and the largest dining room afloat.

In his 1929 novel *Dodsworth*, Sinclair Lewis chronicles the European vacation of a pair of well-off Midwesterners, Sam and Fran Dodsworth. As the SS *Ultima* steams out of New York, the Dodsworths explore their floating home. There's no shortage of scope for the imagination. Sam "was pricked to imaginativeness, standing outside the wireless room, by the crackle of messages springing across bleak air-roads ocean-bounded to bright snug cities on distant plains."[23] There's a smoking room with a Tudor fireplace, a music room, a swimming pool with Roman pillars — even, reportedly, six Brazilian cougars in shipping crates in the hold.

And then, of course, there are the fellow passengers. As Fran and Sam stroll the decks, they get:

> A racing view of all their companions of the voyage, their fellow-citizens in this brave village amid the desert of waters: strangers to be hated on sight, to be snubbed lest they snub first, yet presently to be known better and better loved and longer remembered than neighbors seen for a lifetime on the cautious land.
>
> Their permanent home, for a week; to become more familiar, thanks to the accelerated sensitiveness which is the one blessing of travel, than rooms paced for years.

Every stippling of soot on the lifeboats, every chair in the
smoking-room, every table along one's own aisle in the
dining salon, to be noted and recalled, in an exhilarated
and heightened observation.[24]

The Dodsworths would never have suspected it, but war would
soon once again overtake the devil-may-care world of the transatlantic liner. Between 1939 and 1945, leisure passenger travel ground
almost to a halt. Anyone heading to Europe on a ship during those
years was likely in uniform.

The Île de France was one of many famous ships pressed into
service in aid of the war effort. After ferrying supplies to Europe
and the Far East in 1940, the liner was rebuilt in New York as a
troopship in 1941. The luxury fittings were removed and the whole
ship repainted battleship grey. Its capacity was also increased sixfold
with the installation of berths for 9,706 soldiers.

GRAND LINERS SAIL INTO THE SUNSET

Once the Second World War was over, travellers were eager to return to normal. When it came to transatlantic ocean liners, however,
things would never be quite the same.

At first, it looked as though these classic voyages would be even
more glamorous than ever before. The Île de France, for instance,
was completely refurbished in a two-year retrofit that decreased its
pre-war passenger capacity by almost two hundred. Yet, as a sign of
these new times, on the redesigned ship there were proportionally
fewer spaces for first-class and third-class passengers (the latter now
euphemistically renamed "tourist class"), while spaces for second-class
("cabin") passengers increased from 408 to 577. The middle-class
takeover of the luxury liner had begun. A 1949 ad promoting the
ship's first post-war passenger voyage appears aimed squarely at this
growing market segment:

Now Paris begins on the reborn "Ile"! For you're in Paris
the moment you cross her gangplank. You sense it in
her Continentally suave atmosphere. You see it in the
elegance of her lovely and airy staterooms, her brilliant
salons and exquisite décor. You savor it in the superb
meals created by the masters of the French cuisine.

This part of the ad flatters potential passengers and appeals to
their aspirational tendencies. Who wouldn't want to be part of a
"Continentally suave atmosphere" and savour the creations of "masters
of the French cuisine"? However, unlike the first-class travellers of
pre-war days, who often learned French in their elite prep or finishing
schools, the new breed of traveller wanted an experience that was
glamorous but not *too* exotic. Thus, the ad goes on to note that there
would be "English-speaking stewards nearby to cater to your every
wish."

Four years later, an ad for American Export Lines' Mediterranean
ships made the point even more bluntly. Under the headline
"Traditional American Friendliness" is a drawing of a group of fresh-
faced kids holding Raggedy Ann dolls, climbing ropes or playing
cowboys and Indians. In the background, a cheerful nurse hovers.
As well as promoting the three playrooms available in cabin (second) class, the ad notes that "easy-going informality" aboard "makes
friendship easy." Far from being exotic, these ships were destinations
for people who didn't like to dress up and who wanted safe playrooms for their growing families.

Despite the promises of both safety and sophistication, however,
ocean liners simply could not compete with the airplane. By 1957,
more people were crossing the Atlantic by air than by ship, the grand
liners of the 1920s and 1930s were showing their age and it didn't
make economic sense to build new ones. Some were retrofitted to
serve as cruise ships. Most met the fate of the *Île de France*, which
made its last transatlantic voyage in 1958, less than a decade after
its hopeful relaunch; a year later, the grand ship was sent to Japan
to be scrapped.

THE CRUISE SHIP INDUSTRY IS BORN

The day of the transatlantic ocean liner might have been waning, but the day of the pleasure cruise ship — where the trip itself was more important than the destination — was just beginning.

Pleasure cruises have been around for some time: in 1929, novelist Evelyn Waugh spent several months researching a guidebook aboard the *Stella Polaris*, a Norwegian cruise ship serving a wide range of Mediterranean ports. While some passengers used the ship as a means of practical transportation, others simply stayed aboard and soaked up the sun.

But the idea of spending one's vacation living aboard ship didn't really become popular until the late 1950s. The boom was due partly to the sudden availability of ocean liners — the *Queen Elizabeth*, for example, was removed from transatlantic service and began providing cruises from New York to the Bahamas in November 1963 — and partly to the rise of mass tourism. Before the war, the number of customers with the time and money to spend on a week at sea had been limited. In the post-war boom economy, millions of people suddenly had legislated vacation time at their disposal and well-paying jobs to fund their vacation dreams.

Bermuda, the Bahamas and the Caribbean were the first destinations for these leisure cruises. The new middle-class tourist still couldn't manage a month in Europe. Such destinations also had the advantage of partial familiarity. On British and US possessions, new travellers could rest easy in the knowledge that the locals would speak their language and that the surroundings wouldn't be too "foreign."

The new cruise industry differed from the transatlantic liners in other ways as well. As their numbers grew, middle-class passengers became increasingly important to ship owners, who eventually realized that their bread-and-butter customers didn't like being relegated to "second-" or even "tourist-" class status. Cunard's *Queen Elizabeth 2* led the way in 1974 when it introduced single-class cruising. No longer would certain passengers on the luxury vessel be barred from particular dining rooms, decks and facilities; everyone would have free run of the ship.

But the idea that a cruise vacation was well in reach of "ordinary" people had already been planted almost two decades earlier when television producers realized that life at sea had a potent fantasy appeal for a wide audience. The result was *The Gale Storm Show* a popular sitcom that ran from 1956 to 1960 and was later syndicated under the title *Oh! Susanna*. Storm played social director Susanna Pomeroy on the SS *Ocean Queen* (which, in real life, was the American President Line ship the *President Cleveland*). As the ship pulled into a different port every week, wacky adventures ensued among the crewmembers, who also included the captain, a steward, the ship's doctor and the proprietor of the ship's beauty salon. The program's direct descendant was a better-known series that ran from 1977 to 1986 with a very similar cast of main characters, supplemented by a purser and a bartender.

A MEGA-INDUSTRY EMERGES

Today, we are used to product placements smuggled into the TV shows we watch, but with *The Love Boat*, ABC launched a product placement for an entire industry. Every week, viewers imagined themselves on a boat where the hip bartender knew their favourite drinks, the cruise director knew their names and there was always room at the captain's table. Cruising wasn't just for rich guys in top hats in anymore.

The show, although not formally designed as an ad campaign, worked spectacularly as one. Princess Cruises, which allowed ABC to use its ships for the series, made *The Love Boat* a key part of its marketing. Although the show can hardly take full credit for the explosive growth of the cruise ship industry — in North America, the number of cruise ship passengers soared from 1.4 million to almost seven million per year between 1980 and 2000 — its popularity certainly didn't hurt the cause.

In 2003, Princess merged with Carnival Cruise Lines to create the world's largest cruise company. By 2006, it was operating 80 ships, with 15 more to come by 2009. And Carnival was far from the only company to boom. In 2004 alone, the North American industry as a whole grew by eight ships and almost twenty-five thousand single beds. That year, 10.85 million people worldwide — more than three-quarters of them Americans — took a cruise ship vacation. A fancy cruise was finally within reach of the average family. Everyone, it seemed, could take a ride on the *Love Boat*.

Of course, by this time, Isaac and Julie and Captain Stubing were long retired. The reason cruising became affordable was that the industry was finally able to benefit from economies of scale. Ships in the *Love Boat* era would have felt cramped with just fifteen hundred people on board. But by the 1980s, cruise ships were starting to swell, almost as if they were gorging on their own midnight buffets.

The first mega-ship was Royal Caribbean's *Sovereign of the Seas*, launched in 1988 with room for 2,800 passengers. From there, the ships kept getting bigger and bigger. Carnival launched a new fleet of ships with room for 3,400 passengers apiece. Royal Caribbean saw Carnival's 3,400 passengers and raised the stakes: *Voyager of the Seas*, launched in 1999, could hold 3,840 passengers.

At one time, the first *Queen Mary* seemed like the monster of the seas, at just over one thousand feet long and weighing 81,237 gross tons. But just as the Empire State Building may still be tall, the *Queen Mary* may still be big, but it is by no means the biggest. Her successor, the *Queen Mary 2*, built in 2003, was the longest, widest and tallest cruise ship ever built, edging past the original at 1,132 feet and weighing in at 151,400 gross tons.

The *QM2* promises "time for all the things you never have time for." Experts from *Condé Nast Traveler*, *Gourmet*, *Architectural Digest*, *Departures* and *The New Yorker* offer seminars on everything from picking out the right wine to mastering the perfect dance floor moves. There are even people from Oxford aboard, if your tastes run to the more esoteric and academic. You can study the Renaissance masters one day, then try your own hand at some watercolours the next.

The *QM2* got off to a gala start, docking at Piraeus for the 2004 Athens Olympics and serving as lodgings for Tony Blair, Jacques Chirac and George W. Bush. But by this time, it was already being displaced in the ooh-and-ah buzz by the *Freedom of the Seas*, a Royal

JUST KEEP MOVING

Today's cruise ships have become so luxurious that people don't just want to enjoy one for a week or two — they want to live aboard one permanently. The *ne plus ultra* of cruise ships is *The World*, a floating condo that takes its wealthy residents (studio apartments start at $825,000, and sizes and prices rise from there) on an endless vacation around the world. Many owners rent out their apartments for at least part of the year to short-term passengers.

As befits a ship that is a literal home away from home, *The World* has a bit more space for people to move around in than does a standard cruise ship. The ship is 644 feet long and has twelve decks, but a passenger capacity of only about two hundred — one-sixth the capacity of a typical budget cruise ship of similar length — meaning that apartment sizes can be much bigger than a standard cruise cabin. Of course, all this room doesn't come cheap. Apartments available in May 2006 ranged in price from $1.3 million to $3.6 million, with maintenance fees extra.

Caribbean vessel that busted the scales at 158,000 gross tons, more than three times that of the *Titanic*. Even that record is headed for a fall, as Royal Caribbean plans to launch its behemoth Genesis-class ships in 2009.

A ship the size of the *Freedom of the Seas* has a lot of room for press-release-worthy features: a water park with a wave pool for simulated surfing, a planetarium, volleyball and basketball courts, a rock climbing wall, a bookstore, even a skating rink. And there is room for 4,370 passengers, more than double the 2,139 people that the original *Queen Mary* could accommodate. That's more drinks than even Isaac the bartender could remember.

Cruise ships still market themselves as affordable luxuries, but the ships are essentially floating factories of fun. There's nothing wrong with fun, of course. But if you're expecting five-star dining, forget it. Writing for *Cruise Industry News Quarterly* in the mid-1990s, Nancy Huie estimated that cruise ships spent an average of $12 per passenger *per day* on food. That's breakfast, lunch, supper and snacks.

Cruise ships also inculcate a slight but palpable fear in their passengers, many of whom are journeying abroad for the first time. Passengers are told which stores are "reputable" and warned away from people offering freelance shore excursions at the piers. As many as eighty percent of passengers will select from the ship-approved list of excursions, but the cost of these sanctioned trips includes the profit margins of all the intermediaries, from the concessionaire to the tour operator, each of whom gets a cut. While more convenient and undoubtedly less risky, these official excursions are also considerably more expensive than a jaunt an adventurous traveller might be able to negotiate privately.

Any modern cruise ship has many ways to separate you from your money, even on an "all-inclusive" trip. Alcohol, for example, is a huge money-earner, especially since about eighty percent of the cost of a drink at the ship's bar is pure profit. You can also lose money at the casino, buy art at the auction, shop in the onboard mall, get framed pictures of yourself, make calls home and treat yourself at the spa and beauty salon. In 2005, Royal Caribbean reported that, in the preceding year, it had made $703 million from ticket revenue, but an extra $261 million from onboard revenue, an increase of $23 million from the year before. In 2006, the news was even better, with the company posting a record profit, despite hurricanes and escalating oil prices.

NEW YORK, AS ALWAYS, MOVES WITH THE TIMES

 In his 1980 book *Abroad*, Paul Fussell wrote a lovely elegy for what must have seemed like the final days of New York as a passenger ship port city.

When you entered Manhattan by the Lincoln Tunnel twenty years ago you saw from the high west bank of the Hudson a vision that lifted your heart and in some measure redeemed the potholes and noise and lunacy and violence of the city. You saw the magic row of transatlantic liners nuzzling the island, their classy, frivolous red and black and white and green uttering their critique of the utility beige-gray of the buildings. In the row might be the *Queen Mary* or the *Queen Elizabeth* or the *Mauretania*, the *United States* or the *America* or the *Independence*, the *Rafaello* or the *Michelangelo* or the *Liberté*. These were the last attendants of the age of travel, soon to fall victim to the jet plane and the cost of oil and the cost of skilled labor.[25]

But the rumours of New York's death as a romantic port city may have been exaggerated. True, few of the new ships simply convey passengers from point A to point B, as the transatlantic liners used to do. But New York was the fourth most popular cruise-ship embarkation port in the United States in 2004, with almost a dozen cruise lines using the five-thousand-foot berths at the New York Cruise Terminal on the Hudson, just a few blocks from Times Square. That year, 845,778 passengers passed through the terminal, nearly a third more than in 2003, and traffic is expected to grow to 1.5 million passengers by 2020. Facilities are also being built on the Hudson to accommodate much larger ships, such as the *Queen Mary 2*, which, in the interim, has had to dock at a former cargo pier in Brooklyn.

All Aboard
OUR ENDURING LOVE AFFAIR WITH TRAINS

*Sam never lost the adventurousness of seeing on
a railway car a sign promising that the train was
going from Paris to Milan, Venice, Trieste, Zagreb,
Vinkovci, Sofia and Stamboul...the names of foreign
towns always beckoned him.*
> — *Sinclair Lewis,* Dodsworth

"Bear!"

The cry echoed up and down the glass-domed Park car, as the train travelled through the Rockies. Instantly, everyone crowded around the picture windows on the right-hand side of the train, and I wondered briefly if the car might tip over from the sudden shift in weight. Then I saw him: a smallish (but large enough, thank you very much) black bear, munching berries near the railroad right of way. Digital cameras beeped, but otherwise silence reigned. We stared at the bear and the bear ignored us. As the clacking wheels of the train passed by, he turned and ambled into the brush.

Both delighted and deflated, we ambled back to our seats. A murmur grew to a dull roar as we discussed the sighting. "Never seen one before...so close to the train...amazing to think they're still in the wild...glad I was on *this* side of the windows!"

I recalled that, earlier in the day, I'd been ensconced in my single bedroom on *The Canadian,* the famous train that hums the rails between Toronto and Vancouver three times a week in each direction. I was fascinated by the roomette, with its ingenious brushed steel fixtures: tiny foldout shelves and coat hooks, a clever reading lamp, a miniature closet and a microscopic bathroom. Best of all, I thought, was the bed, which the steward converted each morning into a small, comfortable divan. Holed up in my little room, I had a private, personal view of the passing Rocky Mountain scene. No tinny rap wafting from the headphones of an iPod halfway down the public car. No children kicking the back of my seat. And no fellow passengers attempting to strike up a conversation.

It's not that I'm a misanthrope. I like people. In general, I love meeting strangers on vacation. But I have rather bad luck with seatmates on public transportation. Not quite as bad as Farley Granger's in the 1951 Hitchcock movie *Strangers on a Train*, who has the spectacularly bad fortune of running into a sociopathic killer. But bad enough.

The worst example was a bus trip I took to Montreal as a university student. For two solid hours, my seatmate described his artistic career in minute detail. He specialized in pictures of pigs, and confided late in the trip that he'd love to paint my portrait.

So, when offered the opportunity to spend part of my trip in glorious isolation in my cozy roomette, I jumped at the chance.

There were, however, drawbacks to that plan. After my morning in the roomette, I went to the dining car.

"Did you see that moose?" someone asked me over lunch.

"Moose?" I'd spent ages gazing out my private picture window. "No."

"Big one. Not very far from the train. You couldn't miss it."

I must have been reading my book or in the bathroom, I mumbled, achingly disappointed. How could I have missed it?

That's the problem with privacy in travel. It's relaxing. It's quiet. It's blessedly free of pig portraitists. But you do miss something when not travelling with a group. The eagle eyes in the Park car — a carriage with big windows and a glass dome designed specifically to give passengers a great view of the landscape — would have made certain I didn't miss the moose.

After lunch, I foreswore my private digs and headed to the Park car. And, in the company of others, I saw more than I would have alone. When all is said and done, the company is still one of the greatest advantages of train travel over car travel. I think that's why the romance of the rails will never truly die. A plane will get you between two places faster, and a car will do so more conveniently.

But the modern long-distance train is a more communal experience. And meeting new people is half the fun of travel — even for a quasi-hermit like me.

BRITANNIA RULED THE RAILS

I spotted my bear on the second of two transcontinental routes that opened up the Canadian West to settlement. Railroads in the United States, Australia and other New World countries played similarly vital roles in connecting wild, sparsely populated land masses. Despite its importance to the New World, however, the passenger train — like so many Industrial Revolution innovations — was an Old World invention.

It didn't get off to a glorious start. September 15, 1830, was to be the grand opening day of the Liverpool and Manchester Railway, the first railway in the world to carry both passengers and freight. As would later be the case with air travel, passengers were very much an afterthought in the early days of rail.

It was a cold, rainy day, but that didn't stop crowds of the curious from gathering at Oldfield Lane in Manchester to watch for the arrival of the mighty locomotive carrying Napoleonic War hero the Duke of Wellington. Huddled on the cloth-covered benches of the temporary reviewing stands were the rich and famous, including actress Fanny Kemble and an assortment of lords and business magnates. Milling about the surrounding area were thousands of workers and farmers, who did not have the special cards that admitted the powerful to the reviewing stands.

The scheduled time for the arrival of the festive procession came and went, but no train arrived. Skeptics in the crowd began to tell anyone who would listen that this whole passenger railway idea was rubbish and poppycock. Then, a lone engine, the *Northumbrian*, steamed along the track.

The spectators were puzzled. Where were the other cars? Where was the duke? Was this it? Bad show, if it was.

The engine stopped just long enough to pick up a surgeon, then headed back down the track. The bad news quickly spread: William

Huskisson, MP for Liverpool and prominent supporter of rail expansion, had fallen under the wheels of the new train and been grievously injured (he would die later that night). By the time the Duke of Wellington finally arrived, borne on a huge railway car festooned with red velvet and waving sombrely to the crowd, a bit of the fizz had gone out of the festivities.

It really wasn't the sort of thing to give the average traveller much confidence in rail, and promoters quickly realized they needed celebrity endorsement to overcome public reluctance to travelling on the "dangerous" machines. They scored an early coup when Prince Albert travelled by train as he courted Queen Victoria, but the icing on the cake came in 1842, when the twenty-three-year-old queen herself deigned to travel by rail, from Slough to London. At the engine's controls was none other than our old friend, Isambard Kingdom Brunel. Nervous commentators worried that the queen shouldn't risk her life on such a dangerous contraption, but Victoria liked the trip so much she took the train back to Slough and brought along the infant Prince of Wales. If it was safe enough for a royal baby, many observers concluded, it was safe enough for them.

Their optimism was a bit premature. Although the queen and prince travelled in style, for ordinary passengers, train travel could be a harrowing experience. Passenger carriages weren't even required to have roofs or seats until 1844, when Gladstone's government passed a law to that effect. Before cars were enclosed, passengers were showered with soot and sparks from the smoky locomotive. Carriages that did have roofs were often drafty, unheated and candlelit. Early brakes were prone to failure and couplings had an annoying habit of becoming uncoupled, leading to a series of serious accidents. Early cars were simply chained together, so that when the train stopped and started, passengers were tossed about like the bridge crew on the Starship *Enterprise*.

There were other dangers. In December 1879, the world's longest railway bridge — a brand new span over the Tay River in Scotland — collapsed as a train was traversing it during a storm.

Despite the risks and discomfort, however, increasing numbers of passengers were travelling by rail. By 1848, Britons were taking 100 million train trips a year; half a century later, that figure cracked one billion. And although many of those excursions were commuter or business jaunts, tourists were responsible for a significant number of journeys. As early as the 1840s, large parties of leisure travellers were journeying by train from the Midlands to nearby coastal areas.

It can't be disputed that the British got the passenger rail industry rolling. But to understand the next stage in its expansion, we need to look into developments on the other side of the Atlantic.

BIG COUNTRIES, BIG IDEAS

The first American steam passenger train, the *Best Friend of Charleston*, took 141 people on a six-mile trip on Christmas Day 1830, a few months after the Liverpool and Manchester Railway staged its unlucky opening ceremonies. Within a decade, the US had more than 4,400 kilometres (2,800 miles) of track; by 1861, those numbers had climbed to 48,000 kilometres (30,000 miles), spurred by government subsidies. By 1869, travellers could go by rail all the way to the Pacific coast, and in the 1880s, an additional 112,000 kilometres (70,000 miles) of track were laid. The years from 1880 through 1920 were the heyday of American railroads. In 1910, for example, about 95 percent of all intercity traffic travelled by rail, and by 1920 Americans were taking 1.2 billion passenger trips a year.

In Canada, the colony of British Columbia wouldn't agree to join the fledgling confederation until the feds in Ottawa promised to build the Canadian Pacific Railway. The job took ten years and was mired in corruption, but the Last Spike was hammered in at Craigellachie, BC, on November 7, 1885. The new railway both literally and metaphorically tied the huge, empty country together. Canadians have been in awe of the achievement ever since.

Along with hockey, "eh?" and beer commercials, the CPR has become part of the Canadian *Zeitgeist*. In fact, on January 1, 1967, it scored a rare Canadian-identity hat trick when the CBC (first point) commissioned ubiquitous folkie Gordon Lightfoot (second point) to write "The Canadian Railroad Trilogy" as part of its year-long celebrations of Canada's Centennial (three points and the crowd goes wild!).

Lightfoot's song perfectly captures the emotion that pops up
again and again in nineteenth-century accounts — the feeling that
the railway represented a watershed between the pre-industrial past
and the exciting future. "We gotta lay down the tracks and tear up
the trails," he sings, going on to observe that the railroad would
bring new energy to the Prairies in a way that older, slower modes
of transportation just couldn't.[26]

All that enthusiasm, though, didn't mean that the average
nineteenth-century passenger rail trip was a journey in the lap of
luxury.

GETTING THERE WAS NOT HALF THE FUN

In the years since Gladstone first required railroads to provide roofs
and seats for their passengers, train technology had improved immensely. George Westinghouse had invented the air brake, and others
had developed shock absorbers and mechanisms to reduce derail-
ments. But throughout the nineteenth century and into the twentieth,
train travel could still be unpredictable and unpleasant.

Kate Field, an American journalist travelling through Spain in the
1870s, caught a train from Santander to Madrid with just moments
to spare and settled gratefully into a small railway car called a coupé.
Due to a previous altercation with a customs inspector, her trunks
had been confiscated and she was travelling with all her possessions
tied up in large bundles. Not surprisingly, she had no intention of
moving anywhere once she had ensconced herself in the coupé.
Unfortunately, she didn't have the proper ticket. In desperation, she
asked one of the train officials if she could book the whole coupé,
but that didn't work out so well: "The polite young man sat down
and did sums for ten minutes, at the end of which time he presented
a bill that staggered my intellect and frightened my purse."[27]

Despite her offer to pay for the whole carriage, the conductor
assumed Field was poor because of her ersatz luggage. "Yes, a woman
is known by her trunks," Field commented acerbically. The clerk's
assumption worked in her favour, however; he took pity on her

and allowed her to stay in the coupé until a carriage specifically earmarked for single women travellers was added to the train, and then he helped her move all her bundles there.

Aside from bureaucratic hassles, train travel was fraught with mechanical difficulties, such as those that beset immigrant Frank Rowbottom on a trip to Saskatchewan in late 1906. His woes began with a slow start leaving Winnipeg:

> Boarded train at C.N. station just after 8.30, but she did not move out until about 11.30...The engines on this line are continually "drying" as they call it here, that is, the steam gives out and then the whole affair freezes up, causing a delay of something like 8 hours until fires are again lighted and everything thawed. Fortunately our engine did not die this journey, but the one in front had died two or three times in a 24 hour journey.

Later in the trip, he found accommodations on the train through Saskatchewan less than ideal but maintained a stiff upper lip:

> Caught the 8:30 train for Marshall and prepared for the most trying part of the journey, for we could not get sleeping berths without paying a great deal for them, so had to extemporize a couch for the little ones at night as well we could, and sit up ourselves. The train was very crowded, which made it still more unpleasant.[28]

A few years later, a traveller named Teresa Girardi had less-than-fond memories about travelling on the Coal Branch line of the Grand Trunk Pacific between Edson and Mountain Park, Alberta, during the First World War:

> The train, it must be a museum coach now — old wooden coach, wooden slat seats, coal oil lamps nailed to brackets on coach walls, and an old wood and coal stove for heat.

If you wanted air in the coach, the brakeman would come along with a long handled stick with a hook on the end to open the vent in top of the coach. I won't forget that as I still have the scar from one of the vent windows which was jerked too hard, fell out and crashed down and the glass cut my arm.[29]

As in the days of the Grand Tour *diligences*, over-exuberant passengers could also make the journey trying for folks who liked a bit of peace and quiet. An anonymous New Englander travelling on the Quebec Central Railway in the 1880s noted with tight-lipped Yankee reserve that his fellow passengers "show a strong desire to express themselves in song."[30]

Given the undeniable discomforts of rail travel, it isn't surprising that one bright entrepreneur would build a better train carriage, hoping that the railroads and the wealthy would beat a path to his door. But if it hadn't been for the untimely death of a president, George Mortimer Pullman might have gone bankrupt in the attempt.

PAMPERING ON THE RAILS

When Abraham Lincoln was assassinated on April 14, 1865, Pullman knew a good promotional opportunity when he saw one.

Pullman had had a chequered career to that point. He had sold cabinets in New York state, devised a system to build new foundations under existing buildings in fast-growing Chicago and run a ranch and various other enterprises in Colorado. In between, he'd developed some rudimentary sleeping cars for trains, but passenger indifference and the Civil War put a crimp in those ventures. Pullman refused to give up on the idea, though. After racking up a reported $20,000 in profits in Colorado, he returned to Chicago partway through the war and sank every cent into developing a luxurious sleeping car that would far outstrip the uncomfortable cars currently on the rails.

It took Pullman a year to build the car, which he christened the *Pioneer*. With its panelled interior, silver-trimmed lamps and thick red carpets, it was more like a room in a Victorian mansion than a train car. The only problem was that railroad companies deemed it too tall, too wide and too heavy for existing railroad tracks. Pullman realized to his horror that he had built a very expensive failure.

Then John Wilkes Booth fired his fateful shot at Ford's Theatre. Lincoln's widow decided he would be buried in Springfield, Illinois, and a slow cortege train was arranged to bear the president's body westward from Washington. Pullman offered to donate use of the *Pioneer* to carry dignitaries through Illinois to the funeral. The historical record differs on whether the car was actually attached to the funeral train itself in Chicago or to a separate train headed to Springfield for the ceremony. Lincoln's widow and son may even have used it for the 480 kilometres (300 miles) from Chicago to Springfield.

Part of the problem is that Pullman was an inveterate publicity hound, and his claims about who was aboard and when may have been inconsistently embellished. After all, the man was trying to drum up interest in a $20,000 white elephant and thus avoid bankruptcy; it wouldn't be surprising if he exaggerated a tad.

In any case, the car's inaugural run brought *some* combination of VIPs to Springfield to join a national day of mourning that was the focus of intense media coverage. The event proved that Pullman's car — which, after all, was only a foot wider and two feet higher than other railcars — could be carried perfectly well on existing tracks, although a few tunnels might have to be widened just to be on the safe side.

Railroad magnates, it turned out, weren't sticklers for accuracy. They knew the *Pioneer* had played some role in the Lincoln funeral. They'd seen pictures of its luxurious interior. And now, finally, they wanted a piece of the action. Orders for Pullman cars flooded in. Most of Pullman's customers were railroads, but Pullman and his competitors also began crafting immensely opulent private carriages for Victorian royals, celebrities and business titans.

ALL THE COMFORTS OF HOME

In 1869, the London and North Western Railway built a private saloon car for Queen Victoria. To modern eyes, it looked more like the interior of a casket than a comfortable sitting room. Walls, chairs and an ornate sofa were upholstered in royal blue. Swagged blue drapes were suspended beneath fringed blue pelmets. Crystal floor lamps and wall sconces shed light on a richly patterned red carpet. The piece de resistance was the ceiling, completely upholstered in ivory silk.

Less noble personalities soon followed the queen's lead. For her 1881 tour across the United States, opera diva Adelina Patti travelled in a private car appointed in satin and leather, with a hand-carved piano and leopard-skin rugs. As the train crossed the Midwest, Patti requested frequent stops so that her three chefs could jump out and hunt prairie chickens for her dinner.

In the same decade, English actress Lillie Langtry toured the US in a private railroad car called the *Lalee*. The car included a salon, a bedroom with padded silk walls, a maid's room, a pantry, a kitchen and a bathroom, the latter equipped with solid silver fixtures. The brocade for the salon walls was specially commissioned in France, and the outside of the car was painted blue with gold and white lilies.

Railroad executives, not surprisingly, were some of the most enthusiastic purchasers of private cars, which allowed them to survey their sprawling holdings in relative comfort. Secretaries would board the train laden down with boxes of correspondence, to which the busy president would dictate replies as the train chugged across the open prairie. At each station stop, the secretary would pick up important new messages for the boss at the telegraph office.

In his memoirs, D.B. Hanna, the first president of Canadian National Railways, imagined how a Saskatchewan farmer might feel on encountering a well-lit private car on a siding on a cold October night.

to reach Brindisi almost a day earlier than Nagelmackers' trains. By then, Nagelmackers was surely ready to throw in the towel — until he met a big-talking American named Colonel William d'Alton Mann.

Mann's career had been even more chequered than Pullman's. He'd dabbled in oil speculation, politics and publishing, and become a colonel in the Union Army before settling on building railroad cars. Deciding to go head to head with Pullman, he claimed that his "boudoir cars" were more spacious and comfortable than Pullman's "palace cars." Unfortunately for Mann, Pullman responded to the upstart manufacturer by slashing his prices. Pullman won that battle, and Mann started looking for better prospects abroad. On a trip to England he met Nagelmackers, and the two briefly formed a partnership. The Belgian soon bought out his somewhat disreputable partner (who moved back to the States to become a celebrity blackmailer) and formed a new venture, the Compagnie Internationale des Wagons-Lits.

The new firm continued, however, to look to America for inspiration. Pullman had introduced his first dining car in 1867, so that passengers could enjoy fine, fresh cuisine rather than gnawing on whatever they could scrounge during quick stops at remote stations. Nagelmackers followed suit, commissioning Europe's first custom-built restaurant car in 1881. Two twelve-seat salons with padded leather walls enclosed a kitchen with a coal-fired stove and a cold-storage pantry. As well as pampering passengers, the dining car allowed Nagelmackers to reduce the number of station stops. His trains were suddenly faster *and* more pleasant than his competitors'.

He was now ready for his next luxury venture, the *Orient Express*, which officially debuted on October 4, 1883. Between Paris and Giurgi, Romania, passengers rode in comfort in luxury carriages, but after that things got a bit dicey. After crossing the Danube by ferry, they transferred to creaky old Austrian coaches for a bumpy ride across what is now Bulgaria, then boarded a ship in Varna for a queasy eighteen-hour trip across the Black Sea and through the Bosporus to Constantinople.

Nobody seems to have complained, though. Fashionable Parisians crowded into the Gare de l'Est to wave the train on its way. Passengers, including the Paris correspondent for *The Times* (a man with the memorable handle Henri Opper de Blowitz), stuffed themselves with fine food and wine, enjoyed concerts by Hungarian minstrels and a meeting with King Charles of Hohenzollern and relaxed in private compartments with two benches that converted into bunks. Nagelmackers didn't skimp on a single detail; unlike most hoteliers of the period, he even provided soap.

By the end of the 1880s, Wagon-Lits had negotiated an all-land route to Constantinople, avoiding the inconvenient journey across the Black Sea. And, contrary to popular belief, the firm ran many other "Orient Express" routes besides the famous one from Paris to Constantinople, serving much of eastern Europe.

In the years to come, the *Orient Express* and Wagon-Lits would play some curious roles in the public imagination. On November 11, 1918, the Armistice ending the First World War would be signed in a Wagon-Lits car in Compiègne, France. More than two decades later, Hitler's troops extracted the car from a museum and brought it to the same spot to receive France's 1940 surrender during the Second World War. The SS blew it up in 1945 so that the Allies wouldn't get the bright idea to use it to accept the German capitulation at war's end.

The *Orient Express* was also immortalized in a number of books and movies. Graham Greene throws together passengers ranging from a chorus girl to a socialist agitator in his 1932 book *Stamboul Train*. In the 1934 Agatha Christie novel *Murder on the Orient Express*, detective Hercule Poirot grills passengers on a snowbound train. In 1957's *From Russia With Love*, Ian Fleming has James Bond escape Istanbul on the *Orient Express* with a Russian decoder and a beautiful girl (of course). Along with movies of the latter two books, there is the 1938 Hitchcock film *The Lady Vanishes* (based on a 1936 novel) and the 1979 Sherlock Holmes flick *The Seven Percent Solution*.

TIME CHANGE

To describe the next major influence of the railroads on the wider culture, one has to backtrack a bit. In the first fifty years of passenger railroads, the trains rarely ran on time. This fact was annoying enough for VIPs, but they could simply open their wallets and extend their stay at a nearby hotel. Those on meagre budgets, however, would likely weather the delay on a hard station bench. Looking back on Canadian train travel in the late 1800s, a cleric named James Carmichael remarked without regret:

> The day has passed when express trains pulled up to allow officials to pick blackberries or to "liquor up," when travellers waited five to ten hours at leading stations, or built up fires in a box stove in the waiting-room of a way station, or lay full-stretched on a form, with a portmanteau for a pillow.[33]

Fruit-loving, alcoholic railway executives may well have been part of the reason behind the delays, but a more influential factor was that each town kept its own time, based on the position of the sun. When the sun was directly overhead, it was noon, and all other times of day were calculated from that point. People synchronized their own watches from a central clock, positioned on a town hall or church steeple.

This wasn't a problem when the fastest travel speed widely available to humans was the pace of a fast horse. When Paul Revere galloped from Boston to Lexington, it didn't matter that the clock in Lexington was a few minutes off the one in Boston. No one was on a schedule, and revolutionaries had bigger things on their mind than synchronizing their watches.

But when trains started moving goods and people at speeds of twenty-nine kilometres (eighteen miles) an hour and more, things got a bit confusing. Passengers wanted to be certain they could make their connections, which was a particularly thorny issue when they needed to navigate a welter of competing railways for any long-distance journey. Even more important, railway employees needed to have an accurate estimate of the arrival and departure times of various trains, to avoid delays and accidents.

And yet a train passenger making a trip from New York to Boston in the 1860s needed to move his watch twelve minutes ahead when alighting in Beantown. Similarly, someone travelling from Montreal to Toronto would need to set his watch back by twenty-five minutes upon arrival. Some frequent travellers coped with the problem by travelling with multiple watches, each set to the local time in major cities they were due to pass through. Jewellers even sold watches with multiple faces.

A few small countries addressed the issue by imposing a single time zone on the whole nation. Britain was the first to try it and, not surprisingly, railways led the way: the Great Western Railway was the first to impose Greenwich Mean Time on all its schedules, in November 1840. Most other British railways adopted the system by the end of that decade, and many public clocks were set to GMT by the end of the 1850s. Not everyone was thrilled with the loss of local autonomy, however. One of the clocks at Oxford University was fitted with two minute hands, one to show GMT and one to show local time. The legal system clung to the local time concept until 1880, when a national law forced it to catch up to the rest of the country.

If the concept was a hard sell in Britain, it was an almost impossible sell internationally, as a Canadian engineer would soon find out.

Sandford Fleming was something of a renaissance man. By the age of thirty, he had already invented an inline skate, founded a scientific society called the Royal Canadian Institute and designed Canada's first adhesive postage stamp (the Threepenny Beaver). He went on to become one of Canada's leading surveyors and engineers, working for a variety of Canadian railways, including the CPR. So, when he missed a train in the west of Ireland in 1876 due to inconsistent, conflicting timetables, he decided he was the man to address the issue head on — a decision that would see him branded a communist, among other things.

Within a few years, Fleming developed a basic proposal for a system of international time zones based on meridians of longitude. The world would be divided into twenty-four equal portions, each fifteen degrees wide, and everyone within each portion would set their clocks to the same hour. Simple, really, when you think about it.

Except for the fact that people were really, really attached to their local time zones. Fleming's proposal was seen as yet another example in a long line of scientifically rational but emotionally cold ideas that had transformed noble farm labourers into sooty factory workers and charming villages into urban slums. Sure, it was progress, but did we really want progress? More to the point, did we really want to cooperate with all those other countries? Remember, this was long before the League of Nations was a glint in Woodrow Wilson's eye.

Despite legions of doubting Thomases, Fleming persisted, and in late 1883, several major North American railroads adopted his plan. The following year, delegates to the International Prime Meridian Conference in Washington, DC, finally agreed to the proposal, and on January 1, 1885, standard time came into effect.

Of course, ever since then, "standard" time has been anything but standard. Some jurisdictions adopt variations such as daylight savings time (even as their neighbours, such as renegade Saskatchewan, abstain). Others insist on distinctions of less than an hour. Newfoundland Time is half an hour later than Atlantic Time. People in Nepal set their clocks fifteen minutes ahead of their neighbours in India, who themselves are just half an hour ahead of the folks in Pakistan. And some countries refuse to have anything to do with time zones at all — China, which by strict geographical standards should have at least four, maintains a single time zone across the country. So much for those Victorian claims that international standard time was a "communist" notion.

In a tourism-related crisis that Fleming could hardly have been expected to foresee, a fracas broke out among various South Pacific islands in the late 1990s over which speck of land could claim the distinction of being the first place to witness the dawning of the new millennium in 2000 (which, technically, would not dawn until 2001, but I am *not* delving into that battle).

The problem was the International Date Line, which has a nasty habit of zigzagging in that part of the ocean. In particular, at the time, it cut right through the assorted islands of the tiny nation of Kiribati, with some islands on either side. In late 1994, Kiribati announced that its islands on *both* sides of the date line would observe the later date that until then had been observed only by islands west of the line. It claimed the decision was based on administrative convenience — after all, it was a bit awkward to have two different dates observed in different parts of the country — but it seems likely that the government must have also sensed a potential tourism bonanza. So, with one sweep of a bureaucratic pen, an uninhabited bit of Kiribati called Caroline Island would be the first place on earth — aside from an even more inaccessible section of eastern Antarctica — to see daylight in the twenty-first century. Kiribati, in a bit of savvy branding, renamed the spot Millennium Island.

Needless to say, this hijacking of the End of Days didn't sit well with some of Kiribati's island neighbours, such as New Zealand's Antipodes Island (which had dibs on first place until Kiribati started messing with the meridian) and Tonga (whose long-time tourist slogan was "the place where time begins"). As competition seemed poised to get truly ugly, calmer heads prevailed and a South Pacific Millennium Consortium was set up to promote New Year's Eve travel to the entire region. After all, what are a few minutes between island friends?

IMPORTING THE TOURISTS

The long-term consequences of railroad innovation range far beyond time zones. In an effort to keep their trains filled, late-nineteenth-century railroad magnates almost single-handedly created tourist industries in thinly populated areas across North America.

Take the CPR, for instance. It did a booming trade in moving settlers into the Prairies, but by the time its trains reached the Rockies, passenger numbers had dwindled significantly. After all, why would anyone go to the mountains? In Canada, the concept of the long vacation was still in its infancy, and the Romantics' fascination with travelling to wild landscapes had never really caught on. In the 1880s, the vast majority of Canadians *lived* amid wild scenery. They had little interest in spending a lot of money to see more of it.

CPR general manager William Cornelius Van Horne set out to change that mindset. As he famously put it, "If we can't export the scenery, we will import the tourists."[34]

Between fall 1886 and early 1887, the railway opened three "dining station stops" along mountain sections of the line, where train travellers could stretch their legs and get a meal before clambering back aboard. Each stop also offered half a dozen guest rooms. Moreover, the stations solved a logistical problem for the CPR: the fact that the dining cars were too heavy to be moved along the steep grades through the Kicking Horse and Rogers passes.

But Van Horne had more grandiose ideas. For decades, huge railway hotels had been springing up in cities near the termini of major rail lines. People in transit needed somewhere to stay, after all, and railway magnates were only too happy to squeeze a few extra dollars from them at the beginning and end of their trips. Indeed, the CPR's first hotel, the Hotel Vancouver, fit this mould, opening at the railway's western terminus in 1886. The genius of Van Horne — and a few other North American entrepreneurs, as we shall see — was to build large hotels in isolated places, as destinations in themselves. Van Horne primed the pump by commissioning advertising billboards in eastern Canadian cities with corny slogans like "Said the Prince to the Duke: 'How high we live on the CPR'."

The first link in the CPR resort chain was the castle-like Banff Springs Hotel in Alberta, which opened on June 1, 1888. As the old saying goes, location is everything in real estate, and the Banff Springs had snagged one of the best spots in the Canadian Rockies: ringed by mountains, at the conjunction of two rivers, with a convenient hot spring to draw long-stay guests. Inspired by the architecture of Loire Valley chateaux, New York architect Bruce Price created a solid stone building replete with towers and pitched roofs that initially provided luxurious accommodation for 250 guests (the hotel now has 770 guest rooms). The Banff Springs set the standard that the chain's other hotels — such as the nearby Chateau Lake Louise, built two years later — would soon follow.

The company also continued to show a flair for picking great locations; its Chateau Frontenac, on a promontory overlooking the St. Lawrence River in Quebec City, eventually would become the city's best-known landmark.

And if someone got to the best site first, the company wasn't shy about buying them out. In 1903, CPR purchased the Algonquin, a luxury resort on the Bay of Fundy in New Brunswick, and in 1970 it acquired a huge hunting lodge on the Ottawa River between Ottawa and Montreal and transformed it into the Chateau Montebello.

THE INVENTION OF THE SUNSHINE STATE

On the other side of the continent, another entrepreneur was using rail to open up a completely different sort of tourist landscape.

Henry Morrison Flagler first saw Florida as a tourist. Flagler, one of the founders of Standard Oil, had by that time made a fortune trading grain and salt as well as petroleum. But none of his money had been sufficient to cure his wife Mary's tuberculosis, and their doctor suggested an extended visit to warmer climes for her health. The Flaglers arrived in Florida in 1878, but the trip did not succeed — Mary died in 1881.

Two years later, Flagler returned to the state for a honeymoon with his second wife, Ida. He quickly realized that Florida wasn't particularly well set up for the convenience of tourists. There were few hotels, and railroads ran on a variety of gauges, requiring travellers to switch trains frequently. Sensing that large numbers of snow-weary northerners might someday be captivated by the idea of spending the winter surrounded by palm trees and orange groves, Flagler set about remedying both problems.

His first step was to buy the Jacksonville, St. Augustine and Halifax Railroad in 1885. He then hired two up-and-coming architects, John Merven Carrère and Thomas Hastings, to create a grand 540-room hotel in St. Augustine. It was the opportunity of a lifetime for Carrère and Hastings, who would go on to design such famous Manhattan landmarks as the New York Public Library. Drawing on Florida's Spanish heritage, they designed the Hotel Ponce de León as a festive confection of cloisters, fountains and arcades. From the moment it opened in 1888, the place was a magnet for the rich and famous. Novelist Henry James declared it "the most amusing of hotels."

In the meantime, Flagler was busily extending his railroad south. In the 1890s, to give his leisure passengers somewhere new to visit, he developed two luxury hotels in the new resort community of Palm Beach. The grounds of his 1,150-room Hotel Royal Poinciana, once the world's largest wooden structure, sprawled so widely that employees ferried guests around on bicycle-propelled rickshaws. The Palm Beach Inn, meanwhile, set such a standard for luxury that it survives today as The Breakers.

Gilded Age New Yorkers, never slow to spot a trend that benefited them, soon decided that "wintering" in Palm Beach was a very civilized thing to do. By 1903, there were enough moneyed folk in town that Flagler and his third wife decided to hold a "Bal Poudré" at their Palm Beach mansion to mark George Washington's birthday. The *New York Herald* proclaimed the event "one of the most sumptuous social affairs ever attempted south of Washington." Palm Beach has been synonymous with the idle rich at play ever since.

Flagler, however, was far from idle. Throughout the 1890s he continued to extend his railroad, to allow visitors to conveniently travel further and further south. In the small outpost of Fort Dallas, he built another hotel and supported the development of roads, churches, a school, a hospital, a power company and a newspaper. Grateful citizens wanted to rename the newly incorporated city "Flagler," but in a burst of modesty he convinced them to name it after the river that flowed through town. The townsfolk agreed, and "Miami" it became — one of the modern world's first major cities founded to support tourism.

At first, Miami grew so quickly that tourist facilities were rudimentary. As late as the 1920s, *Vogue* writer Viola Tree reported that there was no proper railway station ("they have not had time for one") and that piles of chopped-down palm trees littered the streets of the still-small town. "Flagler Street is nothing but eating shops, real estate offices, and a few Riviera shops for pretty clothes, stockings and bags," she noted. She added, however, "The big hotel never ceases to charm you by the iced water which you drink out of cups you throw away."[35]

Mildly obsessed with expansion, Flagler soldiered on. His *coup de grâce* was an engineering marvel few doubted could succeed: a series of bridges that finally brought his railroad to Key West, the tip of the United States, in 1912. For this accomplishment, Tree, who took the train from Key West to Miami, had nothing but praise: "[Y]ou are flung into a train over a chain of islands threaded like beads on to the steel thread of the line. A scientific triumph, pictorial in itself — chemical, wonderful, mechanical."[36]

THE GLORIOUS TWILIGHT OF LONG-DISTANCE RAIL TRAVEL

It must have seemed in the early twentieth century as if there was nowhere to go but up for the railroads. In the two decades between 1896 and 1916, US passenger rail traffic tripled. But little did railroad owners know that their industry had already crossed a watershed. Within a few years, as automobile sales soared, passenger rail traffic would plummet by 18 percent.

The railroads rallied bravely. If they couldn't beat the automobile for convenience, they'd try to trump it with glamour. In 1934, the Burlington, Chicago and Quincy line's new streamlined diesel train *Zephyr* wowed crowds at the Century of Progress Exhibition in Chicago. Not only was the train the "star" of a Hollywood movie, *The Silver Streak;* on its maiden trip between Denver in Chicago, it made the trip in thirteen hours, cutting the travel time of its steam-train predecessor almost in half. Everything from cigarette lighters to buildings aped the futuristic shape of the *Zephyr*. Train travel was once again both practical and cool. Under the New Deal, the federal government helped rail companies switch from steam to diesel and passenger traffic rebounded somewhat. But by 1939, numbers were still just half of what they had been in 1920.

The Second World War saw a leap in rail traffic across North America, as soldiers travelled by train to camps and embarkation points around the country. If private citizens could even get a seat, they faced crowded conditions and equipment that was getting more outdated by the day, as resources were poured into more important military materiel. As Frank Lapointe, a CNR employee, recalled:

> They'd brought out a lot of stuff that had been stored for years. Some of the engines were antiques. Breakdowns were pretty frequent, but we tried to do the best we could. It was real busy. The freight trains were running. Freight and passenger cars were coming all the time from the west. Everything was crowded.[37]

But this short-term boom would prove to be part of the railroads' undoing. Washington slapped a 15 percent tax on rail travel for the duration of the war, to discourage private trips and leave seats free for the military. The government didn't get around to lifting the tax completely until 1962, and by that point, federal spending on inter-state freeways and airports had left the railroads in the dust. But the age of cross-country train travel had one last, glamorous cinematic gasp in Alfred Hitchcock's 1959 classic, *North By Northwest*.

When Cary Grant's Roger Thornhill flees the New York police and sets out to track down a mysterious stranger in Chicago, he dismisses the idea of flying. On a plane, he tells his mother in a phone conversation, the risk is too great that someone will recognize him. For some reason — likely plot convenience — he doesn't consider driving. His last option is the train — not just any train, but the fabled *20th Century Limited*, which had already had a moment of movie fame in the 1934 screwball comedy *Twentieth Century*.

Inaugurated in 1902, the express train between New York and Chicago literally treated its passengers like royalty. At each station, a special red carpet would be rolled out for the well-heeled passengers, a custom that can be traced all the way back to the fifth-century BC Greek play *Agamemnon*, (when Agamemnon returns from his travels, his subjects unfurl a crimson carpet for his regal feet). The *20th Century Limited* offered a range of perks designed to lure people away from cramped cars and dusty highways, including an on-board

barbershop, a telegraph operator, elegant dining, and valet and secretarial services.

In Hitchcock's movie, the train seems to have magical charm.
First of all, Roger manages to dodge a series of rather inept cops.
Then, within minutes of boarding, he encounters sultry Eve Kendall
(Eva Marie Saint), who proceeds to throw herself at him with very
un-1950s' abandon. (In a related miracle, their double-entendre laced
dialogue made it past the Hays Office censors.) After foregoing a meal
in the lovely dining car, Roger spends the rest of the trip — including
the night, gasp! — hiding out in Eve's enormous "drawing room."
After various travails, the now-married lovers end up back aboard
the *20th Century Limited*, and the movie ends with the now-famous
cliché of the train shooting into a tunnel as the newlyweds turn out
the lights.

Watching this film makes me long to spend a week on the rails in
style. For years, it was difficult. The *20th Century Limited* was put out
to pasture on December 2, 1967. The original Paris-Istanbul run of
the *Orient Express* expired a decade later. VIA Rail's grand *Canadian*,
inaugurated in 1955, soldiered on, but in the face of schedule and
budget cuts. It seemed the days of the grand trains were over.

But, like those of the death of the luxury ocean liner, rumours of
the luxury train's demise were somewhat exaggerated. Perversely,
public interest in the somewhat derelict *Orient Express* spiked when
it made its last run to Istanbul in May 1977, though by then the
service even lacked a restaurant car. The storm of media coverage
of that final trip and of the subsequent sale of several *Orient Express*
carriages convinced shipping magnate James Sherwood that nostalgia
could make reviving the service to its former standards a lucrative
business proposition. He began tracking down, buying and restoring
old *Orient Express* carriages, and launched the new *Venice Simplon-
Orient-Express* on May 25, 1982.

The company now runs three other luxury trains in the UK, as
well as the Eastern & Oriental Express through Thailand, Malaysia
and Singapore. Marketing materials play heavily on the nostalgia
theme. "Step aboard the Venice Simplon-Orient-Express and you step
back into a more gracious, elegant age," wheedles the company's Web

site. "Your personal steward, instantly available to attend your every comfort, will show you to your compartment of gleaming wood, polished brass, soft towels and crisp linen." Of course, all of this wood, brass, linen and coddling doesn't come cheap — the six-day, five-night journey from Paris to Istanbul was a hefty US $7,690 per person in 2007.

The prices don't seem to be deterring folks. In fact, luxury train services have since popped up in other parts of the world. Canada's *Rocky Mountaineer* takes travellers along several scenic routes in British Columbia and Alberta. The *Blue Train* shuttles well-heeled passengers through South Africa, serving them English high tea and Cuban cigars as the veldt rushes past. In Australia, you can book the entire Chairman's Carriage on *The Ghan* and enjoy meals from your private kitchen and DVDs from the carriage's video library as the train travels between Adelaide and Darwin. And in the US, passengers on the *GrandLuxe* train can listen to jazz standards in a piano lounge as they travel through the national parks of the West.

On the Road

Afoot and light-hearted I take to the open road,
Healthy, free, the world before me,
The long brown path before me leading wherever
    I choose.
Henceforth I ask not good-fortune, I myself am
    good-fortune.
                    — *Walt Whitman,* Song of the Open Road

In 1985, four university buddies and I tried to travel map-less through a winter night from Ottawa to Rochester, New York, for a *Star Trek* convention. Lost, frustrated and too cheap to fork out for a map, we were reduced to begging directions from amused clerks in all-night McDonald's outlets. Once you've heard someone bellow, "You drove all the way from *Ottawa* for a *Star Trek convention?*" to a roomful of the sort of folks who hang out at McDonald's at one in the morning, you never forget it.

Older and, I hope, wiser, I wouldn't think of attempting a trip of any length these days without a good map. But in the days when most of the world beyond one's hometown was a cipher, and when neither printing presses nor cheap distribution systems existed, many people who left home wandered into the void with little better than educated guesses to guide them.

In the pre-modern world, maps of the routes between major, proximate cities weren't as essential as you might think. In many cases, there was just one major road between the two, and it was called something rather obvious, like "Montreal Road." Many of these old nomenclatures survive today in the names of urban streets, such as Oxford Street in London.

These old names die hard, even when the roads in question are replaced by four-lane highways. On a trip to Ireland in 2001, my

123

husband and I became so hopelessly lost trying to drive out of Cork that I feared we'd have to give up, buy real estate and settle in the city permanently. The problem, we eventually realized, was that we were asking passers-by for directions to the N22. Many locals rarely use the official numbers for highways, preferring the informal names that emerged long before the major roads were paved and widened. When we finally started asking, as any good Corkman would, for the Killarney Road, we soon found our way.

However, even in the ancient world, road maps came in handy. One of the earliest surviving road maps is the Peutinger Table — which, for those of you who are sticklers, is actually a *cartogram*, a graphical presentation of information on a map that is often not remotely to scale. It's a thirteenth-century copy of a map dating back to the heyday of the Roman Empire, much of it likely based on a map from the early decades of the first century. It shows the network of roughly 100,000 modern kilometres of roads — from southeastern Britain to Sri Lanka — that led to Rome.

Despite the prominence of military matters in ancient Rome, this map appears to have been designed for merchants and pilgrims, rather than soldiers. Hot springs, trading centres and pilgrimage sites are marked with consistent symbols. The fifty-two spas on the map, for instance, are denoted with a drawing of a square building with an internal courtyard and, often, a tower.

Unlike modern maps, the Peutinger Table makes no attempt to portray its sites in correct mathematical proportion. Travellers trying to figure out the distance between two places had to add up the figures written on each separate small stretch of road between inter-mediate points. Onerous as this task sounds, it was made infinitely more difficult by the fact that distances on different parts of the map were recorded using the local systems of measurement: Roman miles in much of the empire, but leagues in Gaul, parasangs in Persia and Indian miles in India, for instance.

And those of you who have ever cursed the cumbersome nature of a modern folded road map should spare a moment to pity the poor Roman tourist, who had to contend with a scroll almost seven metres long (on the bright side, it was just thirty-four centimetres wide). The odd shape may have been dictated by the need to roll the original papyrus map up so that it could be transported easily in a *capsa*, or toolbox.

By medieval times, road maps had evolved little from their Roman predecessors. One of the best examples is the itinerary that forms the first seven pages of the *Chronica majora*, an illustrated history text written by a monk named Matthew Paris from the Benedictine Abbey of St. Albans in England around 1250. Interestingly, around the same time, a monk in Colmar, in what is now France, was painstakingly copying the Peutinger Table.

Paris's map outlines several routes from England and across Europe to Jerusalem and the Holy Land. One of its most interesting characteristics is its interactivity. Users could unfold various flaps to change the route or find out more information about the places depicted. As several experts on the *Chronica majora* have noted, this structure may have evolved because the map was not designed to be used on the road, but rather was aimed at cloistered monks who would never be allowed to travel outside their monastery to the Holy Land but found imagining such a sacred journey a useful meditative tool. Being able to alter and "experience" the route by choosing different flaps was the closest they would ever come to standing at a foreign crossroads and deciding how to proceed. Paris's monastic colleagues were the medieval equivalent of armchair travellers.

I CAME, I SAW, I SENT A POSTCARD

Soldiers, merchants and pilgrims weren't the only people who needed maps. Among the earliest cartographical clients were the ancient world's equivalents of the modern-day mailman.

"Neither snow, nor rain, nor heat, nor gloom of night stays these couriers from the swift completion of their appointed rounds" — the unofficial slogan of the United States Postal service — actually comes from Herodotus, who was describing Persia's legendary mounted postal service of about 500 BC. The Persians set up a wide network of postal stations a day's journey apart, each staffed by a horse and rider. An arriving courier would pass his message to the next, who would take it along the following section of the established route. It was an efficient system, and part of the reason the Persians did so well is that they knew where they were going.

The Romans — the ancient world's most meticulous bureaucrats — took note and developed a fairly sophisticated system of their own, to give officials access to food, shelter and horses at Imperial Post stations throughout the empire. The emperor sent a batch of signed blank forms called *tractoria* to each provincial governor. If an official could prove he needed the postal service's resources for official government business, the governor would give him a *tractorium* valid for a specific length of time. But woe betide the poor functionary stuck in some backwater province if the emperor died suddenly, as Roman emperors often did — inconveniently, the *tractorium* expired with him, and the bureaucrat would be left to his own devices to make his way home.

Eventually, of course, the whole empire expired, along with its postal system and cartograms, and people in western Europe really didn't travel that much for a while. Of course, it isn't as though the whole world stopped dead.

TIED TOGETHER BY SILK

One of the most famous ancient trade routes stretched from modern-day Xian in China to modern-day Antioch in Turkey. Called the Silk Road, it actually pre-dated — and outlasted — the Roman postal system and the Peutinger Table by centuries.

Its first recorded traveller was a Chinese court official named Zhang Qian. In the second century BC, China was having a bit of trouble with the Xiongnu, nomadic warriors who had managed to subdue a good chunk of central Asia stretching from eastern Mongolia to the Aral Sea, a body of water between modern Uzbekistan and Kazakhstan. Xiongnu raids were so terrifying that they spurred the Chinese to build the Great Wall. But, as usually happens in human history, walls proved insufficient for deterring people who really wanted to get in or out. What the Chinese needed were some allies, and quickly. The most likely prospects seemed to be the Yueh-chih people, whom the Xiongnu had driven from their homeland in northwest China. Needless to say, the Yueh-chih had a bit of a bone to pick with the Xiongnu.

From his capital at Xian, Chinese ruler Han Wu-ti, proceeding on the timeless assumption that the enemy of his enemy was his friend, dispatched Zhang Qian westward to see if he could get the Yueh-chih to launch an attack on the Xiongnu from the west while Han Wu-ti's forces struck from the east.

When Zhang set out with a hundred soldiers in 138 BC, he wasn't exactly embarking on a pleasure trip. First, the Xiongnu, probably suspecting Zhang's motives, captured him and held him prisoner for ten years. It doesn't appear to have been all punishment and no play for Zhang, however, as he managed to marry a Xiongnu woman and have a son with her. He eventually escaped (with his family and a few of his men) and tracked down the Yueh-chih, who had wandered about central Asia before finally settling down in Transoxiana, part of the area now shared by Kazakhstan and Uzbekistan. Zhang pitched the emperor's proposal, but the Yueh-chih liked their safe life and had no intention of annoying the Xiongnu again. He spent a year with them before heading back to Xian to tell Wu-ti he had had no luck with the Yueh-chih. On the way back, perhaps in the hopes of avoiding the Xiongnu, Zhang took what would become the southern route of the Silk Road, rather than the northern route he had travelled earlier. Unfortunately, he was again captured and held for a year before once again escaping — the Xiongnu seem to have been fearsome warriors but incompetent jailers.

By the time Zhang got back to Xian, he'd been gone thirteen years. Despite the failure to make an alliance, the emperor was interested in the news and goods Zhang brought back from the west. The Yueh-chih had been similarly intrigued by the contact with China. Soon, despite the threat from the Xiongnu, caravans of ambassadors, scholars and merchants began making their slow way across the haphazard network of cart tracks and mountain paths that comprised Zhang's two routes. As always, for the ambitious few, the possibility of political, economic or religious gain overrode fears for safety.

Shortly after Zhang's visit, many of the Yueh-chih moved south to

Bactria, an area under Greek control. That move eventually would bring them into contact with the Romans. And once the wealthy, novelty-loving Romans found out about the silk and spices making their way along the Silk Road from China, the route became a trade artery between East and West.

The fortunes of the route ebbed and flowed over the centuries, with the rise and fall of empires and the disruption of countless wars. Once the Persians mastered the silk-making process in the sixth century AD, Europeans had a much closer — and thus more economical — supplier of the rich fabric, so European use of the route declined somewhat. But at least parts of the route were still used by Buddhist scholars travelling between China and northern India, and Xian prospered on the strength of the road's traffic to become a city of almost two million people by 750. When the Tang dynasty ended in 906, the resulting political instability led to increasing raids on passing caravans, as warring factions tried to thwart each other's trade. Even so, in periods of calm, Muslim traders made frequent use of the road to transport goods between China and the Middle East.

But in the early thirteenth century, Genghis Khan's Mongol hordes made travel along the route even more dangerous. Merchants, then as now, sought some kind of magical protection that would keep them prosperous, and built religious grottoes along the road network as shrines to their various faiths — it's possible to trace the spread of Buddhism, Hinduism and Christianity along the road through the grottoes' murals and statues. (The giant Buddhas of Bamiyam in Afghanistan, whose destruction in 2001 by the Taliban caused such distress to historians and archaeologists, were a particularly old and famous link in this chain of artworks created by merchant travellers.)

Although sections of the Silk Road would always be used locally, its importance as a transcontinental trade route ended for good in the sixteenth century, after the Portuguese Vasco de Gama successfully navigated a sea route around Africa to India.

CARTOGRAPHY ON A TRULY GRAND SCALE

Road maps weren't really a big business in the Middle Ages, partly because most roads were so poor. In England, the fourteenth-century Gough map (named after the man who re-discovered it four centuries later) was nothing more than a crude depiction of roads throughout Britain, with information on staging distances. Yet travellers appear to have used it for at least the next two centuries, and few competing English maps emerged.

In Germany, in the 1490s, an instrument maker named Ehrhard Etzlaub developed a road map depicting the region stretching from France to Poland and from Denmark to Rome. It was evidently a one-shot effort designed to complement the Holy Year celebrations in Rome in 1500, and for at least a century few printers or cartographers followed in Etzlaub's footsteps. Instead, publishers produced "road books" — written descriptions of roads and the landscapes they traversed, with numerical tables showing the distances between major destinations. Not until the mid-1600s were "sheet maps" — akin to the documents we use today — produced for large areas of England, France and central Europe.

In 1675, mapmaker John Ogilby published *Britannia: A Geographical and Historical Description of the Principal Roads Thereof*, a collection of a hundred strip maps of England and Wales. The work that went into this popular volume was immense: mapmakers walked 12,000 kilometres (7,500 miles) of road, painstakingly measuring distances with a wheel known as a perambulator. Likely to the relief of many readers, Ogilby used the "standard" mile of 1,760 yards consistently, eschewing competing measurements such as the long, middle and short miles that were still in use in many parts of the country.

Travellers quickly realized the usefulness of Ogilby's invention. A spate of maps and road books was published in the decades that followed, reflecting Britons' greater mobility, spurred partly by an improving road system. Within a century, titles such as Thomas Kitchin's *Post Chaise Companion* (1767) were catering specifically to people travelling by the evolving post chaise system, which used fast-moving, enclosed carriages.

THE CONTINENTAL CARRIAGE TRADE

Though roads were improving, it still wasn't always easy to get there from here. Carriages could be unwieldy. Some Grand Tourists hauled their carriages across the English Channel to begin their trips, but others preferred to buy one once they reached France. A 1787 newspaper ad informed readers that almost two hundred *remises* (high-end carriages) were available for purchase in Calais. Normally, travellers would buy a carriage at the beginning of the trip and then try to resell it in Calais on their way home. (This practice survives today in spread-out places such as Australia, where some long-term tourists buy an RV or car-and-trailer combination at the beginning of their vacation and resell it at the end.)

To English travellers, the carriages for sale in Calais were likely fairly similar to those available back home. But those who went further afield sometimes found foreign carriages almost as exotic as the destinations themselves.

Lady Mary Mortley Montagu travelled to Turkey in the early 1700s with her husband, Britain's ambassador there. Among the many things that fascinated her were Turkish coaches:

> These *voitures* are not at all like ours, but much more convenient for the country, the heat being so great that glasses would be very troublesome. They are made a good deal in the manner of the Dutch coaches, having wooden lattices painted and gilded, the inside being painted with baskets and nosegays of flowers, intermixed commonly with little poetical mottoes. They are covered all over with scarlet cloth, lined with silk and very often richly embroidered and fringed. This covering entirely hides the persons in them, but may be thrown back at pleasure and the ladies peep through the lattices. They hold four people very conveniently, seated on cushions, but not raised.[38]

Even people who could afford a luxury carriage often faced trials and tribulations en route. Carriages were notoriously fragile conveyances, and many travellers were forced to cool their heels for a day or two when an axle cracked or the leather straps supporting the carriage broke. One pothole could hobble a horse — sometimes for life. And in the days before carriage springs, even perfectly working carriages weren't particularly comfortable.

In the eighteenth century, many European governments began paying a bit more attention to road construction and upkeep, mainly as a way to ease the passage of commercial and military vehicles. But many roads were still narrow, uneven and muddy — or non-existent. In some cases, neither the money nor the technical ability existed to build roads that would have been very useful — such as a road between France and Italy.

Until a road over the Alps between Lyons and Turin opened, voyagers to Italy by land had to complete at least part of the alpine section on mule, on foot or by sedan chair. Servants who weren't busy hauling milord over the mountains in a litter would take the carriage apart, pack the pieces onto mules to be hauled over the Mount Cenis pass, then reassemble the vehicle once everyone reached the road on the other side.

Once they arrived in Italy, however, their road traumas weren't over. On the treacherous mountainous roads between Florence and Bologna, tourists sometimes opted for litters — not only for safety reasons, but because some sections were so steep and rocky that horses had difficulty pulling the carriage. Rivers presented another problem, particularly in spring and fall when the waters were high, since most crossings were made by ferry rather than by bridge.

OFF THE BEATEN TRACK

Dangerous thoroughfares weren't the only hardship of life on the road in the early days of leisure travel. Modern readers might wonder why the Grand Tourists stuck to such a limited itinerary: mainly Paris and Italy, with some minor interest in Germany and the Low Countries. To Grand Tourists, of course, few places could hold a candle to the archaeological and renaissance wonders of Italy, the cradle of modern civilization. Why go anywhere else?

But only a few intrepid travellers ventured as far as Spain, eastern Europe, Scandinavia and the Balkans, as there was nowhere to eat or sleep along the way. Those who did make the journey had to make even greater preparations than their colleagues who stuck to the main tourist trail.

In the mid-1770s, for instance, Thomas Pelham travelled across the Iberian peninsula. He was warned by the few English speakers he met on his way through rustic Portugal that conditions in much of Spain were even more spartan, so he had a boiler made to hang under his carriage. Come dinnertime, he would snare a rabbit or buy a chicken in a local village and boil it by the side of the road. The eternally optimistic Pelham claimed he came to love boiled meat on that trip better than any fancy dishes he had sampled in Paris.

Road conditions facing travellers in the New World were, if anything, even worse than those in Europe. A stagecoach passenger travelling between Yarmouth and Halifax, Nova Scotia, recalled:

> To be jolted and tossed about in an inferior vehicle, with lean horses, over a notoriously rough and sometimes dangerous road, for the distance of 200 miles [320 kilometres]; to be exposed during this journey, occasionally in an open conveyance, to the pelting storm, and to be compelled to vacate your seat over and over to help the poor horses drag the coach up the hills... and, besides all, to be asked to hand over for this rough usage a pretty good sum in hard cash — to endure all this requires no ordinary amount of nerve.[39]

PRIMITIVE PUBLIC TRANSIT

In the years of the Grand Tour, many travellers in France boarded *diligences*, lumbering vehicles that regularly shuttled between major cities — particularly along the routes leading from Paris to Calais, Lille and Lyons.

A *diligence* looked like three carriages hooked together and could transport about thirty people, including those who were willing to ride on top with the luggage. It wasn't the fastest way to travel, logging only about six to eight kilometres (four or five miles) an hour, but it was relatively cheap and dependable. A similar but usually more basic service was available in parts of Germany, Switzerland and other countries. By the 1780s, Grand Tourists arriving from England who couldn't afford a private carriage could avail themselves of daily *diligence* service between Calais to Paris. The trip took up to four days, twice as long as by private carriage.

British tourist Sacheverell Stevens took the *diligence* from Paris to Lyons in 1739, travelling 480 kilometres (300 miles) in four days, which was rather impressive for its time although not as fast as journeying by post chaise. Passengers could pay seventy livres for the whole trip if they made their own arrangements along the way for food and lodging, or 100 livres with everything included. It's likely that most visitors, particularly if they didn't speak the language or know the route, would go for the all-inclusive option. Either way, it was a reasonable price. And, as Stevens noted approvingly, travelling by *diligence* brought you into contact with "the odd assemblage of the passengers, such as monks, pilgrims, officers, courtesans, etc."[40]

Author John Andrews waxed even more enthusiastic about the joys of public transit in his 1784 book, *Letters to a Young Gentleman on His Setting Out for France*:

> People that meet on a traveling party, being usually total strangers to each other, and meeting together for the first and last time, are not fettered by any apprehensions of what may happen from the discourse that passes among them: they indulge themselves without any restraint, and speak of men and things with a latitude and freedom, which they would not dare to use elsewhere.[41]

Not everyone shared Andrews' liking for travelling with strangers. In the 1780s, while touring the Continent, a British agricultural student named Arthur Young was horrified when the passengers on

his *diligence* started singing to while away the hours. He grumbled
that he "would almost as soon have rode the journey blindfold on
an ass."[42]

    Diligences could also be dangerous. In November 1848 American
journalist Margaret Fuller, in Italy to cover radical Italian politics for
the *New York Tribune*, planned to travel to Rome. The *diligence* was
due to pass by her inn at between three and four in the morning, so
when an acquaintance offered Fuller a lift in a hired carriage — which
would depart at 6 AM — she gratefully accepted. During the night,
the weather turned bad, with wind and rain lashing the inn. As she
wrote in a letter to her mother, she would be gladder still:

> I rose with twilight, and was expecting my carriage, and
> wondering at its delay, when I heard, that the great *dili-
> gence*, several miles below, had been seized by a torrent;
> the horses were up to their necks in water, before any
> one dreamed of the danger. The postilion called on all
> the saints, and threw himself into the water. The door
> of the *diligence* could not be opened, and the passengers
> forced themselves, one after another, into the cold water,
> — dark too. Had I been there I had fared ill; a pair
> of strong men were ill after it, though all escaped with
> life.[43]

CYCLISTS PAVE A NEW PATH

In the nineteenth century, the invention of a revolutionary new mode
of transportation spurred demand for both better roads and more
accurate maps. I'm referring, of course, to the bicycle.

    The idea of a wheeled, human-propelled vehicle had been around
for centuries — as with so many other ideas ahead of their time,
Leonardo da Vinci sketched out some rudimentary plans for one
but apparently never built a prototype. One of the earliest bicycle
forebears was the *Draisienne*, a bicycle-*cum*-scooter invented by
Baron von Drais and introduced in Paris in 1818. It had two wheels
and a frame, all right, but no pedals. The rider sat on it and pushed

the machine along with his feet. It enjoyed brief, faddish popularity among society gentlemen in France and England — where it was called a velocipede or hobbyhorse — but muddy, bumpy roads made it impractical.

A few determined hobbyists and inventors continued to tinker with bicycle design for the next few decades, but the resulting machines never really took off with the public, quite possibly because some of them lacked brakes or steering mechanisms. Not until the 1860s did French inventor Pierre Michaux come up with a practical way to affix pedals to a large front wheel. This innovation spurred another short-lived cycling craze — a nickname for the bicycle that emerged at this point, "boneshaker," gives some clue as to why the machines didn't really take off.

Fans persisted, though. The addition of rubber suspension wheels around 1870 made the machines more comfortable to ride, and within a decade cycling clubs had sprung up in North America and Europe. The Cyclists' Touring Club, founded in the UK in 1878, had 60,000 members by 1900. Groups such as the National Cyclists' Union in Britain lobbied for better roads, respect for cyclists' rights, improved maps and discounts at boarding houses.

In 1885, the first practical "safety" bicycle was introduced. By using a chain drive, the designers had eliminated the need for a huge front wheel. Three years later, Dunlop started making bikes with pneumatic tires, and by 1891 Michelin had introduced air-inflated tires. Bikes, which had previously appealed mainly to athletic young men, quickly became a mass-market phenomenon.

Given the differences in distances between towns, bicycling became a much bigger craze in Europe than in North America. In more densely settled Europe, it was quickly seen as a practical form of private, inexpensive, mass-market transportation. For the first time in history, people who couldn't afford to keep a horse had a practical alternative to walking if they wanted to travel quickly by their own route and on their own schedule. No longer did they have to squeeze into crowded post chaises or limit themselves to places served by the railway.

Increasing numbers of cyclists also changed the perspective of

people who wouldn't have considered getting on one of the contrap-
tions if their lives depended on it. Suddenly, rural roads and small
villages far off the railway's path were seeing an influx of strangers.
Gone forever were the days when you would recognize every person
you met on your local road simply because you saw them every
Sunday at church or your mothers were cousins or they were the
local tinker who had been selling trinkets in your village since your
father was a child. Like it or not, even people who had no interest in
seeing the world found that the world was coming to see them.

By the late 1890s, an intrepid American couple were exploring
the mountains of India from the seats of their bicycles. Most of the
Indians they met assumed they were selling the odd machines. "They
could not understand otherwise, why we should take the trouble
to travel on cycles," the female half of the couple, Fanny Bullock
Workman, later recalled.[44]

The Workmans were startlingly fit. One day, they cycled 120 kilometres (75 miles) on bumpy roads from Madras to Ranipat. On
another day, they pushed their loaded bicycles uphill for 35 kilometres (22 miles), gaining an estimated six thousand feet. It's no
wonder the Indians were puzzled by their enthusiasm.

But when it came to road travel, bicycles were just the advance
guard. The real revolution was awaiting...just down the road.

FROM TWO WHEELS TO FOUR

In 1885, the same year the first safety bicycle was introduced, a
German inventor named Karl Benz built the first gasoline-fuelled
automobile with an internal combustion engine. People on both sides
of the Atlantic had been tinkering with this idea for years. American
George Baldwin Selden apparently came up with a workable design
for an internal combustion engine in 1876, but due to a protracted
legal battle was never able to profit from it properly.

In 1886, on the heels of Benz's invention, his compatriots Gottlieb
Daimler and Wilhelm Maybach designed a workable four-wheeled
car powered by a four-stroke engine. Within two decades, Henry
Ford had designed a car that could move at the amazing rate of

146 kilometres (91 miles) per hour. The age of the automobile had dawned.

Almost immediately, wealthy risk takers who bought the first cars encountered a major problem: their newfangled machines theoretically could take them across large distances at astonishing speeds, but most intercity roads were little more than bumpy, unmarked trails.

There were some exceptions, of course. In the late 1700s, Scotsman John McAdam had developed a process for surfacing roads with aggregate and gravel that would become known as macadamizing. Governments on both sides of the Atlantic adopted this process for major intercity roads, such as the National Road in the US. Construction on this road into the American interior began in 1811 in Cumberland, Maryland, and continued for more than two decades until the money ran out in Vandalia, Illinois. By the 1840s, the route was well marked with iron mileposts.

Macadam roads were better than dirt tracks for motorists, but not ideal. Moving faster than horse-drawn vehicles, cars created a vacuum that sucked up dust and spewed it in motorists' eyes. Cars also eventually wore down the loose road surface.

In response, motorists vigorously took up the crusade of their bike-riding brethren for better roads and maps. The American Automobile Association was founded in 1902; similar organizations soon sprouted up in the UK (1905), Canada (1913) and Australia (1924), among other countries.

The driving conditions these associations fought so hard to change would seem almost prehistoric to the modern Western road warrior, used to smooth, multi-lane highways studded with handy twenty-four-hour gas stations. On August 27, 1912, magazine journalist Thomas Wilby set out from Halifax, Nova Scotia, in a Reo Motorcar Company wagon, accompanied by Reo mechanic Jack Haney. Their destination was Victoria, BC, and it would take them almost two months to get there. On some sections of the route, there were no roads at all — they had to load the car onto a ship to cross part of Lake Superior, and bundle it onto a train to get through the mountains near Lytton, BC. When roads did exist, they were often dangerous to both driver and car. One particular stretch was so rutted it trashed the Reo's driveshaft, and the pair lost several days' time waiting for a new one. No wonder that Wilby and Haney logged only 298 kilometres (179 miles) on their best driving day, and 19 kilometres (11 miles) on their worst. No wonder, too, that they loathed the sight of each other by the time they put-putted into Victoria on October 17. On the bright side, they were the first people to cross Canada by car.

A NATION OF ROAD TRIPPERS

The automobile would eventually transform travel in just about every spot on the globe, from Albania to Zimbabwe. But it was the United States that embraced the cult of the car with a near religious fervour. "I'm going to democratize the automobile," Henry Ford said in 1909, the year after the first Model T rolled off the assembly line. "When I'm through, everybody will be able to afford one, and about everybody will have one." By 1910, the company was selling twenty thousand of them annually. Three years later, that number had skyrocketed by a factor of ten. By the middle of the 1910s, hundreds of thousands of cars crowded America's roads. The only problem was that most of the drivers had no idea where they were going and few ways to get there. Map making and road building hadn't quite yet caught up to this new consumer craze.

One of the first American publishers to develop road maps for motorists was Chicago-based Rand McNally & Company. The firm's first foray into the field was more like an old road book than a map. The *Photo-Auto Guide* was the brainchild of Anthony McNally II, who had odd taste in romantic destinations and a very patient new wife. On the couple's honeymoon road trip from Chicago to Milwaukee in 1907, McNally stopped at every turning point and snapped a photo. When he got home, he compiled the results into a picture book that drivers could use while travelling the same route. The problem with this approach was that it went out of date as quickly as the landscape changed.

One hurdle early mapmakers had to overcome was what to call the roads. A few major ones, such as the aforementioned National Road, had widely recognized names that mapmakers could use. For other roads, publishers often devised their own numbering system. None of these numbers, of course, was actually marked on the roads themselves, so map publishers also had to provide detailed written instructions for drivers that included landmarks and turns.

In an attempt to solve this problem — and, not coincidentally, divert some traffic and business to their communities — Babbitt-like boosters all over America blithely began promoting "named trails": road systems, overlaid on existing roads, that boasted inspiring names like the Old Spanish Trail (linking St. Augustine, Florida, with San Diego) and the Theodore Roosevelt International Highway (which travelled through Ontario on its way from Portland, Maine, to Portland, Oregon). Often, there was no compelling reason to connect two cities other than the aspirations of their civic leaders and those of the towns in between. As a result, many trails took a meandering route rather than following the shortest distance between two points.

In their defence, the named trail associations did make it easier for early motorists to find their way across the country; often with the help of auto associations, they flagged their trails with route markers painted on any available roadside surface, from rocks to barns. By 1918, however, it was already becoming clear to government officials that the grassroots movement didn't have the finances, authority or vision to maintain the nation's major roads. As Arthur R. Hirst, Wisconsin's state highway engineer, put it sardonically at a National Road Congress meeting that year, "The ordinary trail promoter has seemingly considered that plenty of wind and a few barrels of paint are all that is required to build and maintain a 2000-mile trail."[45]

GET YOUR KICKS ON ROUTE 66

A year earlier, Wisconsin had become the first state to number its highways. And not a moment too soon. By 1920, there were almost ten million cars on America's roads, and by the middle of that decade two hundred and fifty named national trails competed for motorists' attention. At that point, the federal government stepped in, creating the relatively systematic numbering system for long-distance highways that remains in use to this day. This seemingly rational decision nevertheless called up considerable consternation among editorial writers across the land. Named trail associations, not surprisingly, were among the most vociferous opponents of the plan. The *Lincoln Highway Forum* thundered:

> Can an edict from Washington wipe out the name Lincoln Highway and henceforth require that Americans shall know this great and famous artery of transportation as No. 64 or No. 13, or some arbitrary designation, requiring a cross index volume of numbers and locations before it would convey any significance to the public mind? We believe not.[46]

A writer for the *Western Highways Builder* concurred. "I feel that such a move will never waken a popular response. The Lincoln Highway and reputable routes of a like character will never lose their identity.... Romance is the manna on which the Americano thrives."[47]

Perhaps, but "the Americano" managed to weave romance even out of seemingly soulless numbers; it's hard to beat the allure of a lyric like "Get your kicks on Route 66." That highway from Chicago to Los Angeles opened in 1926 and quickly became part of the national fabric. John Steinbeck called it the "Mother Road," because it took Okies to California during the Dust Bowl. After the Second World War, it took GIs home from the conflict and gave them a route to take their families on long vacations, allowing convenient side trips to the Grand Canyon and the Painted Forest. The road even provided the title of an early 1960s' series on CBS, in which Tod and Buzz roamed America in their Corvette.

Route 66 became a magnet for oddball roadside architecture, not to mention the first McDonald's, which opened in San Bernardino, California, in 1940. Travellers found themselves experiencing a collision between America's car culture and retro-futurism, which produced a movement called "populuxe," also known as googie architecture for an LA coffee shop of that name. Populuxe was characterized by boomerang angles, colourful neon signs, large domes, plate glass windows and upswept cantilevered roofs. Think 1950s' diner or gas station and you have it.

Among the icons of Route 66 architecture were giant fibreglass statues that the Web site RoadsideAmerica.com calls "Muffler Men." Steve Dashew, as president of International Fiberglass, built the first muffler man for the PB Cafe on Route 66 in Flagstaff, Arizona, in about 1962. The original mould was of Paul Bunyan, but could be adapted to create all kinds of characters: instead of Paul Bunyan's axe, for example, they could hold anything, even mufflers.

Route 66 was eventually decommissioned, but dedicated nostalgia buffs still try to make their way down the now-abandoned pathways. Today, other highways fill the nostalgic void. US Highway 61 extends from New Orleans through St. Louis to Duluth, and up into Canada as far as Thunder Bay. Running alongside the Mississippi, it soon became known as the Blues Highway, for the purported route blues musicians took on their way to Chicago (and, presumably, Thunder Bay). Robert Johnson was said to have sold his soul to the devil at the crossroads where Highway 61 meets Highway 49, out in Clarksdale, Mississippi. Bessie Smith died in a car accident on Highway 61, and Martin Luther King was killed in a motel along the road. Two geniuses of later music would also grow up within spitting distance of Highway 61. One was Elvis; the other, at the Minnesota end, was Bob Dylan, who wrote the epic song "Highway 61 Revisited."

WHY OWN WHEN YOU CAN RENT?

By the end of the First World War, Americans who didn't have a car at their disposal could rent one. One of the first to think of renting cars was an Omaha man named Joe Saunders, who, in 1916, attached a makeshift odometer to his Model T and charged customers ten cents a mile. Apparently, in a story that seems too perfect not to be apocryphal, Saunders's first renter was a travelling salesman who booked the car to take a girl on a date. Even though Saunders expanded the business quickly — by 1925, he was serving twenty-one states — it failed during the Depression.

A bit more successful was Walter Jacobs, a twenty-two-year-old entrepreneur who opened Rent-a-Ford in Chicago in September 1918 with a dozen or so Model Ts. Within five years, the company had 200 cars and annual sales of $1 million, numbers that soon attracted the notice of John Hertz. Buying Rent-a-Ford, he expanded it into a larger company called the Hertz Driv-Ur-Self System.

Hertz, incidentally, had another important role to play in the history of travel. Before he got into the rental business, he helped save a Chicago car dealership. He did it so well that he soon found himself neck-deep in traded-in used cars. That's when he hit on the idea of running his own taxi company, in itself unremarkable except that Hertz commissioned a local university to figure out what colour potential customers standing on the street would be most likely to notice. Hence, the Yellow Cab and Yellow Truck and Coach Manufacturing Company. Because of Hertz's business acumen, yellow soon became a default colour for cabs in many North American cities.

It's probably a good thing Hertz had other business interests, because car rentals were proving to be a complicated field. During Prohibition, rental cars developed an unsavoury reputation as the vehicle of choice for hookers, bootleggers and bandits; one estimate pegged the percentage of rental cars used for criminal activities during those years at 90 percent.

Things improved a bit when Prohibition was lifted in 1933, but the Depression didn't do the industry any favours. Good news finally arrived in 1940, when a railroad consortium, worried that private car ownership was cutting into passenger rail traffic, founded Railway Extension Inc., which set up car rental franchises in train stations across the Midwest. The railroads even offered passengers free telegraph services for reserving cars, hoping to persuade people that taking the train to one's destination and then renting a car to drive that last little distance, or to use around town, would be more convenient than driving the whole way. (This wasn't such a wild assumption, in the days before four-lane interstates made long-distance car travel fast.)

Hertz set up a competing, if not quite as convenient, system with railroads in the eastern US. It was the right idea, but at the wrong time. After Pearl Harbor, Washington set monthly mileage limits for rental cars, froze rental car rates and forbade rental agencies to buy new cars, all in the interests of preserving gasoline and materials for the war effort.

The car rental business didn't really start to boom until after the war, and it wasn't by working with the railroads. By then, the days of large-scale passenger rail travel in the US were over: by 1950, 80 percent of all long-distance trips in the US were being made by car. Instead, rental car agencies tied their fortunes to another rising industry: aviation.

Before the war, most air travellers had been rich, but by the late 1940s salespeople and other middle-class travellers had begun to take to the skies. In 1948, a Hertz Drive-Ur-Self System ad mentioned the competitive advantages of both rail and air:

> Sales depend on more than a salesman's "genius" for selling! Is there a more important factor in keeping sales' graphs steadily climbing than transportation?...Salesmen, executives, field men, etc. travel fast and luxuriously by train or plane, and when they arrive fresh, unwearied, make more calls in big new Chevrolets or other fine cars rented from Hertz!

It wouldn't be long, though, until the combination of air and rental car left passenger railroads in the dust.

In 1947, Hertz set up rental outlets at airports in Milwaukee and Atlanta, and a car dealer from Detroit named Warren Avis launched the Avis Airline Rent-a-Car System. Avis moved quickly to try to dominate the airline car rental business; by 1949, it had licensed rental booths in eight major airports and had negotiated promotional deals with Eastern Airlines and American Airlines. Hertz immediately beefed up its airport presence, and a third firm, National Rent-a-Car, joined the fray. Throughout the 1950s and 1960s, the three companies would battle for market share. Then, the arrival of discount chains such as Budget spurred serious rate competition. That, along with the

oil crisis of the early 1970s, led companies to start offering a wider
range of small rental cars as well as the huge sedans that had always
been a mainstay of the business.

In the ensuing years, airlines, car manufacturers and other outside
companies have bought and sold interests in car rental firms, as the
industry's fortunes have waxed and waned. Competition intensified
to the point that, by the early 1980s, rental companies were offering customers perks galore, from golf clubs to free plane tickets.
Eventually, they realized they were going to drive themselves into col-
lective bankruptcy if they kept up the cutthroat competition, and the
juicy gift and premium programs were quietly shelved. These days,
perks are more likely to include incentives related to the car itself,
such as satellite radio access or unlimited mileage. Car rental firms
are looking for other ways to increase business, including outlets at
secondary European airports favoured by low-cost airlines such as
Ryanair, and programs to encourage car-less urban dwellers to rent
cars for short-term local trips.

TAKE YOUR HOME ON THE ROAD

In the early days of car travel, accommodation choices were fairly
limited unless you stopped in a big city or didn't mind camping. But
not everyone relished the idea of nights under canvas, as Wally Byam
found out in the 1920s.

Byam was no stranger to living on the road. As a child, he'd travelled with his grandfather, an Oregon mule train leader. As a teen,
while working as a shepherd, he'd made his home in a two-wheeled
donkey cart, cooking on a kerosene stove and washing from a pail.
Despite these modest beginnings, however, he went to Stanford Law
School and eventually became a magazine publisher.

When one of Byam's company's magazines published flawed do-
it-yourself building plans for a car trailer, readers complained. Byam
took a closer look at the plans and decided he could do better. The
resulting trailer wasn't the world's first, but it *was* one of the first
that was high enough to allow campers to stand up inside it. Byam
boasted that anyone could build one for $100. Increasingly mobile

readers responded in droves, snapping up the $5 plans, as well as trailer kits and fully assembled trailers that Byam put together in his backyard. By 1930, he'd made trailers his full-time business. And on January 17, 1936, he launched the product that would make him famous: the Airstream Clipper trailer.

It was no accident that the trailer's name was inspired by the famous Pan American Clipper flying boats that had recently captured the public's imagination, as Byam had drawn extensively on aviation technology to make the little silver trailers light and aerodynamic. With room for four travellers, a dinette that converted into a bed, an enclosed galley, a water system and electric lights, the trailer cost a whopping $1,200; even so, Byam could barely keep up with demand.

The company ran into a temporary roadblock during the Second World War, when the government banned all house trailer construction except for official uses. Byam closed the company and went to work, naturally enough, in the airline industry. After the war and an unworkable partnership with a larger manufacturer, Byam reopened Airstream in 1948. And soon, he had a stroke of genius: why not organize group trips called "caravans" to promote the use of Airstream trailers?

Byam himself led all of Airstream's foreign caravans throughout most of the 1950s. Trips included jaunts to Central America, Mexico and Canada, as well as a six-month European tour and, in 1959, an 18,000-mile, forty-one-trailer trip the length of Africa from Cape Town to Cairo. Byam even designed a special harness used to load the trailers onto ships.

Throughout it all, Byam never stopped extolling the simple joys of life on the open road. Like Thomas Cook before him and Arthur Frommer after him, Byam had an almost religious belief in the right of all people — not just the wealthy — to enjoy an affordable, relaxing, enriching vacation. As he reportedly told a caravaner in 1959:

> Keep right on going. Hitch up your trailer and go to
> Canada or down to Old Mexico. Head for Europe, if
> you can afford it, or go to the Mardi Gras. Go someplace

you've heard about, where you can fish or hunt or collect
rocks or just look up at the sky. Find out what's at the
end of some country road. Go see what's over the next
hill, and the one after that, and the one after that.[48]

Airstream was not the first trailer manufacturer — in 1936, there
were more than three hundred small trailer companies across the
United States. None of those competitors survived the Depression, but
in the post-war boom years, Airstream would face serious competition for travellers' hearts and dollars from the major automakers. The
next step was to combine car and trailer into unit. In 1973, Airstream
and General Motors both launched their first motorhomes.

YOUR PRIZE ... A BRAND-NEW MOTORHOME!

Anyone who watched TV game shows during the mid-1970s will
remember the allure of these vehicles. As the top prize on shows
like *The Price Is Right* and *Wheel of Fortune*, they were built up by
hyperkinetic announcers as rolling mansions for the vacationing con-
noisseur. Whenever I saw one, I wondered why my family lived in
something as boring as a sedentary house. We could have a dinette, a
fully equipped kitchen and — best of all — spinny captain's chairs like
those on *Star Trek*! We could have adventures all day and then curl up
in a lime green bunk at night! What child wouldn't want that?

Many adults, apparently, shared my enthusiasm. After a somewhat slow start, hampered by the 1970s' oil crisis, the popularity of
trailers and motorhomes — brought together under the new rubric
"recreational vehicles" — began to climb. Between 1980 and 2005,
RV ownership in the United States increased by 58 percent — not a
demand spike on the order of, say, DVD players or iPods, but notable
enough when one considers that the price of many large motorhomes
now easily tops $100,000. They aren't usually impulse purchases.

By 2005, almost eight million US households owned an RV, according to the Recreation Vehicle Industry Association (RVIA). The
average RV owner logs 7,200 kilometres (4,500 miles) and twenty-six
days on the road each year.

LET'S STAY AT WAL-MART!

Most RV owners pull into one of North America's thousands of public and private campgrounds for the night, but a sizable minority gets more of a kick out of "boondocking" — staying overnight in their self-contained rigs in the parking lot of a truck stop or big box store. Drifting off to sleep to the noise of traffic on a nearby highway may not compare to being lulled to sleep by crickets at a lakeside campground, but it does have two major advantages: it's free, and it's located in an easy-to-reach urban area. For some travellers, those perks more than compensate for the distinct lack of atmosphere. To find their next piece of asphalt for the night, they check out Web sites that rate various parking lots and their surrounding amenities, such as fast food joints and grocery stores.

Wal-Marts are particularly popular boondocking stops because many are open twenty-four hours and openly encourage RVs to pull in for the night. Some Wal-Mart managers stock extra quantities of supplies RV drivers need, such as maps and compact appliances, and create separate areas of the store dedicated to RV accessories. "We treat them as shoppers who take a while to make up their minds," Tom Williams, a Wal-Mart spokesman, told Time in 2001.[49]

RVers themselves concede that the temptations of staying in the parking lot of an all-night big box store may outweigh the cost advantages of doing so. "We all know an overnight in a Wal-Mart parking lot is likely to cost us more than a campground. Wal-Mart does too! That is why they are happy to give us a place to get off the road," writes Paul Bernhagen on RVHometown.com, a Web site for RV owners.

Not surprisingly, boondocking has its critics, and not just among people who find the idea of waking up under the neon glare of a Wal-Mart sign deeply disturbing on an aesthetic level. Campground owners, naturally enough, aren't big fans of the trend. Civic authorities sometimes frown on the practice, too. Flagstaff, Arizona, for instance, has banned boondocking entirely. In an argument that sounds eerily like the cases made for banning the Roma from European cities in earlier decades and centuries, a Flagstaff police officer told a National Public Radio reporter that legitimate RVers aren't so bad, but some boondockers don't add much to the place: "Sometimes you do have a certain element of people who may be indigent or transient in nature and not only do they camp in the city limits, but they also then commit petty crimes to basically support themselves."[50]

ROLLING MANSIONS

At the other end of the RV spectrum from the folks who camp out in Wal-Mart parking lots are the rising numbers of luxury RV drivers, who are tooling around the country in rolling mansions equipped with flat-screen TVs, side-by-side refrigerators, granite countertops, marble floors, trash compactors and spiral staircases to the rooftop wet bar. According to the RVIA, about three hundred RVs costing more than a million dollars are sold each year. Many are made by specialized companies such as Liberty Coach of North Chicago, which builds fewer than three dozen a year.

If you're vacationing in a forty-five-foot vehicle better equipped than the vast majority of homes, you probably don't want to rub shoulders with just anyone. After all, these motorhomes are known as "Class A" motorhomes, and those who think the class issue in America is passé obviously haven't heard of Pelican Lake, a Florida property that bills itself as "The Exclusive Class A Motorcoach Resort."

If your vehicle isn't at least twenty-six feet long and loaded with luxury goodies, forget about getting past the security gate. "This ain't no KOA, baby," the owner of a $1.3 million custom-built motorhome told a *Chicago Tribune* reporter in 2006. The resort's site manager made the point even more bluntly: "Our residents like to be with the same type of people...It's not that they are looking down on people, but when they come here, they will be with other Class A's. That keeps the park exclusive."[51]

And for the rich RV enthusiast who can't decide between an RV and a boat, two companies — one in the US and one in Britain — have developed an amphibious motorhome. The American version, the Terra Wind, crams a lot of goodies into its forty-two-and-a-half-foot length, including a forty-two-inch plasma TV, a satellite dish, a dishwasher, an eight-jet whirlpool tub and a marble shower. When you get sick of hauling all this on the road, you can just drive it into the nearest lake and motor away (at a top speed of seven knots). And the price of becoming the James Bond of the RV set? The Terra Wind starts at $850,000.

RVS CONQUER THE PLANET

RV-ing might seem to be a quintessentially North American activity, best suited to a landscape of long distances and wide roads. But while the vehicles may be smaller than some of the behemoths cruising along America's interstates, life on the open road is wildly popular in many other places, particularly in Britain and Australia. Britain alone is home to an estimated two million "caravanners," who, according to a 2002 article in *The Economist*, spend a total of eighteen million nights annually sleeping in their little trailers.

One of the field's earliest UK advocates was a dentist named Ralph Lee. When Lee took his new bride Muriel camping in South Wales on their 1930 honeymoon, only to spend the week drenched from constant downpours, he was miraculously inspired to invent a more rainproof shelter for their road trips. (As the old saying goes, behind every successful man is an annoyed woman.) Even though he had never seen a trailer, he had read about them, and invented one built of wood and canvas — sort of a rolling tent.

Over the years he would build ten more, and his family lived in one for part of the Second World War when their house was destroyed in a bombing raid. After the war, Ralph and Muriel logged more than 800,000 kilometres (500,000 miles) by caravan. "I like to do things that other people have never done," Ralph once told a newspaper interviewer.

The Lees' adventures included trips to the Soviet Union (where they were the first-ever RV tourists), Norway (where wolves surrounded their trailer north of the Arctic Circle), Belgium (where they got trapped in an anti-royalist riot) and Romania (where suspicious communist officials locked them up in a steel cage). They hauled one or another of their little caravans across the English Channel seventy-four times. One of the country's leading trailer manufacturers made Lee a technical advisor. In 1999, Queen Elizabeth knighted him for his services to caravanning.

RVs attract their fair share of detractors, particularly in Britain. Perhaps it's because roads there are narrower and thus more prone to traffic jams when a slow-moving car towing a trailer moves into the queue. Or perhaps it's the fact that witty vitriol seems to catapult media figures to fame more regularly in Britain than elsewhere (this is, after all, the country that gave the world dominatrix-like game show host Anne Robinson and sob-inducing *American Idol* judge Simon Cowell, among countless others).

For whatever reason — maybe it's even lingering class consciousness — the humble travel trailer has been the object of scathing ridicule in Britain for years. In 2000, *New Statesman* columnist Andrew Martin caused a minor fracas when he claimed that "no individual has ever simultaneously possessed a caravan and a university degree." Among those who took him to task was his own degree-holding and caravan-owning uncle. But Martin remained unrepentant. "[W]hile I now concede that the odd caravanner may exist in the higher echelons of the middle class, there's no denying that the practice is regarded chiefly as a ludicrous and creepy fetish of the petit-bourgeoisie," he responded.[52]

When it comes to caravan-bashing, though, Martin is strictly a minor leaguer. The leading exponent of caravan hatred in the UK appears to be an automotive journalist named Jeremy Clarkson, who once crushed one with an airborne Porsche 911. (Well, this stunt has to be taken in context — he also once fired a Gatling gun at a Chevrolet Corvette, and trashed a Nissan Sunny by shooting it from a catapult.)

"I know the Caravan Club says its members are considerate but we must never forget that the Ku Klux Klan says its followers are respectable too," he told a British tabloid[53] after getting stuck behind a trailer while test driving a Lotus — a comment that ended up in Ralph Lee's obituary in *The New York Times*. Ouch.

FORGET THE DEPRESSION, GO SEE THE DAM!

Road construction, which had been haphazard throughout the late nineteenth and early twentieth centuries, took off in the US after the passage of federal legislation in 1916 and 1921 that provided states with federal funding for road construction. In the 1920s, the two levels of government spent a combined total of $10 billion to build and improve roads across the country.

By 1936, three-quarters of all American vacationers drove on vacation, while another 5.6 percent took the bus. The railroad's popularity had plummeted to just 13.6 percent. Despite the grinding poverty of the Depression, people still yearned for the open road — in fact, between 1929 and 1933, auto-related vacation spending (on products such as gas and oil) remained fairly steady at about $1 billion annually.

One of the factors spurring travel was novelty. By the mid-1930s, there were more and more places to travel *to*, and they were easier to reach. Under the New Deal, the federal government underwrote scores of public works projects that benefited vacationers, from six hundred shelters in New York's State Forest Preserve to paths at Mammoth Cave. Even infrastructure projects like the Hoover Dam — often called the Boulder Dam in those days — became worthy destinations.

Flight Patterns
A CENTURY OF AIR TRAVEL

Now the world is every man's oyster.
— Time, *about Pan Am's Juan Trippe,*
March 28, 1949

In 1958, Frank Sinatra capitalized on the public's fascination with international air travel with the album *Come Fly With Me*. With songs including "April in Paris," "Brazil" and "On the Road to Mandalay," Sinatra takes listeners on an audio world tour. On the album cover, Ol' Blue Eyes beckons some anonymous lovely (all we see is her hand in his) onto one of the planes in the background. But perhaps best capturing the boundless enthusiasm at the time for air travel is the title track, with its casual references to exotic locales — Bombay, Peru, Acapulco Bay — its promise of romantic adventure involving high-altitude cuddling and the almost irresistible finale: "Pack up, let's fly away!"

In 1964, Sinatra took the airborne concept even further when he recorded a hit version of "Fly Me to the Moon," written a decade earlier. As usual, the Chairman of the Board knew exactly when to capitalize on the *Zeitgeist*. Yuri Gagarin and John Glenn had circled the earth, and airports like LAX were looking more and more like space pods every day. Why shouldn't people dream that they could "play among the stars" and "see what spring is like on Jupiter and Mars"?

And yet, every senior citizen among Sinatra's listeners had been alive before the world's first successful plane ever left the ground.

TWELVE SECONDS THAT CHANGED THE WORLD

On December 17, 1903, Orville Wright was the first human to fulfill mankind's longstanding dream to fly. For twelve amazing seconds, he managed to keep the *Wright Flyer* airborne above Kitty Hawk, North Carolina, before landing 37 metres (120 feet) away. By the end of the day, his brother Wilbur had bested that initial distance seven times over, taking the craft on a 59-second, 260-metre (852 feet) flight.

It wasn't exactly the sort of experience that would appeal to a sophisticated jet-setter — more like hang-gliding, really. The pilot lay face down atop the fuselage of the 6.4-metre-long craft. Operating the elevator control with his left hand, he controlled the wing tips and rudder by wiggling his hips inside a cradle to move a system of wires.

Aviation technology developed quickly, as inventors and amateur flyers in both North America and Europe scrambled to come up with the next innovation. Within two years, the Wrights would set a distance record of 39.2 kilometres (24.5 miles) at Huffman Prairie, Ohio.

Terrified of having their technology stolen before they could properly capitalize on it, the Wrights kept their stunning success largely secret for several years, until they could secure patents and sales contracts. Not surprisingly, word leaked out anyway, and other inventors rushed to duplicate the Wrights' achievement. The brothers hurried to get all their ducks in a row, then demonstrated their latest plane in a series of public flights in Europe in 1908 and 1909, becoming worldwide celebrities.

By summer 1909, public interest in aviation was at a fever pitch. The first major international air show took place near Reims, France, in August. In New York, more than a million spectators lined the Hudson River on October 4 to see Wilbur Wright pilot a thirty-three-minute flight from Governor's Island to Grant's Tomb and back, in celebration of the hundredth anniversary of Robert Fulton's steamboat and the three-hundredth anniversary of Henry Hudson's initial trip up his namesake river. Wright planned ahead for possible emergency by strapping a canoe to the bottom of the plane.

It wasn't long, of course, before people realized that there was money in the skies. However, what appears to be the world's first commercial flight, on November 7, 1910, carried, not passengers, but cargo — two bolts of silk flown from Dayton to Columbus, Ohio, as a publicity stunt sponsored by a department store.

As with long-distance coach travel and transatlantic shipping centuries earlier, growth in the air transportation industry was spurred at first by the desire to move, not people, but goods — especially airmail, with the first official flight taking place on February 18, 1911, when Henri Pequet carried 6,500 letters a distance of thirteen kilometres (eight miles) near Allahabad, India. In many countries, military or civilian government authorities ran airmail services at first, but they were eventually supplanted by private airlines that jockeyed for government contracts.

It would take a decade after the Wright brothers made their first short hop across a North Carolina sand dune before the world's first scheduled passenger aircraft service began shuttling passengers across Florida's Tampa Bay. The St. Petersburg-Tampa Airboat Line used a Benoist seaplane that could carry just one passenger — or two small ones — on a hard wooden seat in the hull.

When the company was planning its inaugural flight, it decided to auction the honour of being the world's first commercial airline passenger to the highest bidder. Competition among local luminaries was fierce, but bidding came down to Noel Mitchell and Abram C. Pheil, both former mayors. With a bid of $400, Pheil topped Mitchell's final offer of $375. On January 1, 1914, in St. Petersburg, as an enthusiastic crowd estimated at three thousand looked on, the forty-six-year-old Pheil climbed into the fragile-looking plane and pilot Tony Jannus scrambled into the cockpit. Soon, they were airborne.

The ensuing trip had a bit more in common with a theme park ride than a modern commercial flight. The plane barely skimmed above the bay, the salty seawater spraying into the plane through the open cockpit. After twenty-three minutes and roughly thirty-two kilometres (twenty miles), they landed on the Hillsborough River at the foot of Lee Street in Tampa. On exiting, Pheil apparently uttered the momentous words "Please unbutton my coat," before heading for a phone to reassure his family he had landed without incident. His next task was to place an order worth several thousand dollars for his wholesale business, thus making this the first business trip by air as well, before bravely heading back to St. Petersburg on the afternoon plane.

From the beginning, the little airline was a boon to businessmen, and a group of backers in St. Petersburg subsidized it to the tune of $25 for each day it flew round-trip. The short flight had definite advantages over the other primary alternative for travel between the two cities: an eight-hour train trip. Business appears to have been brisk — the company later reported that seats had been sold out for sixteen weeks in advance before the airline even opened for business. It suspended operations after three months, when many of the region's visitors returned north for the summer, and intended to reopen the following season with a new, twelve-passenger Benoist flying boat. By late 1914, however, war had been declared in Europe and people in every line of business were proceeding with caution. The world's first commercial passenger airline closed its doors. For the next few years, the primary air travellers would be military.

AVIATION MANIA TAKES HOLD

On the night of May 21, 1927, thousands gathered around the tarmac at Le Bourget Aerodrome, their gazes cast expectantly into the night sky just north of Paris. Ever since telegraph operators had cabled the news that a small grey plane had been spotted off the coast of Ireland, then over Cherbourg, Paris had been fizzing with excitement. Those who couldn't make it to Le Bourget thronged squares and newspaper offices in the city, desperate for news.

Finally, it came: the thrum of an engine high above the airfield. At 10:22 PM, thirty-three and a half hours after leaving Roosevelt Airfield on Long Island, Charles Lindbergh landed the *Spirit of St. Louis* on solid ground once more. In so doing, he ensured that he would win the $25,000 prize that New York hotelier Raymond Orteig had offered for the first person to fly non-stop from New York to Paris.

The crowd surged, bearing the exhausted pilot aloft to cries of

"Cette fois, ça va!" ("This time, it happened!") Back in the city, by-standers shouted "Vive l'Américain!" Such was the celebrity of the first man to fly solo across the Atlantic. That historic night cemented the romantic appeal of early air travel forever. Just twenty-four years after the Wrights had made their first short hop across a North Carolina field, a man had flown across an ocean. Surely everyone would soon be soaring through the heavens as easily as they boarded a train?

Subsequent daredevil feats only cemented this view. In 1930, English aviator Amy Johnson became the first woman to fly solo from England to Australia. Seven years later, Amelia Earhart failed in her quest to be the first woman to fly around the world. Each new advance — and tragedy — in the evolution of long-distance flight captured the imagination of the public in the dark days of the Depression.

THE INFANCY OF AIRLINES

Charles Lindbergh's transatlantic crossing sparked the imagination of entrepreneurs around the world. What if scheduled airline service could shuttle mail, cargo and people across oceans in the fraction of the time it would take to complete such journeys by ship? The economic potential of these dreams was too great to remain unexploited.

The foundation of some of the world's major airlines was already in place years before Lindbergh landed at Le Bourget. In terms of passenger aviation, Europe took an early lead over North America. In the wake of the First World War, airplane manufacturers were eager for new, non-military customers, and roads and railways had been devastated by the conflict. In comparison to less densely settled areas of the world, European capitals were relatively close together. Conditions for the quick development of commercial airplane travel were ripe.

Arguably the world's first passenger airline was the German company DELAG, founded in 1909, which used airships rather than planes. The service was aimed largely at rich tourists, who paid between one hundred and two hundred reichsmarks — more than the average German worker earned in a year — to waft between various German cities.

The world's first regular daily scheduled international flight took place on August 25, 1919, when British Aircraft Transport and Travel flew a converted de Havilland 4A bomber from London to Paris. Entrepreneurs in other countries soon followed Britain's lead: KLM made its first flight, a run from Amsterdam to London, on May 17, 1920.

Soon, governments realized the value of capitalizing on economies of scale. In 1924, the British government formed Imperial Airways — a forerunner of British Airways — from the merger of several smaller companies. Two years later, the German government combined two companies to create Deutsche Luft Hansa (later simply Lufthansa), which boasted of a fleet of more than one hundred and fifty planes. In contrast, in 1927 there were only about thirty commercial passenger planes in the entire United States.

Part of the reason for the faster growth of airlines in Europe was that many European countries were motivated by a desire to travel more quickly to their far-flung colonies. Imperial Airways began flying a route between Cairo and Baghdad in 1927; by 1935, it was serving more than five hundred destinations, including Kuwait, Bahrain, Cape Town, Karachi, Singapore and Brisbane. In the early 1930s, Air France was serving Saigon, KLM served Batavia (now Jakarta), and Sabena had established a route from Brussels to the Congo.

JUAN TRIPPE AND THE RISE OF PAN AM

Of the early tycoons of the air, none prospered so quite spectacularly as Pan American Airways' risk-taking, charismatic founder. Juan Trippe had the raw nerve to take the luxurious elites-only mystique of long-distance travel and make it the mind-numbing aggravation we know and love today.

In other words, Trippe saw a business aimed at travellers, and opened it up to tourists.

Largely unknown today except among business historians and

aviation buffs, Trippe was the Richard Branson of his day — a bit more low key, certainly, but no less willing to risk everything to bring the latest thing in aviation to his customers, and to get rich doing it. He made the cover of *Time* magazine twice, and he was one of the magazine's one hundred "people of the century" in 2000. (Branson, not surprisingly, contributed the essay about his forerunner.)

In the early 1920s, Trippe and some of his Yale buddies launched an airline that shuttled their rich friends between New York and the Hamptons. After blowing an inheritance on that failed project, Trippe raised some money from his friends and invested in the company that snagged America's first airmail contract, for service between New York and Boston.

In 1927, Trippe bought into Pan American Airways Inc., a company that would endure for more than sixty years. So dominant was the company that its 1991 collapse would have been as inconceivable to the average American a few decades ago as the bankruptcy of Microsoft or Coca-Cola would be to people today. In the middle years of the twentieth century, Pan American *owned* long-distance commercial aviation in the Americas. As just one example, from 1930 to 1934, when other airlines struggled and failed to come to grips with the Depression, Pan American enjoyed gross business growth of 150 percent, largely on the strength of its international mail contracts.

It's significant that Pan American's first flight, a mail-carrying trip in October 1927, connected Key West and Havana. When the company launched a daily passenger service on the same 144-kilometre (90-mile) route a few months later, with a tab of $100 for a return ticket, some of its most enthusiastic customers were Trippe's old Yale crowd, attracted by the promise of limitless sunshine, gambling, nightlife and legal rum. But Trippe now had a broader vision: he wanted to dominate aviation in Latin America. And he did, although at times it could get a bit, well, messy.

For example, in 1933, the US government asked Pan American to fly deposed Cuban dictator Gerardo Machado y Morales to safety; the feds returned the favour a few years later, when Trippe needed some help persuading the Guatemalan government to grant him landing rights. In another instance, a revolution suddenly broke out near a remote Pan American refuelling station in Honduras. When the airline expressed its concern about the safety of its planes, the United Fruit Company — which was funding the revolution to depose the Honduran president, who had had the temerity to raise the tax on bananas — simply instructed the rebels to stop bombing the airport.

Pan American's expansion required nerve and a thick skin. At one point, when Trippe was working hard to take over a Colombian airline called SCADTA, local newspapers were decrying the "hateful Yankee air monopoly." But the effort paid off. Within two years, Pan American was flying into seventy-one airports in North, Central and South America, and the company had taken over SCADTA.

Trippe learned to trust his vision and to stick his neck out when few competitors would dare. He was the first to see the possibility of flying, not just across continents, but also across oceans.

The major obstacle to long-distance travel was the technological challenge of building a plane with both the size and the range to complete the journey. Airlines around the world tackled this problem by planning routes that included multiple stops. For instance, Imperial Airways launched service from London to Karachi in 1929, with stops along the way in more than a dozen places, including Paris, Athens, Alexandria and Baghdad. Australia and South Africa were similarly reachable. But when it came to transoceanic travel, there was another problem: even if island stopping points existed (as they did in the Pacific, but not in the North Atlantic), many were tiny places without concrete runways.

Trippe's genius was to realize that he didn't need an airport. Instead of coming down on land, his transoceanic Boeing "flying boats" would land on water. He tackled the Pacific first, using Hawaii, Midway, Wake, Guam, Luzon and other islands as refuelling stops between the west coast of the US and Asia.

Trippe was also one of the first airline owners to anticipate the rise of mass air travel. In 1945, he slashed the round-trip price of his transatlantic trips to $275 — almost $1,700 in today's dollars but still much less than the $750 fare on Pan American's inaugural transatlantic flights in 1939.

This move did not make him popular with the competition. Other airlines flattered themselves that they were the conveyors of the elite — moneyed folks who didn't mind paying for speed, convenience and bragging rights. If people wanted cheap fares, they could get on a ship. In Europe, governments moved quickly to protect their homegrown airlines from this price slashing. Britain, for instance, wouldn't allow Pan American flights with the new "tourist class" seats to land. Trippe didn't blink — he just took his business to more open-minded Shannon in Ireland. He also launched a route between New York and San Juan, Puerto Rico. Passengers stampeded to pay the reasonable $150 round trip fare. By the early 1950s, airlines around the world were grudgingly following Trippe's lead and offering their own cut-rate seats.

Even "cut-rate" long-distance flights were still out of range for most people, though. It would take the arrival of the jet plane to bring air travel to the masses. Again, Trippe was ahead of the curve. Pan Am's first scheduled jet flight, using a Boeing 707, connected New York and Paris in October 1958. Even though this new plane was much faster than its prop predecessors and carried nearly twice as many people, Trippe saw an opportunity to squeeze in more passengers and thereby cut fares. In a move that would haunt economy-class passengers forevermore — but which made it possible for there to *be* an economy class in the first place — Trippe asked Boeing to increase the number of seats in each row from five to six. This alteration helped him drop his fares even further.

But he wanted still more. He asked Boeing to build him a bigger jet, and he promised to buy twenty-five of them. The 747 debuted commercially in 1970. Like the monster cruise ships launched in the past few years, the 747 dramatically changed the scale of air travel. Like ports now scrambling to build longer wharves and deeper harbours, airports raced to build bigger facilities to accommodate the new behemoths.

Ironically, with the 747, Trippe may have finally dreamed the impossible dream. He bought the aircraft and passengers loved them, but the oil crisis of the early 1970s decimated air travel. Pan Am limped along for another two decades, but it was never the same. It stopped leading and started following.

COMING IN FOR A LANDING

Airlines couldn't grow very well without airports. Even Trippe's flying boats needed some sort of terminal where passengers could buy tickets and wait for their flights. And airport expansion had an early champion in Charles Lindbergh.

As soon as he got back from his triumph in Paris, Lindbergh set off on an aviation crusade of sorts across the United States. Inspired by the network of airlines in Europe, he declared that America needed to catch up. He visited every state in the union, touching down in more than eighty cities and logging 35,200 kilometres (22,000 miles). More than thirty million people came to see him, including Henry Ford, Douglas Fairbanks, Mary Pickford and Will Rogers. The celebrity touch seems to have been the spark America needed to get behind the idea of air travel. A year after Lindbergh's promotional trip, hundreds of airports were being planned, built or upgraded.

The first tiny airports bore little resemblance to the sprawling behemoths we dazedly pass through today. For one thing, architects and city planners had little idea how to design them. For the first time in human history, we needed terminals to welcome vehicles from above our heads. It was an engineering challenge, to say the least.

At first, many chose to pave the middle of the property for planes and build the terminal and hangars on the edges of the field — almost the mirror image of today's airports, with a terminal in the middle surrounded by runways. And many early airports were also designed to accommodate dirigibles as well as winged aircraft. Until the *Hindenburg* disaster in 1937, some people were hopeful that dirigibles would become a popular form of air transportation, particularly over long distances.

Like the architects who designed stolid, columned banks to reassure jittery customers that the institution wouldn't fail, early airport architects worked hard to convey an image of solidity and safety in their structures. The grounds of Fairfax Airport in Kansas City, landscaped in 1929, included a fountain, formal gardens and a reflecting pool. The entrance of Swan Island Airport in Portland, Oregon, was a streamlined structure that resembled an elegant office building.

Some architects, particularly in California, opted for a more theatrical approach. One terminal at Mines Field (now LAX) in Los Angeles was reminiscent of a Spanish monastery, while the Moorish-style airport in Van Nuys was so convincing that Michael Curtiz used it for the exteriors of the last scene in the film *Casablanca*.

Still, most passenger terminals were small and dull — cramped, windowless afterthoughts modelled on small-town railway depots. As usual, Juan Trippe was one of the first to realize that air travel had to seem exciting from the moment the passenger arrived at the airport. In 1928, he commissioned William Adams Delano and Chester Aldrich — best known for designing townhouses and private clubs for New York's elite — to design an inspiring terminal for Pan Am in Miami. The resulting building had a curved, vaulted roof and a balcony overlooking the tarmac. Inside, below huge windows, porters in crisp white uniforms ferried luggage, and passengers sat in wicker chairs among potted palms as they listened for the brass bell that signalled each flight's imminent departure. The terminal was such a success that the firm was later asked to design the first terminal at LaGuardia.

Not all the efforts to make airports atmospheric were politically correct. In the early 1940s, a plantation-inspired restaurant opened at Atlanta's airport, complete with murals of cotton fields and an elderly black employee spinning Uncle Remus tales while perched on a bale of cotton.

Meanwhile in Europe, cities were beginning to build ever more stylish airports with a greater range of services. At Leipzig, for instance, diners in the restaurant could gaze onto the runway though floor-to-ceiling windows. In his 1935 novel, *England Made Me*, Graham Greene was able to write lyrically of a character who "knew the airports of Europe as well as he had once known the stations on the Brighton line — shabby Le Bourget; the great scarlet rectangle of the Tempelhof as one came in from London in the dark...; the white sand blowing up round the shed at Tallinn; Riga, where the Berlin to Leningrad plane came down and bright pink mineral waters were sold in a tin-roofed shed."

AIRPORTS IN THE SKY?

In the early days, at least to some people, it wasn't even entirely
clear that the ground was the best place to build an airport. One of
the most famous — and, like all the others, abandoned — schemes
to build an airport in the sky gave the Empire State Building its
distinctive profile.

It started as a Donald Trump-style effort at one-upmanship. The
original plans for the Empire State Building called for a structure just
a few feet taller than the Chrysler Building, which had become the
world's tallest building when it opened in 1930. But former New
York governor Al Smith and financier John J. Raskob, the Empire
State Building's backers, wanted a more decisive triumph over their
rival. They decided to add a two-hundred-foot masonry tower with a
chrome-and-glass cylindrical mooring mast for dirigibles. The day had
come, they declared, for air travellers to arrive directly in Manhattan,
without a long trip in from Long Island.

The problem was that Smith and Raskob hadn't made any serious
plans for accommodating a huge lighter-than-air vehicle that would
exert a fifty-ton pull on their new building. They'd stiffened the
building's framework, reserved space on the eighty-sixth floor for
a ticket office and departure lounge, and installed some rudimentary winches to haul the dirigibles in. But the structure's optimistic
promoters had conveniently overlooked the fact that airship pilots
wouldn't be thrilled by the idea of navigating their puncture-sensitive
craft through a thicket of pointy skyscrapers, which themselves
created nasty wind currents. And then there was the small matter of
getting the passengers out, a task that would have required a system
of walkways and ladders that would have given even a hardy seaman
pause — all suspended a quarter of a mile above the teeming streets
of Manhattan.

Smith blithely dismissed all skepticism of the project, assuring
doubters that all these problems could be worked out with the help of
the US Navy (which, interestingly, had nothing to say on the topic).
Two airships did manage to connect to the building, very briefly, by

rope, but the project didn't succeed. Gradually, Smith and Raskob stopped talking about mooring dirigibles to their new creation — after all, after taking the record for the world's tallest building, the Empire State Building had nothing to prove to anyone. The public eventually forgot the reason for the glittering mast. In an ironic footnote, the mast eventually did serve to bring people together in quite a different way — it made a dandy television and radio transmission tower.

That zeppelins were once considered the high-tech wave of the future suggests just how up in the air (literally, I suppose) the aviation business was in the 1930s. Until the development of winged aircraft capable of crossing oceans, zeppelins were the only aircraft capable of giving the immensely profitable transatlantic ocean liners a run for their money. From beginning to end, German manufacturers and operators dominated the industry.

After launching regular services to Rio de Janeiro, German entrepreneurs extended their reach to North America. Perhaps the greatest zeppelin of all was the *Graf Zeppelin*, launched in 1928. Like its competitors, the transatlantic liners, it had a promenade deck, two-berth cabins and sumptuous public rooms. Astonishingly, given the danger open flames posed aboard an airship held aloft by flammable gas, there was even a smoking room, where ship personnel watched passengers with eagle eyes. (According to a contemporary newspaper article, passengers felt the smoking limitations "keenly.")

Like Lindbergh's arrival in Paris the year before, the approach of the *Graf Zeppelin* to the United States was followed eagerly by thousands of people. Up to sixty-five thousand had made their way to Lakehurst, New Jersey, to await the aircraft. But due to bad weather, the airship took almost 112 hours to make the journey from Germany, and over three days most of the crowd drifted away. About five thousand die-hards remained to greet it when it came to earth at 5:38 PM on October 15, 1928.

They were far from the only people to witness its progress, however; it had captivated Manhattan when it cruised by on its way to New Jersey. "AIRSHIP HYPNOTIZES CITY GAZING UPWARD; Sight of the Majestic Visitor Quickens Pulse of Metropolis, Stirs

Strange Exultation," blared the headline of the normally sober *New York Times* the following day. As the story below breathlessly reported, "The appearance in the skies of the massive Graf Zeppelin, with its 121 assorted tons of mortals; freight and mechanism, halted New York City in its tracks yesterday afternoon." Even the presumably jaded reporters of the great, grey lady were enthralled by the ship's arrival: the paper ran more than forty stories about the event on October 16 alone.

Lakehurst would reappear in zeppelin history, and not in a happy way. For German airships, gas was a particular problem. Due to a military embargo, Nazi Germany was unable to get helium, and instead inflated their airships with hydrogen, which was much riskier. This became a particular problem in the design of the *Hindenburg*, which succeeded the *Graf Zeppelin* as the epitome of airships. After several uneventful trips, the *Hindenburg* exploded on arrival in Lakehurst on May 6, 1937, before the very media reception that had been engineered to greet it. The ensuing circus almost destroyed the entire airship industry.

Except for the Goodyear blimp and similar novelty machines, airships pretty much disappeared from the skies for the half-century after the *Hindenburg* disaster. But beginning in the late 1980s, interest began to revive. In 1988, a Canadian company called 21st Century Airships began developing spherical airships, and a few years later a German company descended from the original Zeppelin firm started manufacturing more traditionally shaped machines. So far, aircraft made by these firms and others are used mainly for advertising, surveillance, sightseeing and aerial photography purposes, but hopes are high among promoters that the airship as a serious form of long-distance transportation isn't quite dead yet.

TRANSATLANTIC FLIGHTS BOOST AIRPORT CONSTRUCTION

The Great Depression slowed, but did not stop, airport construction in the United States. President Franklin Roosevelt authorized construction or renovation of numerous facilities through work relief programs such as the Civil Works Administration and the Work

Projects Administration. Most of these buildings were plain and utilitarian, although several featured artwork funded by the Federal Art Project.

The largest airport built in the United States in the 1930s was LaGuardia on Long Island, named after the determined New York mayor who had pressed for its construction in the face of widespread public skepticism. He wanted to make sure proper facilities were available to welcome visitors to the 1939 World's Fair, held in nearby Flushing Meadows.

The next step now was to connect Europe and North America — to make Charles Lindbergh's heroic trip a matter of plodding routine. Transatlantic air service thus became the holy grail for airlines on both sides of the ocean in the 1930s. Opening up the Pacific, as Juan Trippe had done at Pan Am, was all well and good, but cities on the west coast of North America didn't yet have the economic and cultural importance and size of the cities of the east, particularly New York. And North America's ties to Europe were stronger than those to Asia. Transatlantic sea routes were some of the world's most profitable, and airlines wanted a piece of that very large pie. Lindbergh had proved the ocean *could* be crossed; now they just had to find a way for ordinary people and heavier planes to do it.

Flying across the North Atlantic in a winged aircraft was problematical for two reasons: capricious weather and a distinct lack of refuelling points. Zeppelins seemed poised to dominate the market into the foreseeable future and had already carried thousands of passengers back and forth across the North Atlantic. But this was a German technology, and their competitors in the United States, Britain and elsewhere — particularly Pan Am and Imperial Airways — were reluctant to concede the field.

It was already well known that the shortest route between New York and London passed through Newfoundland and Ireland. The first transatlantic telegraph cable had been laid between Ireland's Valantia Island and Newfoundland's Trinity Bay in the 1850s. So it seemed only natural to use these two points as refuelling stations. In 1935, the governments of Britain, Ireland and Newfoundland agreed to develop a regular transatlantic flying boat service that would carry both mail and passengers. In 1936, Pan Am joined the project, after the British government lifted its restrictions on American planes landing in Britain. A seaplane refuelling station opened at Botwood Harbour in northeastern Newfoundland in 1937. On July 5, 1937, Pan Am and Imperial Airways began two years of experimental seaplane flights between Foynes, Ireland, and Botwood. At that time, the average flight took almost a day.

Meanwhile Trippe — an old hand at begging, cajoling and otherwise persuading foreign governments to let him land his planes on their soil — was negotiating landing rights agreements with other possible refuelling points, including Bermuda, Greenland and the Azores. Then, in December 1937, he asked eight US aviation companies to bid on a contract to manufacture what seemed at the time like an impossible dream: a long-range flying boat that could seat 100 passengers. Boeing won the contract, and by early 1939 Trippe was the proud owner of a fleet of B-314 flying boats. Each $500,000 plane could carry up to seventy-four passengers and fly up to 5,633 kilometres. The B-314's record as the world's largest commercial plane would stand until the first jumbo jets (also built by Boeing) took to the skies in 1970.

In a brilliant marketing move, Trippe christened the flying boats "clippers," recalling images of the swift, romantic sailing ships that had set oceanic speed records in the nineteenth century. On March 26, 1939, Pan Am's *Yankee Clipper* made a trial flight from Baltimore to Foynes, and only three months later, on June 28, the world's first scheduled transatlantic flight took off from New York. The passengers each paid $375 one-way for the trip. After refuelling, the *Yankee Clipper* glided into the harbour at Marseilles, France. The following month, Pan Am began its service between New York and Southampton.

Pan Am soon made the new LaGuardia Airport its New York base, launching regular service to Lisbon, which was a major European gateway at that time (remember all the trapped refugees in *Casablanca* enviously eyeing the daily flight to Lisbon?).

The Second World War put a long crimp in transatlantic passenger service, but as the war drew to a close, the US Civil Aeronautics

Board gave three airlines — American Export, Pan Am and fledgling TWA — permission to run commercial flights on the North Atlantic route. American Export would run the first regular landplane passenger services in the North Atlantic, beginning with a fourteen-hour route from New York to Bournemouth, England, in October 1945. American Export's DC-4s would stop at Gander, Newfoundland, and Shannon, Ireland — two new airports built in anticipation of the replacement of flying boats by landplanes.

Pan Am launched its regular DC-4 transatlantic passenger service a few days after American Export (it must have galled Trippe to be second, for a change). TWA followed suit in February 1946, but it used the Lockheed Constellation, which offered a significant advantage over the DC-4: its pressurized cabin made it possible to fly as high as 6,100 metres. Other airlines quickly adopted the Constellation and the later Super Constellation. By August 1947, Pan Am was offering regular, non-stop service between New York and London with the Lockheed planes.

US airlines had the early advantage in post-war transatlantic travel; unlike their competitors in Europe, their airfields and fleets weren't in ruins. But Europe quickly caught up. In the immediate aftermath of the war, busy airports sprang up in some unlikely places to serve as refuelling points for the fledgling transatlantic air services, which did not use the flying boats that had been popular before the war.

Shannon Airport opened in the west of Ireland in 1942 and received its first commercial passenger flights in fall 1945. As the closest European airport to North America, it was soon booming (its heavily publicized duty-free shopping opportunities were an added bonus). On the other side of the ocean, Gander Airport in Newfoundland had opened just before the outbreak of the war, as an air force base; by the 1950s, this unlikely spot on the rural east coast of Newfoundland was one of the busiest airports in the world.

By 1950, almost a dozen airlines — including KLM, Air France, Sabena, SAS and Swissair — were plying the North Atlantic route, which, in a little over a decade, had become the world's busiest air route. In a few years, when the combination of post-war prosperity, longer paid vacations and jet airplanes brought air travel to the masses, there would be few more hotly contested routes on earth.

In the 1960s, airlines began to see their departure lounges as an extension of the brand itself. To complement sexy new stewardess uniforms and racy advertising campaigns, Braniff redesigned its terminal at Love Field — a double entendre in itself — with mirrored ceilings and op-art murals, seemingly trying to make passengers feel as though they were about to take off into a James Bond movie. Dubbed "the Terminal of the Future," it opened in December 1968.

The futuristic feel of the terminal got another boost in April 1972, when, with much fanfare, Braniff launched its $2 million Jetrail. In the days before security checkpoints, this monorail ferried passengers right from the parking garage to the Braniff terminal, three-quarters of a mile away. They could even check their luggage through to their destination before boarding the monorail. The Jetrail was the predecessor of dozens of "people-mover" systems at airports around the world, but ironically its own life was short: Braniff moved to the new Dallas-Forth Worth airport a few years later, and the monorail was dismantled in 1978.

PIONEER PASSENGERS

What was it like to be one of the brave passengers on these early commercial flights? It seems to have been a strange, heady combination of thrills, discomfort, embarrassment, fear and smugness.

The earliest air travellers, particularly in the US, were basically afterthoughts. The primary commercial business of aviation was moving mail. If passengers didn't mind sitting on top of a mail sack in a cabin that was neither heated nor air conditioned, they were welcome. Fortunately, planes in those days didn't fly nearly as high as modern jetliners, so the cabin air was merely unpleasant rather than life threatening.

The fears many travellers brought with them to the airport, however, were solidly based in reality. In the US in 1928, one in every hundred air passengers died: fourteen of the fourteen hundred people who took to the skies that year. In comparison, from 1980 to 1996, there were 0.37 and 0.52 fatal accidents per *million* flights respectively for North American and European operators.

Like airport designers, airlines and tour companies worked mightily to dispel the fears surrounding early air travel. In a 1920 brochure, the Thomas Cook company tried to reassure potential customers that flying on repurposed military bombers was perfectly safe. After all, the brochure pointed out, these aircraft had been built to fly long distances and to keep valuable military pilots safe. Since many people's main impressions of aviation were the antics of stunt flyers, the brochure's author felt compelled to add that "the pilot will not loop the loop or perform any other spectacular but useless and dangerous stunts."

Airlines did what they could to allay travellers' fears, but they couldn't quite cover up the somewhat demeaning aspects of early air travel. Before boarding, passengers had to stand with their luggage on a freight scale. If the combined total was more than 180 pounds, they had to pay a higher fare.

Despite such indignities, many early flyers were quite conscious that they were among society's most privileged members. For conspicuous consumption, few things could be more conspicuous than literally soaring over the heads of one's compatriots. When a character in F. Scott Fitzgerald's *The Last Tycoon*, flying from New York to Los Angeles, is temporarily grounded in Nashville due to bad weather, she remarks: "In the big transcontinental planes we were the coastal rich, who casually alighted from our cloud in mid-America." They weren't the only ones who knew it. Ingenious entrepreneurs erected illuminated billboards under flight paths to hawk their products to the magnates flying overhead.

These early flights were really practical only for the rich. In the early 1920s, it cost £10 to fly from London to Paris with Thomas Cook at a time when the minimum wage for a week's work was roughly £1 and 11 shillings. Then, as now, tourism promoters were eager to court the richest travellers, and airlines competed by offering perks such as limousine transportation to the airport (possibly to make up for the fact that until the late 1920s, most passenger planes provided neither washrooms nor food).

Thomas Cook ran its first charter aircraft tour in 1929, a surprisingly upscale jaunt from New York to Chicago to see Jack Dempsey fight Gene Tunney for the heavyweight boxing championship. The rich sports fans dined on lunch boxes from Sherry's Restaurant as they made their way to the Midwest.

LIFE IN THE AIR

Whenever someone tells you things are just getting better and better, cast your mind back to the Pan American's heyday. The interiors of at least some of its flying boats in South America featured walnut panelling and silk window curtains. On the transatlantic clippers, passengers settled into spacious armchairs in private compartments for four, where they'd be served their meals on a collapsible table. They could stretch their legs on the promenade deck, or stretch out completely in a berth to sleep.

Think we make up for those with other amenities now? Some have been around longer than one might imagine. The first in-flight movie — a lightweight Harold Lloyd flick called *Speedy* — was screened during a flight over LA in 1928. But other things remain the same. When I get on any flight, I usually bring enough books and magazines in my carry-on to last me a week, so deathly afraid am I of being bored. Perhaps because they were used to thinking of air travel as so much faster than sea travel, early passengers sometimes forgot to take this precaution. During a ten-day flight (with thirty-five stops!) between London and Brisbane in 1935, a British businessman grumbled: "There are five passengers in this plane, and every one of them is reading one of my books...No one else has come with sufficient literature to get them even as far as Baghdad."[54]

Of course, some routes were more thrilling than others. Travel to developing nations could be even more exciting in the 1930s — in good and bad ways — than flying in Europe and North America. In some Middle East locations, airlines built airfields that were actually miniature forts manned by armed guards.

AIRPORT BELLS AND WHISTLES

As airlines and travel agents began urging passengers to arrive at the airport early to avoid missing their flights, people began spending more time than ever before milling about on both sides of the security checkpoints. It took a surprisingly long time, however, for facility managers and retailers to realize that these crowds of bored, restless, affluent people constituted the very definition of a captive market. At one time, most airline terminals had little more than a couple of restaurants and a newsstand.

Greater Pittsburgh Airport, though, was different. In the 1950s, it had a dozen shops, a full-sized movie theatre and a nightclub. In 1992, its successor, Pittsburgh International, opened the Air Mall, where nationally recognized names such as the Body Shop and Victoria's Secret predominated among the thirty stores, and as many as sixty-thousand passengers a day shopped. When word got out that sales per square foot were as much as 400 percent higher than those at non-airport malls, retailers and airport authorities sat up and took notice. "If you have 15 million or 20 million people going through your gates...it's a tremendous retail opportunity," Larry Berg, president and CEO of the Vancouver International Airport Authority, told *Canadian Business* in 1998. "Passengers are really looking for a high-quality retail and food-and-beverage experience, good service and prices competitive with downtown pricing."[55]

Britain was another leader in the airport retail field, spurred by the profitability of Harrods outlets at Heathrow and Gatwick. A company called BAA manages commercial facilities at these two and five other British airports, as well as eleven other airports around the world, including Pittsburgh. On average, 10 percent of each BAA's airport floor space is devoted to retailing, but the company claims the revenues these stores bring in help the airports keep airline landing fees competitive.

There could be something to that. Lester B. Pearson International Airport in Toronto once made its comparative dearth of retail services something of a point of pride. In 1998, just after announcing what would eventually become a C$4.4 billion airport expansion, Greater

Toronto Airports Authority president and CEO Louis Turpen told the same *Canadian Business* reporter that he had no intention of following the lead of airports such as Vancouver International and Amsterdam's Schiphol:

> "Some airports sell diamond rings," [Turpen] says. "I'm not sure what the market is for three-carat diamonds on the way to Acapulco, but who knows?" According to Turpen, glitzy airport shopping is really just a gimmick pushed by "retail gurus." ... As for food service, Turpen adds, "It's not a revenue generator. I can't build terminal buildings selling hot dogs."[56]

As the airport expansion went on, however, the airport's managers changed their tune. By the time it opened in April 2004, a shopping area had been incorporated into the new terminal.

Yet, hinging the profitability of an airport on its retail propositions has its drawbacks. As airports have come to rely more and more on profits from shops and other ancillary services, they've had to work harder to encourage passengers to spend, spend, spend instead of just sitting around in the departure lounge, reading a book.

When air traffic around the world dropped after 9/11, the shops at Singapore's Changi airport felt the pinch. To bolster sales, the airport launched what it billed as "the first and only game show in an airport." Between December 15, 2001, and March 15, 2002, passengers who made a purchase in the airport's shops or restaurants could compete in a computerized trivia game to win their share of the daily jackpot of S$10,000 in shopping vouchers. Buy something, and we'll give you a prize to buy more! Pure genius.

But there's much more to the new breed of airport amenities than shopping and game shows. Vancouver International Airport proudly displays numerous pieces of West Coast art, including a six-metre-long bronze sculpture by Bill Reid, "The Spirit of Haida Gwaii: The Jade Canoe," which appears on the back of the Canadian twenty-dollar bill. Passengers can also buy time in pod-like napping chairs, get a manicure or chair massage or watch movie trailers and behind-the-scenes footage from current films in a screening lounge. Calgary International Airport has the SpacePort, an interactive space and aeronautics museum, while San Francisco International Airport has a multidisciplinary museum, a small aquarium and a Christian Science reading room.

FROM STEWARDESSES TO FLIGHT ATTENDANTS

In 2003, a Gwyneth Paltrow vehicle called *View From The Top* told the story of a small-town girl who dreams of becoming a jet-setting stewardess. The stewardesses on the fictitious Royalty airline wear pillbox hats and nary a discouraging word is heard about shoe bombers or box cutters. There's even a character, played by Candice Bergen, who has written a memoir about her glory days as an air hostess.

No discussion of the glamour of air travel in the 1950s and 1960s would be complete without some attention to the most glamorous of its ambassadors: the stewardess. But stewardesses didn't spring out of thin air, like Aphrodite from the sea, sometime around 1957. They'd actually been flying the bumpy skies since 1930, when an American nurse named Ellen Church decided she wanted to be a pilot.

Around the time she applied to Boeing Air Transport, a predecessor of United Air Lines, company traffic manager Steve Stimpson had recently returned from a long, boring flight. During that trip, he'd decided the company should provide some sort of cabin service. He had, in fact, already hired three men for that purpose. But when Church showed up, he realized that hiring nurses would be an even better idea. Surely having a nurse on board would ease the fears of jittery passengers, he reasoned. And, as a bonus, she could serve coffee and sandwiches! Stimpson talked his bosses into the idea, and they agreed to hire eight nurses for a three-month trial period. At 8 AM on May 15, 1930, Church left Oakland on a flight for Chicago.

The initiative was an immediate publicity coup for Boeing, but not everyone liked the idea. Some pilots resented having their personal fiefdoms invaded by a bunch of females — some initially refused to speak to the women who greeted them on the tarmac with a snappy military salute. Perhaps they were afraid of the reaction on the home front if word got out that they'd been at all friendly with these unmarried young women. At least one group of jealous pilots' wives bombarded Boeing with letters demanding that it discontinue the stewardess program.

One would think that the easy solution to that problem would have been to hire married women. Instead, Boeing and the airlines that followed its lead required stewardesses to resign if they married. One of the original eight Boeing stewardesses, Ellis Crawford, had neglected to mention the fact that she was married when she was hired. When Boeing found out, the company fired her. ·

In a speech on the twenty-fifth anniversary of the stewardess program, Stimpson explained why the airline didn't want the bother of dealing with panicky husbands (although it didn't seem to be concerned about handling pilots' wives): "Miss Crawford would be out on a trip and be delayed by bad weather and/or other causes, sometimes for several days, and her husband would phone me around 3 o'clock in the morning and say, 'Mister, where is my wife?'"[57]

Such glitches aside, a number of American airlines followed Boeing's lead. American Airlines hired its first stewardesses in 1933; Trans Canada Air Lines, formed in 1937, followed suit in 1938.

In the early years, a stewardess had a wide range of responsibilities. Before the flight took off, she took tickets, handled baggage (paying particular attention to the pilot's luggage) and helped fuel the plane. En route, she was something of a tour guide, letting passengers know what cities, mountain ranges or other interesting things were spooling by below the windows. On some airlines, she also carried a wrench to tighten the nuts securing wayward wicker seats to the floor. Once on the ground, she bent her shoulder to the task of helping roll the plane into the hangar — which would have been particularly difficult for attendants on Boeing, which required stewardesses to be no taller than 5'4" and no heavier than 115 pounds, due to the narrow aisles and low ceilings on early aircraft.

Even in the years when stewardesses were required to be nurses, the airlines preferred them to be *pretty* nurses. Once the nursing requirements disappeared in the late 1940s and early 1950s, the beauty issue took centre stage. As flight attendant Nina Morrison once recalled her 1954 interview for a position with Trans Canada Air Lines: "I still remember I had on a red dress with a white bib. I had to lift my skirt so he could look at my legs; walk back and forth; show him my hands, my nails, my hair and my teeth. You were being studied like a horse."[58]

After Morrison was hired, she was asked to sign a contract promising that she would quit by age thirty if she hadn't married (which was still cause for automatic dismissal). She managed to avoid signing the contract, but she still put up with other requirements: wearing the right colour of nylons and lipstick, keeping her hair to a certain length and wearing a girdle, among other things.

Despite such constraints, women were beating down the doors to get the job. "Don't forget, in the fifties there weren't a lot of options for women to do a lot of other things," Morrison told CBC-TV in a 1995 interview. "But flight attendant — or stewardess, at that time — was really quite something to aspire to."[59] By the late 1950s at some airlines, only four percent of applicants made the cut.

In a curious aviation footnote, in April 1953 United Air Lines launched a men-only flight between Chicago and New York. (Interestingly, that was also the year that Hugh Hefner started publishing *Playboy* from his Chicago apartment.) This testosterone club in the sky featured free cocktails, steaks and cigars — the latter often lit by the only women on the plane, the stewardesses. The service ran until January 1970, brought down by changing mores and a boycott launched by the National Organization for Women.

By the late 1960s, the coy allusions to the Mile-High Club in Sinatra's "Come Fly With Me" had morphed into open sexual innuendo in airline advertising, at least when it came to stewardesses. "She only wants what's good for you," claimed one American Airlines ad. "We really move our tail for you," claimed Continental. (In 1961, the airline rolled out the slogan "Proud Bird with the Golden Tail" — and outfitted its stewardesses in gold uniforms.) "Does your wife know you're flying with us?" asked Braniff slyly. "I'm Mandy, fly me," trumpeted one of the most famous come-ons.

The ads rankled many stewardesses. "I thought they were the most degrading things I'd ever seen," Morrison told her 1995 CBC-TV interviewer. "I mean, 'Fly me.' The inference was so obvious."

And then there were those uniforms. Gone were the days when stewardesses wore military-style caps and sensible shoes. In 1965, Italian couturier Emilio Pucci designed a multi-layered uniform for Braniff's infamous "Air Strip." At the beginning of the flight, each Braniff stewardess sported an apricot-coloured coat. During the course of the flight, she would gradually remove layers, moving from a pink gabardine suit to a tunic and culottes. "When a tired businessman gets on an airplane, we think he ought to be allowed to look at a pretty girl," Mary Wells of Braniff's advertising agency told *Business Week* in 1967.[60] In what may have been a publicity stunt, Braniff installed extra-high railings on the balconies of its steward-esses-in-training dormitory at Love Field in Dallas, claiming too many men had been trying to climb in.

Once Braniff played the Pucci card, all bets were off. Stewardess uniforms became more and more inventive. National tried tiger prints and promoted its head-to-toe fake fur outfits as "uniforms that purr." TWA decked out its stewardesses in capes, boots and striped scarves. Pacific Western Airlines had its stewardesses wear leather hot pants and cowboy hats on flights during the Calgary Stampede. Not surprisingly, the sex-drenched vibe spilled off the planes and into the airports themselves. In the mid-1960s, dancers in skimpy tiger costumes and gold pumps gyrated at either end of the bar at the San Francisco airport's Tiger A-Go-Go lounge.

Sexual tension in the skies soared even further after the publication of *Coffee, Tea or Me?*, a 1967 novel with the provocative subtitle "The Uninhibited Memoirs of Two Airline Stewardesses." Purportedly written by "Rachel Jones" and "Trudy Baker," it was a raunchy (for the time) look into an airborne world populated by randy, booze-fuelled playboys and sexy stewardesses in ever-shorter miniskirts. Years later it was revealed that the blockbuster novel had actually been ghostwritten by Donald Bain, an American Airlines PR rep, based on interviews with two pseudonymous stewardesses and Bain's own experiences as a frequent flyer.

But the stewardesses would have the last laugh. Throughout the

1960s and 1970s, they fought winning battles to remove discrimina-
tory rules. United Airlines, which had introduced the "no-marriage"
rule when it invented the stewardess job in 1930, finally abandoned
it on November 7, 1968.

Travelocity UK recently ran a TV ad spoofing the sexist airline
promos of the 1960s — this time, featuring male flight attendants
spouting double entendres, including "I can get you off first thing
in the morning," "Heathrow, Gatwick — I go both ways" and "I'm
direct, I'm not into stopovers, but I will do the red eye."

Recently, open sexism attempted a return to the open skies. On
March 6, 2003, Hooters Air launched its first scheduled flights from
Myrtle Beach to Atlanta. However, despite being accessorized with
buxom women in tight white T-shirts and short orange shorts, the
airline never blossomed (so to speak) and closed its doors in 2006.

AIRPORT INSECURITY

On May 22, 1962, Thomas Doty ignited dynamite in a lavatory of
a Continental flight bound from Chicago to Kansas City, bringing
down the plane and killing forty-five people. He was apparently
hoping that his family could collect the insurance money. Six years
later, Arthur Hailey based part of the plot of his pulpy novel *Airport*
on Doty's desperate move.

In the equally campy 1970 movie version of the book, passengers
simply walk through an open terminal, show a paper ticket to a gate
agent, cross the tarmac and board their plane. Not once do they pass
through a scanner, have an electronic wand waved over them, remove
their shoes or have their carry-on luggage X-rayed. It wasn't until
January 1973, nearly eleven years after the Thomas Doty bombing,
that the Federal Aviation Administration required airlines to search
every bag and passenger, in response to a spate of hijackings. The
airlines were given only a month to come up with a workable system,
so they adapted metal detector technology used by loggers to spot
nails and other bits of log-lodged metal that could damage sawmill
equipment.

By this time, other measures were in place. In November 1971,

a man travelling under the name "Dan Cooper" successfully sky-
jacked a Northwest Orient Airlines flight from Portland, Oregon.
After Cooper informed a stewardess he had a bomb, the flight landed
at Seattle-Tacoma International Airport. Cooper then released the
thirty-six passengers in exchange for $200,000 in ransom money
and ordered the crew to take the Boeing 727 up again. Somewhere
over Washington state, he lowered the rear stairs of the aircraft and
parachuted into history. Aside from about $5,800 in decomposing
currency unearthed in 1980, neither Cooper nor the loot was ever
seen again. The US government responded by requiring all 727s to
be fitted with a Cooper Vane, a device to prevent the rear stairs
from being lowered in flight. Hollywood, as usual, responded by
making a movie: *The Pursuit of D.B. Cooper*, a 1981 flick starring
Treat Williams and Robert Duvall.

After Palestinians hijacked four planes in September 1970, Richard
Nixon had sky marshals assigned to selected flights. One of the first
sky marshals, David Leach, recalled those jittery times in a 2000
segment of the public radio program *The Savvy Traveler*:

> In those days, the lavatory was at the front of the air-
> plane adjacent to the cockpit door. And these people
> would walk down the aisle; they'd grab the cockpit door
> and start shaking it. And my partner and I, we'd put our
> hands on our guns and look at each other and say, "Oh
> no. Don't tell me this is it. This is it. The guy's trying to
> get into the cockpit." And then they'd inevitably see the
> sign "Lavatory," go in there, and we'd just kind of sit
> back and say, "Wow."[61]

Security measures were increased again in the wake of the
December 1988 bombing of Pan Am flight 103 above Lockerbie,
Scotland, which killed 270 people. Since investigators later determined that the bomb had been concealed inside a radio-cassette
player packed in a suitcase in the cargo hold, security checkpoint
personnel began paying closer attention to electronic equipment
brought aboard. Eventually, passengers would be asked to switch on

electronics in their carry-on luggage to prove to inspectors that they worked. As of 2006, passengers were also forbidden from bringing liquids and gels onboard, as a way to deter would-be chemists from mixing explosives in flight.

Sequels to the original *Airport* appeared in 1975, 1977 and 1979. Soon, there was a series of parodies of *Airport* — *Airplane!* became a comedy classic. Our insecurity in the air continues to inspire Hollywood. In *Air Force One*, even the American president, played by Harrison Ford, finds himself dealing with hijackers. And in 2006, Samuel L. Jackson found himself dealing with *Snakes on a Plane*.

Perhaps the most chilling of them all, though, is the 2006 movie titled simply *United 93*. When trailers for the movie, which tells the story of the hijacked flight that crashed in Pennsylvania on 9/11, were first shown in New York theatres, horrified patrons cried out, "Too soon!" Nevertheless, the low-key docudrama was widely hailed by critics for its realism and sensitivity.

The events of 9/11, though, were more than just grist for the cinematic mill. North American airspace was completely shut down for four days after the attack, and fear of flying produced an unprecedented, but temporary, decline in demand for air travel. By one estimate, in just the first week after 9/11, the US airline industry lost between $1 billion and $2 billion. Alongside rising gas prices, airlines found themselves teetering.

Airports felt the pain, too. In 2000, Atlanta's Hartsfield-Jackson Airport — the world's busiest — handled more than eighty million passengers. The next year, in the wake of September 11, that number had fallen to fewer than seventy-five million — a 5.4 percent drop. Traffic tumbled at most American and many worldwide airports that year, sometimes precipitously. San Francisco, Newark, JFK and St. Louis airports all saw decreases of more than 10 percent in 2001. Since then, passenger traffic has slowly rebounded.

GETTING THROUGH THE TERMINAL

In another Hollywood movie, *The Terminal*, a man caught in a bureaucratic morass is trapped in a New York airport, unable to get past security, but unable to go home. He ends up living in the airport, much like Iranian refugee Merhan Nasseri, on whose true story the movie was based. Anyone who has endured innumerable line-ups and security checks to board a plane can sympathize.

British novelist David Lodge sums up the now-hellish airport experience in the opening chapter of his 1991 novel, *Paradise News*. Tour operator rep Leslie Pearson is glumly surveying the crowd at Heathrow's Terminal Four, trying to determine what sort of day it's going to be. At the moment, despite extra security checks prompted by a recent plane crash, departing passengers look relatively fresh and cheerful.

> But if an additional cause of serious delay should occur — a work-to-rule by air traffic controllers, say, or a go-slow by baggage handlers — then, as Leslie Pearson knows from experience, it wouldn't be long before the veneer of civilization began to show cracks. He has seen this concourse, and the Departures Lounge beyond, choked with delayed passengers sleeping under the fluorescent lights in their soiled, crumpled clothes, sprawled promiscuously all over the furniture and the floor, mouths agape and limbs askew, like the victims of a massacre or a neutron bomb, while the airport cleaners picked their way through the prone bodies like scavengers on a battlefield. Things aren't nearly as bad as that today, but they are bad enough.[62]

Sometimes, it seems as if airport terminals are designed to punish you for interrupting their busy day. At check-in, you're asked, "Did you pack this bag yourself?" as if, perhaps, it might not be your valet's day off. Once you've been interrogated and your luggage weighed, the clerk adroitly wraps a bar code around the handle and sends your

suitcase on its lonely way down the conveyor belt. You cross your
fingers as it slips into the rubber-flapped maw behind the check-in
counter. Will you have a happy reunion on the other side, or will
your baggage become one of the disappeared?

Given the elaborate system of hub airports that airlines are using to
economize, you also have to worry if, unseen, your baggage will make
every one of those connections. Worse, in January 2007, five men were
arrested on organized crime charges for stealing hundreds of pieces of
checked luggage in Houston, the latest in a rash of such rings at major
airports. No wonder more people are shoving as much of their luggage
into the overhead bins as carry-on restrictions will allow.

The good news: SITA, a Swiss baggage-tracking firm, reports that
airlines worldwide lost just 1 percent of all checked baggage in 2005,
and that 93.3 percent of those lost bags were eventually returned
to their owners. The bad news: since airlines worldwide handled
a mind-boggling three billion pieces of luggage that year, 300,000
bags got lost in translation and 200,000 of those never made their
way home.

Airlines and security agencies are understandably cagey about what
happens to your bag once you part company at the check-in desk.
However, a recent article in *The Globe and Mail*[63] revealed some
basic facts about the process at Montreal's Pierre Elliott Trudeau airport, which handles about twelve thousand checked bags a day. Since
the author, Lisa Fitterman, had checked her bag through to Orlando,
it was shunted to the international outbound baggage room. There,
it headed along a red conveyor belt for its first screening, which
checked for signs of bombs and explosives, as well as less ominous
but still dangerous goods, such as aerosol cans that can explode. If
that screening had revealed anything worrisome, a security agent
might have decided to put the bag through a second screening. The
passenger might also have been paged to witness a manual search of
the luggage, which only happens to about two out of every fourteen
thousanad bags. At any point, if the bag had been deemed an immediate threat, it would have been hastily wheeled outside to be defused
— a very rare occurrence.

Once it was deemed safe, Fitterman's bag was popped onto its

CANADA'S AIRLINE TAKES OFF

Canada did not get its own nationwide airline until 1937, when Trans-Canada Air Lines was formed from the merger of several smaller companies, as a subsidiary of Canadian National Railways. As had happened in many other countries, the airline immediately caught the imagination of the public. When TCA made its first long-haul airmail flight, on March 25, 1939, CBC Radio sent along a reporter to keep listeners apprised of the flight's painstaking progress from Victoria to Montreal, which included stops in Lethbridge, Winnipeg and North Bay.

Nine passengers — including Vancouver's police chief and an army colonel — joined the historic flight. In typical Canadian fashion, they had nothing but praise for the airline. "If you wish to sleep, you can recline in your chair, and if you wish a cup of coffee or a sandwich, they'll bring it to you," said one passenger admiringly. "There's nothing that you can wish for that they will not give you." No one, apparently, longed for in-seat entertainment consoles and a selection of fine wines by the glass.

A spirit of levity appears to have animated the long flight. At one point, the colonel asked a stewardess when they would hit the next stopover point. As he later told the CBC, "She replied that it was not customary for TCA to hit anything."

In the 1960s, TCA became Air Canada, and in the 1970s, it was split from CNR, becoming its own Crown corporation. The Canadian government had an ownership stake in the aviation business until 1989, when Air Canada was fully privatized.

own tray and set on a blue conveyor belt. When it reached its proper departure gate, the system tipped it into a luggage chute. (Apparently, this system works about 85 percent of the time; in the rest of the cases, baggage handlers have to read the bar-coded tags and re-direct the bags.) Then a baggage handler threw it into a cart, which was later driven across the tarmac to the plane, where other handlers threw the bag onto another conveyor belt that deposited it in the plane's cargo hold.

There may be hope in sight for the hundreds of thousands of passengers whose luggage goes astray every year. Airlines are considering replacing bar-coded tags with radio frequency identification (RFID) microchips, similar to the electronic tags used to track warehouse inventories and identify cars at highway tollbooths. The main hindrance right now is cost, as the RFID tags are much more expensive than the paper tags they would replace. But since airlines worldwide spend $2.8 billion dealing with lost luggage, the hope is that the system might pay off in the long run.

What happens to the 200,000 bags lost every year that are never claimed? In Canada, they're held at a central depot for three months, then they and their contents are donated to charity. In the US, airlines sell off permanently unclaimed stuff to the Unclaimed Baggage Center (UBC) in Scottsboro, Alabama, which resells most of the goods. (Others are discarded, given to charity or returned to their original owners — the store once sent an unclaimed guidance system for an F-16 fighter back to the US Navy.)

The 50,000-square-foot store, the size of a city block, is one of the state's largest tourist attractions, luring about one million shoppers annually from across the US and many foreign countries. Since many people lug nice clothes and new electronics with them when they travel, there's some good stuff to score: Ralph Lauren sweaters, Juicy Couture purses, Sharper Image pillows — you name it. Among some of the more exotic finds: a 40.95-carat natural emerald, an eighteenth-century violin, ancient Egyptian artefacts and a reproduction suit of armour. One customer bought a Barbie doll and discovered $500 stuffed inside the head. And staff unpacking bags at the Scottsboro store once discovered a live rattler.

CUTTING CORNERS AND CUTTING FARES

One of the biggest stories in leisure travel in the past decade has been the rise of discount airlines. Forget any pretence to white-glove service, which most big airlines have long since discarded anyway. These upstart airlines boast they will get you where you need to go for rock-bottom prices — and, often, you'll have fun getting there.

Competition has been fiercest where volumes are greatest. The US domestic market has seen the rise of Southwest, JetBlue and WestJet, as well as low-cost airlines affiliated with the big boys, such as United Airlines' Ted and Air Canada's Tango. And as competition in the skies has intensified, the days of the national airline seem to be waning: Belgium's Sabena has gone under. Air France has merged with KLM, the Dutch national airline, and Brazil's Varig was desperately trying to stay in business. In Europe, with so many cities so close together, competition has been so cutthroat that British travel magazines now consider destinations such as Rome and Stockholm affordable week-end getaways.

I have the feeling Juan Trippe would be delighted to see that.

To Your Health
SPAS AND OTHER CURES

*Healing is a matter of time, but it is sometimes also
a matter of opportunity.*
— *Hippocrates,* Precepts

On a trip to Turkey in 1999, I was beginning to despair that I would
ever get to experience an "authentic" *hamam,* or Turkish bath. Of
modern spas, there were plenty. Just about every swishy hotel had
one. With their piped-in harp music and glass shelves of hair "product," they looked no different from their competitors from Tokyo
to Tampa.

Finally, I found out about a *hamam* on a non-touristed street in
the old section of the port city of Antalya. As I made my way through
the tattered curtain swathing the door and down the worn stone
steps, I rejoiced. From the dank interior, lit solely by sunshine pouring through stars and moons cut in the domed ceiling, to the modest
price (about C$7.50 for a bath and massage), this place was as far
from the yuppie surroundings of a modern spa as one could get.

Eagerly, I paid my fee and accepted a small, threadbare towel
from the attendant. Through hand signals, she indicated that I was to
take off all my clothes. At least, I prayed I'd interpreted her gestures
correctly, as I slipped into one of the tiny changing cubicles. Moments
later, having realized that the towel was sadly not up to the task of
providing even a modicum of modesty, I scuttled across the foyer
like a streaker at the Super Bowl. I relaxed slightly when I got to the
steam-filled bath chamber. No one there seemed to be paying the

slightest attention to me or my shyness, until the masseuse caught my eye.

Let me explain that she was no Enya-playing, hemp-wearing, honey-voiced "spa attendant" barely out of her teens. Rather, she looked as though she could have given Arnold Schwarzenegger a good run for his money in an arm-wrestling match. She wore a black thong, a gold chain and a scowl.

The next twenty minutes passed in a bit of a blur. Biker Masseuse doused me with hot water from a bowl, washed my hair with what smelled like Lemon Pledge, scrubbed the rest of me (including my face) with a wicked loofah and olive oil soap, threw some more water at me, slapped me down on a marble slab and gave me what might have been a massage but might also have qualified in some countries as unaggravated assault. By the end of the proceedings, my hair looked like a badly trimmed topiary hedge and small grey flecks covered my body.

"Skin!" she announced proudly.

As I hobbled back to the change cubicle, I seriously wondered whether authenticity was all it's cracked up to be.

MASSAGES FOR THE TOGA SET

As it turns out, I was far from the first traveller to become a bit obsessed with having the ultimate Turkish spa experience. Back in the days of the Roman Empire, Asia Minor was famous for its health spas, particularly the luxurious mountainside resort of Pergamum, located in what is now the Turkish city of Bergama.

Along with the standard magical fountain and excellent thermal baths, Pergamum had facilities even the modern guest at Canyon Ranch or the Golden Door would envy, including a famous library and an amphitheatre that could seat thirty-five hundred. The place was also crawling with yellow snakes — a small drawback — but they were harmless and supposedly lucky. The rich patients strolling through the cool colonnades paid them little heed, distracted as they were by the prospect of getting cutting-edge treatments such as bloodletting and enemas. There were also appointments to keep with dieticians, astrologers, masseurs and a huge range of other health experts. So famous was Pergamum that one of history's most theatrical hypochondriacs, an orator named Aelius Aristides, once travelled the fifty-mile distance from Smyrna (modern Izmir) to Pergamum in the middle of a heat wave in less than twenty-four hours.

Spas are one of the oldest forms of tourist destination. The Romans were famous for their love of hot springs, and cities from Bath to Aix-les-Bains and beyond sprung up across the empire around the baths they built.

For the Romans, baths weren't only tourist destinations. Every neighbourhood had one, and everyone from slaves to emperors was allowed — expected, really — to participate. As well as bathing, visitors could have a meal, be seen by a doctor or, according to some archaeologists, arrange a lunchtime quickie with a handy hooker. (Other archaeologists believe the erotic mosaics found in the ruins of many ancient baths are just decoration — not an advertisement of services provided on the premises.)

The nice thing about Roman baths for the average Roman tourist was that they were laid out in roughly the same configuration, no matter where you travelled in the empire. So if you were in Ephesus to see the Temple of Artemis (Diana) or Greece to watch an athletic contest or Gaul to inspect a new aqueduct, you could be fairly certain of feeling at ease in the local bath, where everything from the layout to the customs would be familiar. (The Romans were big on standardization and they had the power to make it stick: until Vatican II shook things up in the early 1960s, a Roman Catholic could walk into virtually any Catholic church on earth with the assurance that the major prayers and rituals would be conducted in Latin.)

After paying one's entry fee to the *balneator* (door clerk), visitors would exchange their street wear for wooden sandals and light cotton bathing tunics in the *apodyterium*, stashing their goods in overhead cubicles and praying to Apollo that they'd still be there when they returned, combination locks not having been invented yet. The next stops would be, in order, the *frigidarium* (cold bath), *tepidarium* (warm bath) and *caldarium* (hot bath), followed by another bracing dip in the cold bath.

As visitors made the circuit, they had an unparalleled opportunity to trade news, get tips on what to see and do while they were in town and just generally learn about life in the destination and the hometowns of other visitors. In short, the bath was the perfect place to get an "authentic" local experience — of the sort travellers two millennia later would go to great lengths to acquire.

BRITONS TAKE THE WATERS

Like everything else, from roads to communication systems, the network of baths fell into ruin when the barbarians swept into Rome and ushered in the Dark Ages. People bent on survival didn't worry that much about keeping clean. In some cases, hot springs were allowed to silt over, while other baths were purposely filled in so that new buildings could be constructed on top of them. The ancient bathhouses were left to crumble, their original purpose long forgotten.

In the Middle Ages, however, there was a revival of interest in the healing properties of warm water. The spa town of Karlovy Vary in central Europe, for instance, was founded in the fourteenth century to serve tourists drawn to its hot springs. By the early 1500s at the latest, baths had been reconstructed at several Roman sites, such as Bath in England; in 1537, widely travelled cleric and scholar John Leland relaxed in them after a long journey from London. At that point, the baths served a strictly medicinal function; Leland related that they were seen as efficacious cures for diseases ranging from "great aches" to leprosy and smallpox. Two of the baths were joined to St. John's Hospital, which provided shelter and additional services.

For the next two centuries, baths would retain their medicinal atmosphere. But by the time the pleasure-loving Georgians took to the stage in the 1700s, "taking the waters" had become a clever excuse for journeying into scenic, luxurious surroundings to relax and cavort with other rich folks with more time and money on their hands than ways to occupy it. In 1702, just before the Georgian age kicked in, Queen Anne and her courtiers paid a visit to Bath, propelling it into fashion. In subsequent decades, new assembly halls and theatres would be built to amuse the growing numbers of fashionable

Londoners who came to take the waters. By the time Daniel Defoe wrote his *Tour through the Whole Island of Great Britain* in the 1720s, he could say of Bath:

> In former times this was a resort hither for cripples; and we see the crutches hang up in several baths, as the thank-offerings of those who have come hither lame, and gone away cured. But now we may say it is the resort of the sound rather than the sick; the bathing is made more a sport and diversion than a physical prescription for health; and the town is taken up in raffling, gaming, visiting and, in a word, all sorts of gallantry and levity.

That doesn't mean that travellers didn't still *say* they were travelling "for their health." In fact, some of the most devoted fans of baths and hot springs claimed they were travelling to relieve various aches, pains and nervous conditions. Nor were their claims wholly bogus: the plague- and cholera-infested streets of Europe's growing cities weren't exactly the healthiest places to live, particularly in summer. A bit of a fresh breeze — and, more to the point, less-crowded conditions — was bound to do the traveller a bit of good, even if only to relax his mind. Of course, those who were perfectly healthy often clamoured to accompany sick relatives to the increasingly popular baths. While Cousin Harriet or Uncle William hobbled off to sit in a smelly sulphur bath or choke down cloudy mineral waters, their less-afflicted kin could simply enjoy the pleasures of resort life.

Throughout the 1700s, any pretty spot with a mineral spring might try to bid for this increasingly mobile, rich tourist traffic. In Britain, health seekers went to Bagnigge Wells, Tunbridge Wells and a host of other spots in addition to Bath; on the Continent, they gathered in Aix-la-Chapelle (now Aachen, Germany) and Spa (in modern-day Belgium). The latter resort was so elegant and popular that, almost three centuries later, its name would still be lending glamour to a whole new range of "treatments," from sea-salt scrubs to mud wraps.

SPAS CROSS THE ATLANTIC

Across the pond in America, fewer people had the means to travel, and roads were more rudimentary than those in Europe. But that didn't mean the emerging elites didn't long to echo the style of the rich and leisured back in the Old World. But without a few thousand years of history behind them, America's new "spas" were even more rustic than the roads. In 1761, George Washington had to bring his own tent when he visited Berkeley Springs, in what is now West Virginia.

In the years after the American Revolution, spas enjoyed slow but steady growth in the new country, as doctors began to extol the virtues of hot springs. Mineral waters supposedly could cure everything from rheumatism to respiratory infections. As a bonus, the fresh air surrounding many spas was thought likely to heal gout, asthma and that great scourge of the nineteenth century, consumption (tuberculosis). It might have been wise for some patients to take the good doctors' advice with a grain of skeptical salt, though, since many physicians had a financial stake in spas, which just may have coloured their judgment.

Whether it was for the air or for the water — or, just as likely, for the fashionable company — rich Americans were soon flocking to spas. The fact that the "cures" were not as miraculous as they had hoped didn't bother them as much as we might think. They might still be afflicted with gout, but at least they were suffering in pleasant surroundings.

One of the most famous American spas, Saratoga Springs in up-state New York, began to grow in the 1820s. In 1821, it had two hotels with a capacity of at least one hundred and fifty people each; five years later, the resort was becoming known for its nightly balls and other festivities. Within two decades, local entrepreneurs had built amusements like a miniature railroad and a bowling alley. And by the late 1870s, there were at least two hotels with more than eight hundred rooms each.

Not all observers looked fondly on the glittering life of Saratoga Springs and its ilk. Christian reformers throughout the Western world were beginning to worry about the emerging amusements of the nineteenth century, and to fear that perhaps people were getting a bit caught up in glamour and thrills. And nowhere was this worry deeper set than in the United States, where debates about the relative merits of good "recreation" versus bad "amusement" went back to the country's Puritan founders. Particularly in New England and the Midwest — the South having sprung from different religious roots — pastors and reformers debated which activities were uplifting and which would lead participants into sin. Reading moral tracts and going for long nature walks generally fell onto the "good" side of the ledger, while gambling and waltzing fell onto the "bad" side. Even travellers themselves were not immune from worrying about the merits of their leisure pursuits. In 1826, a guest at Saratoga wondered whether the fashionable resort "will prepare more souls for destruction than these efficacious waters will heal infirm bodies."

Despite such concerns, Saratoga and its kindred continued to grow. Interestingly, the arrival of the railroad did not cause previously fashionable resorts to fall out of favour with the middle and upper classes, as happened at some English resorts, such as Blackpool. At places such as Saratoga, the most luxurious hotels were already charging rates that put them effectively out of reach of most of the middle and all of the working class. As the railroad made it possible for more people to reach the resort in a reasonable time, more moderately priced hotels emerged to serve a growing number of clerks, teachers, clergymen and other middle-class professionals who wanted to visit.

After the Civil War, the rise of the robber barons and their accumulations of fabulous wealth laid the groundwork for America's ongoing fascination with celebrity. The doings of the leaders of the Gilded Age became regular fodder for newspapers and magazines, and their vacations at places such as Saratoga were no exception. Reporters detailed the life of morning trips to the spring, afternoon carriage rides, the daily stroll along the wide sidewalks of Broadway and the obligatory visit to a nearby native village to buy trinkets, as well as the festive dances and parties that took place every night. By the 1870s, life at these resorts had settled into such a regimented round of activity that some people found themselves ironically bored, even though they were on the move almost every minute of the day. A *New York Times* writer complained in 1875 about the "well-established currents of happiness into which everyone is dragged as into an eddy, and we have now the exquisite satisfaction of being miserable in company and trying to believe that we are enjoying ourselves hugely."[64]

THE WONDERFUL WORLD OF HYGIENE

The world was still wide open, though, for daring travellers interested in sampling bathing and other health practices far beyond the genteel treatments of Spa and Saratoga. One of the most cheerful nineteenth-century adventurers was an Englishwoman named Edith Tweedie, who published her impressions in a series of books under the name Mrs. Alec Tweedie.

During a trip through Finland in the 1890s with her sister and some friends, she gets it into her head that she would like to experience a traditional Finnish bath, and nothing will satisfy her until she gets one. Disappointed that she can't arrange to have one with the local peasants — for reasons that are unclear, but probably have something to do with the fact that the locals aren't keen on sharing their ablutions with a stranger — she eventually manages to arrange for a woman named Saima who understands the traditional rituals to come and give her and her friends a group bath.

Difficulties arise almost as soon as the Englishwomen enter the *bastu*, or bathhouse. Saima gleefully begins tossing water onto hot bricks, and the visitors are soon roasting. Gasping for breath, they plead with Saima in broken Finnish to stop. The problem is that Saima is Swedish and doesn't understand a word they're saying, so she continues to steam them like a bunch of pale, damp clams. Finally, through hand signals and a general aura of panic, they make their wishes known. Saima obligingly stops pouring cold water on the bricks and starts scrubbing the bathers with soft soap and a bundle of rags. Once she deems them clean, she sluices them with pails of hot water, then flails them with a birch switch for a while. "It was an awful experience!" Mrs. Tweedie exclaims. Nonetheless, the Englishwomen persevere. Finally, Saima signals that the bathers should head for the cold bath. They take a quick, frosty dip before wrapping themselves in piping hot towels and scurrying back to the room where their clothing is stored.

In retrospect, far from the birch switch and icy bath, Mrs. Tweedie is exhilarated by her adventure:

> Whether it was the heat, or exhaustion, or the loss of one skin or many, we know not; but after a glass of *mjöd*, that most delicious and refreshing of Finnish drinks, we slept splendidly, and felt fit next morning for any amount of hard work, even for a journey to Russia through Finland, though we did not speak or understand the language of either country.[65]

It's hard not to get into the spirit of the adventure as Mrs. Tweedie recounts her Finnish journey; she's a splendid raconteur and game for just about any adventure. Her quest to explore Finland from a watery perspective leads her to try an "ant-heap bath," which she has heard is good for rheumatism. Traditionally, an entire anthill would have been tossed into the bathwater, but in deference to the visitor's presumed delicate sensibilities, her Finnish bath attendant bundled the ants into a little linen bag before pouring boiling water on them. To Mrs. Tweedie's dismay, when she entered the bathhouse she saw the bathwater was brown. "Did I shiver at the thought?" she asks the reader. "Well, a little, perhaps; nevertheless, I tumbled into the warm water."

She also attempts a "waterfall bath," where she and her friends enter a small structure built around a waterfall and simply let the cascade wash over them. "[T]he water, simply thumping on our back and shoulders, came with such force, that we felt exactly as if we were being well pummelled with a pair of boxing-gloves, or being violently massaged, a delicious tingling sensation being the result," she reports. One wonders how a genteel Victorian lady would know what it was like to be pummelled with boxing gloves, but Mrs. Tweedie does seem to have led an adventurous life.

Even when she and her sister try the more usual amusement of swimming in the lake, hilarity ensues. Since no bathing suits are available in the local shops, they buy some fabric and sew their own. The locals, who swim in the nude, immediately assume the crazy Englishwomen have fallen into the lake.

For Mrs. Tweedie, her adventures with waterfalls and birch switches were the essence of her trip. Simply observing historic buildings and sipping tea with friends would not have been nearly as illuminating. "[B]aths in Finland are an art, and Finland without its bath-houses would not be Finland at all,"[66] she concludes.

FROM SULPHUR SPRINGS TO SEAWEED WRAPS

The quest for healthful vacation surroundings helped spur the economic growth of western North America. In the early 1880s, workers building the Canadian Pacific Railway stumbled across two hot springs at the base of Sulphur Mountain in what is now Banff, Alberta. In 1885, the Canadian government declared a twenty-six-square-kilometre parcel of land surrounding the springs Canada's first national park — later expanded to become today's much larger Banff National Park. Hot on the heels of that development came the opening of the CPR's massive Banff Springs Hotel.

Meanwhile, far to the south, promoters from Texas to Nevada were touting the healthful properties of hot springs and dry desert air. In 1882, the Atchinson, Topeka and Santa Fe Railroad opened the Montezuma Hotel in Las Vegas, New Mexico, to draw tourists to a nearby hot springs. That early effort was soon duplicated by many others, ranging from hoteliers and religious orders to legitimate scientific organizations and certifiable quacks.

Promoters eagerly used anything from scientific studies to quotations from famous authors to lure travellers to their enterprises. A brochure from the 1910s for the Desert Inn in Phoenix borrows some lustre by quoting Robert Louis Stevenson on the benefits of fresh air: "What seems a kind of temporal death to people choked between walls and curtains, is only light and living slumber to the man who sleeps afield. All night long he can hear Nature breathing deeply and freely, even as she takes her rest, she turns and smiles."

In Texas, a now largely deserted settlement with the self-explanatory name of Sanatorium grew up around a tuberculosis treatment facility that opened in 1912. By the 1930s, the facility had grown to encompass about a thousand acres, including everything from a dairy to a school, and was home to about two thousand patients. By the time it closed in 1971, it had treated some fifty-five thousand people.

The baths at places like Pergamum may have long ago crumbled or been paved over, but humans remain devoted to their bodies and spas — in all their weirdly varied glory — are as popular as ever. In the US alone, the industry is worth an estimated $11 billion and employs about 280,000 people. According to the International Spa Association, there are now about 12,100 spas in the US and 2,100 in Canada. While many of these are "day spas" — some little more than beauty salons under a different name — many others offer facilities to rival those of Pergamum and even more imaginative treatments with even more exaggerated health claims.

At the Sanctuary on Camelback Mountain spa in Scottsdale, Arizona, a wild lime blossom massage — carried out using "a special recipe of hazelnut, avocado and macadamia oils...blended with wild lime blossom, sandalwood and ginger" — is supposed to be just the ticket for overcoming jet lag.

Or perhaps your skin is looking a little peaked? Head to the Beyond Wrapture day spa in Kelowna, BC, where the red or white wine vinotherapy massage (incorporating wine, grapeseed oil and shea butter) has "anti-aging properties."

Seething about cellulite? Head to EuroSpa in Ottawa, where a $1,500 course of treatments with a machine that looks like a pint-sized vacuum will massage your fatty deposits while bombarding them with infrared light and radio waves, supposedly leaving you firm and sleek again.

I like a good massage as much as the next desk jockey, but as for the claims that grapeseed oil can get rid of my crow's feet...well, I have the feeling the astrologers at Pergamum were feeding that same line to their clients.

THE NEXT STEP: EVERYTHING OLD IS NEW AGAIN

Garth Roberts and Doug Plummer couldn't resist the potential of Sharon Springs, a once-grand spa town about an hour west of Albany, New York. The two ex-Manhattanites — a Broadway conductor and an actor, respectively — moved to the village of 550 people in 1992 to start a café. But it was the vacant shell of the American Hotel, built in 1847, that really caught their interest.

"We always had our eyes on this building," says Roberts. He and Plummer would toss silver dollars onto the long, galleried porch of the American at night and dream of restoring the white clapboard inn. Finally, in 1996, they bought the building for $18,000, then sank another $600,000 into the restoration project — redoing the foundation, stabilizing floors, replacing the shattered roof. In May 2001, the once-derelict building reopened. Energized, other entrepreneurs opened or expanded nearby cafés and shops. Within a couple of years, *The New York Times* and *Spa Finder* had made it official: Sharon Springs was on the cusp of a renaissance.

The renaissance has been somewhat slow in coming. But in August 2006, a consortium of New York City investors announced plans to spend $33 million to redevelop three vintage hotels and the Imperial Bath House into a luxury spa that would employ up to 250 people. Despite the existence of more luxurious spas in more convenient locations, the allure of rebuilding history appears hard to resist.

It seems we humans are surprisingly reluctant to let a good thing go. Even though modern medicine has largely debunked the spectacular health effects once claimed for hot springs and mineral water, heritage activists are often eager to reclaim the elegant status of their now-faded spa towns.

If You Build It, They Will Come
RESORTS AND THEME PARKS

*If you go on a behind-the-scenes tour of Walt Disney
World in the hopes of catching one of those happy
cast members with his smile down — spitting on the
break-room floor, maybe, or being mean to some
kittens — you'll be disappointed. Disney's Cult of
Cheerfulness survives even in the no-go zones.*
— *Steve Hendrix,* The Washington Post

In the nineteenth century, odd as it may seem today, many Americans
were deeply suspicious of leisure. Not for nothing did sober young
ladies embroider samplers with slogans like "The devil makes work
for idle hands."

Some preachers railed against dancing. Others warned against
cards. But few warned their flock against revival meetings, with the
result that these travelling religious festivals became popular travel
destinations for huge swaths of the American population. Those who
wouldn't be caught dead gambling at Saratoga or flirting at Newport
could take a few days away from the farm, save their souls and maybe
even meet a pretty girl under the revival tent.

A similarly uplifting form of "recreation" (as opposed to senseless
"amusement") was the Lyceum Movement, which gave people from
all walks of life an opportunity to learn about the latest scientific,
literary and political advances.

From these two social trends sprang a related, but wholly new,
non-denominational tourist destination that would quickly become
a nationwide sensation.

In 1874, a Methodist minister named John Vincent and an entrepreneur named Lewis Miller set up a training centre for Sunday
school teachers on the shores of Lake Chautauqua in western New
York State. It was an immediate hit; in its first year, it drew some five

hundred students from twenty-five states. It quickly expanded beyond Sunday school teachers to include anyone who wished to spend a week in a pretty lakeside location, opening their minds and enjoying genteel pleasures — as long as they didn't mind teetotalling. Visitors stayed in tents, rented rooms or small cottages. Within a decade, the original Chautauqua was attracting up to 100,000 people a year, and other "chautauquas" had popped up in various parts of the country. It was all very admirable and Puritan. In fact, Vincent had to remind participants to take time to relax during their vacations: "But be careful not to overtax yourself. Do not go to every thing."[67]

If middle-class Americans were leavening their vacations with a heavy dose of self-improvement, their working-class counterparts on the other side of the Atlantic had no such qualms. Indeed, for several decades, they'd been heading to the seashore to revel in a week of dancing, drinking and fairground games.

THE WORKING CLASS GOES TO THE SEASHORE

Some of Thomas Cook's earliest rail excursions had brought Midlands factory workers to the seaside. Victorians had a strong belief that bracing sea air was good for body and soul.

During the course of the nineteenth century, it became more common for British factory owners to close their plants for a week or two at a time each summer. Their workers had quickly acquired a taste for holidays, and owners soon learned that they needed to give their employees guaranteed time off (without pay) or workers would haphazardly take it themselves, playing havoc with production schedules and requiring increasingly onerous disciplinary measures.

In many small towns and urban neighbourhoods, a sizable number of locals worked in the same factory or mill, so when it closed down for the week this huge crowd of people would suddenly be looking for amusement all at the same time. Railroads and tour operators were quick to capitalize on this new mass market, wisely realizing that, unlike the middle class and the rich, working-class Britons had developed a very communal culture. They worked at the same mills, lived in the same neighbourhoods, joined the same clubs, relaxed at the same pubs, attended the same churches. Why should they not travel to the same locations, en masse, for their holidays?

That is, in fact, exactly what they did, and a sturdy infrastructure evolved along the coastlines of the English Midlands to accommodate the predictable — and somewhat lucrative — annual onslaughts. Mill workers from Manchester and Birmingham made Blackpool England's fifth-largest resort by 1911; workers from Yorkshire flocked to Morecambe.

As the working class moved in, their richer compatriots fled. And even though some in the emerging tourism business would have pre-ferred quieter, better-heeled visitors, they pretty much had to adapt to whatever whim struck the working-class masses. If factory workers decided your town was fun, affordable and accessible, they would come — and richer tourists would head somewhere else, preferably a spot the rail lines didn't reach.

It's hard now to imagine the change the railroads wrought to the west coast of England. In the late 1700s, on poor roads in expensive coaches, it took a whole day to travel from Manchester to Blackpool; the journey from Birmingham to the coast took three days. The train reduced the travel time to hours and time, even more than cost, made it possible for factory workers to escape to the sea. During Whit Week (a traditional late spring holiday) in 1848, more than 100,000 people travelled by train between Manchester and the coast; two years later, more than twice that number boarded trains. Most went to Blackpool: by 1865, the seaside town was receiving 285,000 visitors annually.

The middle class, predictably, reacted with alarm, but then, the English middle class had been alarmed about the working class for hundreds of years. Seaside resorts were just the latest incarnation of unwanted public rowdiness that could be traced back to coun-try markets and medieval fairs. "Unless immediate steps are taken, Blackpool as a resort for respectable visitors will be ruined," was a typical mid-1800s' comment from worried genteel travellers. But it was too late. Blackpool landladies saw where the money was, and it wasn't to be made in catering to the genteel families of doctors and lawyers — who soon wouldn't touch Blackpool with a fifty-foot

pole anyway. Instead, landladies formed long-term relationships with
factory workers' families, who would come and stay year after year.
They might not pay as much, but they were steady customers.

Soon, Blackpool had surpassed all other English seaside resorts
in popularity. Between 1870 and 1910, it acquired a range of attractions few other English resort towns could match, including three
piers, a fun fair, a zoo, a pleasure garden, cinemas, carousels, Britain's
first electric streetlights and a landmark tower modelled on Eiffel's
masterpiece in Paris. Children could watch Punch and Judy shows,
while their mothers had their fortunes told and their fathers crept off
to the penny peepshows. One visitor's memories reveal a touching
gratitude for the smallest pleasures:

> We're lucky, we can come in and go out of the house
> whenever we like, and the landlady will make sandwiches
> for us. We sit on the beach and rent a deckchair. Ice cream
> cornets are a halfpenny each for the girls. Then Herbert
> goes up for a beer, and we go to watch the beach races.[68]

Meanwhile, however, wealthier Britons needed to find a more
exclusive bit of seashore.

THE BIRTH OF THE RIVIERA

In 1834, a few years before the railway began bringing the masses
to Blackpool, Lord Chancellor Brougham built a villa in Cannes.
He was one of a small group of rich English ex-pats who came to
the south of France every winter to escape London's cold and rain.
For a couple of decades they kept a fairly low profile, but when
Brougham built his elegant Italianate holiday home, he kicked off
several decades of competitive construction. Mansions and shimmer-
ing white-stucco hotels sprang up in Cannes and Nice.

Then, in the 1860s, a railway was built along the shoreline from
Marseilles to Monaco. Now those lovely mansions with their pretty
sea views were within easy reach of the glittering casino of Monte
Carlo. When the raffish Prince of Wales showed up in Monte Carlo in

1875, the die was cast: there was no better place in Europe that the south of France and Monaco for the idle rich. Playboys, artists, dilettantes, poets, second sons, outcasts, gamblers, socialites, and anyone else with the money to live life on the stylishly wild side came to the Riviera — or, as a guidebook christened it in 1887, the Côte d'Azur. When a later Prince of Wales, the disgraced Duke of Windsor, became a bit of a fixture around the place, its reputation was made.

Despite the railway, prices in Cannes and Nice had risen quickly enough to ensure that they would never become as rowdy as Blackpool or as respectable as Britain's middle-class resorts. The Riviera would remain a bit of a Bloomsbury-by-the-sea, and upper-crust Britons would find it ever more appealing as their own seaside back home became ever more crowded. Thomas Cook had fired the first volley of working-class tourists towards the coast; an ambitious South African-Canadian entrepreneur named Billy Butlin would fire the next round.

HI-DE-HI, CAMPERS!

On Easter Sunday 1936, Butlin opened his first "holiday camp" in Skegness on the coast of Lincolnshire, within striking distance of the industrial cities of the English Midlands. With snow sifting down from a grey sky, it wasn't the most auspicious opening for a summer resort. But Butlin, who owned a popular fun fair in Skegness, had high hopes for his new venture.

Butlin's background made him uniquely equipped to launch the new venture. Descended from a family of travelling showmen, he had spent his early years shuttling between South Africa, Canada and the UK. While living with his mother and stepfather in Toronto, he dropped out of school at fourteen and went to work for Eaton's department store. He didn't particularly take to retailing, but he was intrigued by the summer camp the store operated for its employees. It was one of the first opportunities he'd ever had to take a summer vacation, and the experience influenced him for the rest of his life.

After moving back to the UK, Butlin launched and operated several "fun fairs" — amusement parks featuring slides, haunted houses,

bumper cars and game stalls. They were successful but relatively modest affairs, and he had bigger dreams. While running a fun fair at
Skegness, he'd concluded that there was a living to be made in giving
working-class vacationers an alternative to the often-cheerless boarding houses that were the only seaside accommodation they could
afford. Why not provide purpose-built chalets, where families could
stay, enjoy the beach and be entertained — and full board as well?

Butlin didn't invent the idea of the communal summer holiday
camp. In the 1920s, several bare-bones commercial ventures opened,
often with accommodation in tents. Organizations such as the Co-
operative Holidays Association (founded in 1893) and various church
groups had been working for several decades to help workers take
country holidays. In Canada, a similar burst of reforming zeal resulted
in the *Toronto Star*'s Fresh Air Fund, founded in 1901 to give poor
children the opportunity to go to summer camp; the fund still exists
today. On the other hand, the propagandists of Hitler's Third Reich
were extolling the virtues of communal fresh air and sunshine through
a program called *Kraft durch Freude* ("strength through joy").

But Butlin was one of the first to envision a wide network of
commercial summer camps, and from the beginning he set out to
create a destination that offered more than sunshine and sea breezes.
He eagerly courted celebrities — famed aviator Amy Johnson cut the
ribbon on opening day at Skegness.

He also reduced some of the hassles vacationers faced in resorts
like Blackpool, while retaining all the elements they enjoyed. At a
Butlin's camp, travellers didn't have to worry about appeasing a
temperamental landlady with her long list of rules. No one would
throw them out each morning, whatever the weather, so that the
boarding house could be cleaned. When they reserved a chalet at a
Butlin's camp, it was *theirs* for the duration of the holiday, and they
could come and go as they pleased. It was a concept that had long
been familiar to the wealthier classes, who could stay in grand hotels
in Switzerland or rent entire flats in Rome. For the British working
class, it was revolutionary.

Butlin offered another extremely popular service that had been
hard if not impossible to arrange in traditional seaside resorts: baby-

sitting. Granted, it wasn't the type of babysitting that would sit well with nervous parents today. After the parents had left their offspring for a night of dancing or singalongs, a nurse simply patrolled the walkways between cottages, listening for sounds of crying. Apparently, kids could have pillow fights and read comics until the wee hours, as long as they were quiet about it.

As well as offering popular new services, though, Butlin was careful to retain the common areas that travellers adored in traditional seaside resorts: huge dining halls, enclosed swimming pools, dance halls, cinemas and pubs. He hoped that his holiday camp would quickly become a convivial place where travellers would easily make new friends.

Shortly after opening day, however, Butlin realized that his customers were hesitant to introduce themselves to strangers or to be the first to try out the range of entertainments he'd laid out for them. Clearly, a bit of encouragement was in order. He asked one of the engineers who had built the camp, an outgoing chap named Norman Bradford, to get up on the dining room stage after dinner and warm up the crowd. Bradford complied, telling jokes, answering questions about the camp facilities and encouraging people to introduce themselves to their tablemates.

The ploy worked, and Butlin decided that the camp needed a permanent squad of bubbly employees to keep things lively. He hired several, outfitted them in scarlet blazers and sent them into the crowd to encourage visitors to check out the beauty pageant, enter their kids in the sandcastle contest or come to that night's concert. As the concept evolved, the "redcoats" also became entertainers — singing, dancing, telling jokes — and became the camp's signature feature (and inspired countless descendants, from perky cruise directors to the GOs — *gentils organisateurs* — of Club Med).

Two years later, buoyed by the success of the Skegness operation, Butlin opened a second camp at Clacton-on-Sea in Essex, within easy reach of the huddled masses of London's East End. The price was reasonable: a week's holiday could be had for between thirty shillings and three pounds, at a time when the average annual working-class salary was about £250. Ten thousand people applied to get in.

The holiday camp business got a shot in the arm in 1938, when Parliament passed the *Holidays with Pay Act* to ensure minimum paid holidays for many Britons. Even though most of its provisions wouldn't kick in until after the Second World War, it would eventually create a truly mass market for substantial vacations.

During the war, Butlins camps were pressed into service as military training bases. But once the war was over, Butlins and its competitors prospered. People were desperate for fun, but rationing, fuel shortages and international travel restrictions made it difficult for Britons to travel far in the first few post-war years. Butlins camps conveniently filled the bill. In 1948, one in every twenty vacationing Britons stayed at a Butlins.

Entertainment was a key aspect of a Butlins holiday, and not a few English stars got their start performing at one of the camps. A 1950s' brochure promotes a young singer named Julie Andrews, while Ringo Starr performed at a Butlins with his first band, Rory Storm and the Hurricanes. Shirley Henderson, who appeared in the *Bridget Jones* movies, got her first break when she won a talent competition for guests at a Butlins camp.

Another aspect of the camps was their regimentation. Every moment of the day had some planned activity, and each morning redcoats would walk through the camp crying out "Hi-de-hi!" — the cry became such a catchphrase in Britain that it inspired the name of a 1959 BBC TV series set at a holiday camp. From the Knobbly Knee and Glamorous Granny contests to the evening singalong, there was always some sort of group entertainment on the go.

A holiday at Butlins wasn't designed to appeal to everyone; travel historian Fred Inglis calls it "a life one would not, speaking for the bourgeoisie, have turned up for after death."[69] Butlin, who was knighted in 1964, likely wouldn't have given a flying flip that the upper and middle classes thought his camps common. He was too busy raking in the profits.

By providing a self-contained spot where all the travellers' needs, from food to entertainment, could be taken care of in one place for one fixed price, Butlin presaged the rise of the post-war holiday resort that would, ironically, almost wipe out the company he had created.

The next step in the evolution of the resort would be to move the concept to further shores.

SUN, SAND AND SURF

In 1950, a former Belgian water polo champion named Gérard Blitz opened a resort called Alcudia on the Balearic Island of Majorca and dubbed it Club Méditerranée. It wasn't fancy. Vacationers, who paid a fee of 300 francs to join the club and 15,900 francs for a two-week holiday, shared lavatories and stayed in tents. But it was two weeks of affordable, reliable sunshine, and the concept took off.

The company expanded throughout the next few decades, opening its first ski resort in Leysin, Switzerland in 1957, its first Caribbean resort in Guadeloupe in 1968 and branching into Asia with a village in Malaysia in 1979. As time went on, its facilities became a bit more luxurious and the idea of paying one price for everything — even alcohol — expanded into what we now know as the all-inclusive resort. And Club Med and other European operators expanded their reach into other countries. Anywhere that was accessible, sunny, cheap and relatively politically stable was fair game: the coasts of Spain and Turkey, the Greek islands. The first package tour flight arrived on Spain's Costa Brava in 1954, when there was little more than a couple of villages, some tiny hotels and a few bars to welcome visitors. The main attractions were two sun-drenched beaches; in the half century to follow, they would be almost the only element of the Costa Brava that would remain unpaved.

Europeans didn't jump on the package tour bandwagon immediately; such trips were still expensive in relation to average incomes, and local holiday traditions died hard. As late as the mid-1970s, a British travel agent recently recalled, middle-class and working-class Britons were still somewhat suspicious of sunshine holidays. "Then, the idea of travel abroad was outrageous," he told a BBC reporter. "I remember one boy's family went to Spain. I asked my mum if we could go, and she said: 'Oh no, it's rather common. They're just trying to show off.'"

But soon, the allure of sunshine and falling prices captivated a wide swath of Europeans. By the late 1970s, 2.5 million Britons took a package holiday annually; by 1986, that number had quadrupled.

A similar story was playing out elsewhere in the world. Bali began to draw Australian sun seekers. Hawaii and Arizona were developed as winter getaways for western North Americans. Florida, Mexico and the Caribbean became the destinations of choice for snowbirds from Ontario, Quebec and the US Northeast. (Of course, wealthy playboys had flocked to Havana from the 1920s through the 1950s, but that wasn't exactly mass tourism.)

UNCLE WALT RESHAPES THE WORLD

It started as a modest idea that Walt Disney sketched out in a memo in 1948: Mickey Mouse Park, a small amusement park across the street from Disney's Burbank studio. Walt — who liked to ride on a miniature train that snaked through the grounds of his Los Angeles home — realized that most playgrounds, zoos and other kid-friendly attractions had little to offer adults. He thought it might be fun to build a place that people of all ages could enjoy. His initial idea included a turn-of-the-century village, a carnival and a Western section.

Walt's problem, however, was that he had too many ideas on too many burners. There was *Cinderella*, a major animated movie then in production that would make or break the studio's increasingly expensive animation program. There were also plans to branch out into full live-action features and television.

Despite all the other projects in progress, in 1952 Walt went public with his idea to build the park, rechristened "Disneyland," on a sixteen-acre parcel of land in Burbank. He realized almost immediately, however, that the property wasn't big enough for his rapidly growing idea. He started looking for a bigger site and founded WED Enterprises in December 1952 as a separate company to start developing the park in earnest.

By the end of 1953, Walt had settled on a site in Anaheim and lined up funding for the project from ABC, an upstart TV network all too glad to pay money to bask in the reflected glitter from the Disney name. In exchange for a $500,000 loan and guarantees on $4.5 mil-

lion in additional loans, ABC would get a one-third ownership in
Disneyland and a weekly Disney TV show. (Forty years later, Disney
would repay the favour by taking over ABC for $19 billion.)

For those who think product placement in TV shows and movies is
anything new, the resulting ABC show — which debuted on October
27, 1954 — might provide a wakeup call. Along with Davy Crockett
serials and other stories, "Disneyland" featured extended coverage
of the theme park slowly rising out of a California orange grove.
Walt himself introduced viewers to Frontierland, Adventureland,
Fantasyland and Tomorrowland, along with films showing the
progress of construction.

Supervising that construction was a retired admiral, Joe Fowler,
whose previous employment had included a stint running the San
Francisco Navy Yard. From the very beginning, the Disney company
saw the amusement park as a place that would combine fantasy and
fun with behind-the-scenes hard work and military precision.

It took only a year and $17 million to build Disneyland, which
opened its gates on July 17, 1955. ABC covered the event with a
ninety-minute live special hosted by Art Linkletter, Bob Cummings and
Ronald Reagan. (In a weird twist, Reagan's second presidential inaugural parade thirty years later would be held at Disney's EPCOT Center
in Florida, after bad weather cancelled the Washington event.)

In our more cynical times, it's almost touching to read some of
the gee-whiz press reports about the new park. In the *Minneapolis
Tribune*, a writer named Will Jones raved, "If it's an amusement park,
it's the gosh-darnedest, most happily inspired, most carefully planned,
most adventure-filled park ever conceived."[70]

Within seven weeks of its opening, Disneyland would host its
one-millionth customer, Elsa Marquez. But almost immediately, the
park launched an aggressive campaign to refresh the attraction con-
tinually, cannily realizing that if people liked something once, you
can persuade them to come back if you offer something new. In its
second year, the park opened twelve new attractions.

The park's success spurred Walt to dream of an even bigger park,
closer to the population centres of the east coast. He considered
Miami and St. Louis but eventually started quietly buying land in

central Florida, where it would be possible to accumulate enough land to buffer his dream park from the kind of development that had sprung up around Disneyland: cheap motels and fast food shops that had crept right up to the California park's gates.

Luckily, he had a golden opportunity to test new technologies and eastern interest in theme parks when he was hired to develop four attractions for the 1964–65 New York World's Fair. The previous year, Disneyland had introduced its first Audio-Animatronics robots, but they really came into their own in New York with the debut of the endlessly annoying "It's a Small World" attraction and the "Great Moments with Mr. Lincoln" show. Other Disney attractions at the fair helped the company hone its people-moving systems; the Carousel of Progress, for instance, rotated the audience past a series of non-moving stages (where they were regaled with vignettes about the importance of electricity, courtesy of sponsor General Electric).

By the mid-1960s, however, some of the bloom was off the Disney rose. When the company won a bid to develop a resort in the Mineral King area of California's Sierra Nevada Mountains, environmentalists protested. To be fair, any plan to develop the wilderness site probably would have drawn criticism, but fear that the wilderness would be "Disneyfied" likely added fuel to the fire. The plan was eventually nixed, and the land became part of Sequoia National Park.

Meanwhile, Disney had bigger fish to fry. In late 1965, the company officially announced its plans for an amusement park near Orlando — a massive project Walt Disney would not live to see completed. Its construction would consume $400 million before the park opened on October 1, 1971. The Disney company negotiated deals with local and state authorities to make the new Magic Kingdom almost completely self-governing; to this day, it runs its own police and fire stations, water-treatment plants, zoning board and road-building authority.

From the early 1970s onward, the Disney "brand" expanded with astonishing speed. It opened EPCOT Center in Orlando on October 1, 1982, followed by Tokyo Disneyland a little more than six months later, on April 15, 1983. The parks also expanded to include upscale restaurants and hotels. Disney-MGM Studios opened in Orlando in

1989, a year in which both Disneyland and Walt Disney World each logged their 300-millionth customer — a goal Walt Disney World reached in a little over half the time it had taken Disneyland. Euro Disneyland (now Disneyland Paris) opened on April 12, 1992. Four years later in Florida, the first families moved into Disney's planned New Urbanist community of Celebration and the first students signed up for one of sixty learning vacation options at The Disney Institute. In 1998, not content with land-based fantasy, Disney launched its first cruise ship, *Disney Magic*, and to capture even more dollars from passengers, pointed it toward Castaway Cay, Disney's private island in the Bahamas. And in 1999 the company opened its fourth Orlando park, Animal Kingdom, a five-hundred-acre attraction that includes a recreated African savannah stocked with zebras, lions and imported plants (although a fourteen-storey steel and concrete baobab tree, home to a movie theatre, came straight from the minds of Disney). Noisy open safari vehicles bound down roads that have been artfully rutted to resemble real African bush roads — but without resentful locals, unpredictable rhinos or pesky bug-borne diseases. The company even imports Africans to serve as "authentic" game park guides.

By 1999, Walt Disney World was the world's top tourist attraction, drawing thirty million visitors a year. And even with more than eleven thousand hectares (forty-three square miles) to play with, it's not easy to keep an annual crowd roughly the size of the population of Canada happy, fed and, most important, moving. Few organizations in the world are as skilled at crowd control as Disney. At WDW, visitors regularly stand in line for half an hour or more for each attraction. Amazingly, they *know* in advance how long they will wait, since helpful signs are posted at the entrance to each attraction. Yet, even though the lines include countless small children and their frazzled parents, open rebellion rarely breaks out. The waiting areas are constructed with lots of twists and turns, so it's impossible to see most of the hordes of people further ahead in line. Piped-in music and video screens distract the huddled masses.

Behind the scenes, Disney uses computerized turnstiles to keep a close eye on crowd volume. It urges "cast members" — the company's

preferred term for employees — to keep customers moving at bench-
mark volumes, such as two thousand people per hour through the
Big Thunder Mountain ride. Throughout the park, fountains and
flowerbeds are placed at angles precisely calculated to keep people
walking in the direction Disney wants them to go. If that doesn't do
the job and people wander off script, recorded voices, animatronic
robots and employees steer visitors back on the right path.

SHOPPERTAINMENT GOES GLOBAL

The concentration of all these people, all this concrete, all that
money can't help but make the thinking person stop and, well,
think. Writing in *New Internationalist*, Wayne Ellwood remarks that
techniques first honed to lure and amuse tourists have now filtered
into just about all mass-market aspects of Western life — and it's not
an improvement:

> Critics argue that the theme-park model which Disney
> invented has escaped its tether and now mediates so-
> cial relations around the world. Shopping malls, chain
> eateries like McDonald's, the logo-mania of Nike and
> Reebok, all these are influenced by the Disney model
> which offers what some have called "shoppertainment"
> as a replacement for citizenship.[71]

As Ellwood points out, the phenomenon has spread far beyond
North America and far beyond Disney. There is a Universal Studios
theme park in Osaka, a Sega World in Sydney and a Ripley's Believe
It or Not! attraction in Thailand. Hard Rock Cafés — microcosmic
theme parks — have sprung up from London to Kuala Lumpur; there
are now 122 throughout the world.

That being said, I have an abiding soft spot for the safe, plastic
world of Disney and its spawn. I've been to Disney parks four times
in my life — and I don't even have kids. My husband and I spent part
of our honeymoon — I am not making this up — at the Disneyland
Resort in Anaheim. One of the first things I bought in my married

life was a Mickey Mouse watch, to replace the watch I'd mislaid at our wedding reception two nights earlier.

Sure, the Disney parks are full of elegant fakery, ingeniously designed to separate you from as much of your money as humanly possible. But they're only the latest, biggest, most sophisticated version of the Victorian fun fair. Deep down, we secretly love to be delighted by the sheer audacity and scale of the Disney experience, even if we're justifying our interest by taking an "improving" course at The Disney Institute. In a recent newspaper article, a Toronto twenty-something confessed that he headed to the Disney-MGM Studios to escape the drudgery of adulthood: "I try to be as much of a kid as possible...when I'm at work, I have responsibility, I make decisions and I have people to answer to."[72]

As many academics have pointed out, part of the appeal of places like WDW is the abrogation of responsibility they offer. Critics focus on the fact that it's not real, but for many visitors that's the *point*. We get enough reality every day, juggling unreasonable demands from remote bosses, wading through piles of bills, trying to figure out how to give the kids a decent dinner somewhere between piano lessons and soccer practice. We want to go somewhere we all know is fake — but also safe and relaxing, with no need to use our brains if we don't want to. You don't have to worry about running into danger, dirt or crime, and you don't have to decide among multiple entertainment options competing for your attention. Sure, there are lots of rides and lots of shops, but in the end they are all run by Disney, providing similar levels of pleasure, safety and boasting rights.

The Well-Packed Bag
DON'T FORGET YOUR...

*A souvenir carries a little magic charge which whisks
its owner back from dark, north-west Europe to the
sunny spot below the olive trees and beside the vines
where it was purchased. It is a promise that one will
go back and find the place again.*
— *Fred Inglis,* The Delicious History of the Holiday

As British travel historian Fred Inglis has noted, in the days of the
Grand Tour, painters set the parameters of *what* people should see,
while guidebooks told them precisely *how* to see the celebrated sites.
Guidebooks to England's Lake District, for example, told readers
precisely which rock or tree they should stand by to enjoy a famous
scene.

These days, the mechanisms have changed a bit but the general
idea is still the same. Movies like *Shirley Valentine*, along with glossy
travel magazines and memoirs such as *Under the Tuscan Sun*, paint in-
delible images of exotic locales and inspire people to visit. Sometimes,
though, the inspiration horrifies even its instigators — Peter Mayle,
author of *A Year in Provence*, had to move from his French farmhouse
after he was inundated by admiring readers who wanted to see his
lovely retreat for themselves. But once we've decided where we want
to go, increasingly specialized guidebooks and Web sites point us in
the right direction.

...GUIDEBOOK

Travel accounts, in various forms, are a very old form of literature.
Whenever people have travelled, they've felt the urge — if they could
write, of course — to record their impressions. Christian pilgrims

215

began writing records of their travels called *Peregrinationes* as early as the fourth century. An author known to history as Roger of Sicily gathered information from merchants and pilgrims and, in 1154, compiled *The Book of Roger, or the Delight of whoso loves to make the Circuit of the World*. About 150 years later, Marco Polo used his time in a Genoa prison to dictate the story of his time in Asia.

One of the first modern guidebooks was *Some Observations Made in Travelling Through France and Italy &c in the years 1720, 1721 and 1722*, by Edward Wright. Published in London in 1730, the book would go through thirty-one editions. Other authors followed suit with books such as *Grand Tour containing an exact description of most of the cities, towns and remarkable places of Europe*, by Thomas Nugent, published in 1749. (It would be several centuries before publishers realized the marketing power of snappy titles like *Let's Go* and *Europe on $5 a Day*.) These books complemented travel articles that began appearing with greater frequency in publications such as *The Gentleman's Magazine* in Britain.

In many eighteenth-century guidebooks, particularly those aimed at the Grand Tour, the implicit assumption was that the reader was travelling for more than just recreation; with their frequent digressions into matters historic, artistic and architectural, these books were akin to textbook, designed to help readers improve themselves.

By the early nineteenth century, British tourists had also begun to celebrate the joys of travelling within their own country, and few domestic destinations were as popular as the Lake District. By happy coincidence, William Wordsworth, one of the country's pre-eminent men of letters, who just happened to be a lifelong resident of the area, fell into guidebook writing almost by accident. In 1810, a friend and amateur artist, Rev. Joseph Wilkinson, published a collection of his drawings, *Select Views in Cumberland, Westmoreland, and Lancashire*, and asked Wordsworth to write an introduction that described the region for readers. Wordsworth, who liked the good reverend but didn't particularly care for his artwork, complied but did so anonymously. He liked his own words enough, though, that he updated and repurposed them (as publishers would say today) as an annex to *The River Duddon, a Series of Sonnets: and other Poems*,

published in 1820. Travellers found Wordsworth's tips on what to
see and how to see it so useful that Wordsworth — not too proud a
poet to follow the money — published a stand-alone version of the
guide in 1822.

The immensely popular book would go through several more
editions and titles. Wordsworth's introduction to the fifth and last
edition, published in 1835, includes a pithy summary of his purpose
in writing the little guidebook that wouldn't seem out of the ordinary
for a guidebook writer today:

> In preparing this Manual, it was the Author's principal
> wish to furnish a Guide or Companion for the *Minds* of
> Persons of taste, and feeling for Landscape, who might
> be inclined to explore the District of the Lakes with that
> degree of attention to which its beauty may fairly lay
> claim. For the more sure attainment, however, of this
> primary object, he will begin by undertaking the humble
> and tedious task of supplying the Tourist with directions
> how to approach the several scenes in their best, or most
> convenient, order.[73]

Books like these appealed to people's high-minded self-concept
by promising details of art, architecture and culture. At the same
time, they weren't so exalted that they neglected the practical little
details — like how to get there, or, in later books, where to eat, stay
and shop. Nevertheless, Wordsworth, as did the guidebook writers
to follow, had an uneasy relationship with the world of tourism. In
the spectrum of travellers and tourists, Wordsworth was definitely
not a tourist.

Although Wordsworth's book and similar guides were popular in
their day, it would take the Industrial Revolution — with its trains,
efficient printing presses and distribution systems and rising middle
class with the money and time to travel — to make the travel guidebook a truly mass-market phenomenon. And one of the first people
to realize its potential was John Murray, son and namesake of a
London printer.

His father's company had for some years published guides to Italy and the rest of the Continent by a prolific writer named Mariana Starke. Over the first three decades of the nineteenth century, however, her books had slowly morphed from the classic lyrical memoir of a Grand Tour adventure to hybrids that also included some information on inns, exchange rates, shops and so on, to allow readers to replicate Starke's lovely trip if they so wished.

When the younger Murray tested the book during his own Grand Tour in 1829, however, he found parts of it — those Starke had based on information from others, rather than her own on-site research — wildly inaccurate. Murray decided to improve on the concept and, after years of research, wrote his own book, *Hand-Book for Travellers on the Continent*, published in 1836. Unlike earlier guides, his minimized the historical details and stylistic flourishes, concentrating instead on the nuts and bolts: the most important sights to see, recommended inns and restaurants, transportation details and money matters.

Encouraged by the book's success, Murray launched a line of similar titles. A century before Eugene Fodor produced his eponymous branded guidebooks, Murray developed the hallmarks of the genre. The title of each pocket-sized volume began with the words *Hand-Book for Travellers*, and each book had an easy-to-spot red binding. Inside, readers were guaranteed a consistent product, with an introduction, practical information, suggested itineraries and maps. Like the Victorian industrialists whose factories produced identical chairs and bolts of cloth, Murray realized that standardization was the key to efficiency, customer satisfaction and profits.

It didn't take long for others to take note of Murray's success. In Koblenz, Germany, a young publisher and bookseller named Karl Baedeker was already publishing a small guidebook to the Rhine when he first spotted Murray's guides in the hands of British tourists. Using the English books as a model, he published a new Rhine guide in 1839, then built on its success with subsequent guides to other European destinations. These books were among the first to use a star system to rate the worth of various museums — a gimmick that proved so popular with readers that Murray later copied it. In fact, the two publishers openly built on each other's innovations at every opportunity, Baedeker going so far as to start using red bindings for his own books in 1854.

Baedeker was a stickler for accuracy. According to one story, he ensured a correct count of the number of steps in the tower of Milan's cathedral by dropping a pea on each twentieth step on his way up, while keeping count in his head. On the way back down, he collected all the peas and checked his count against them.

These guidebooks were essential to the development of mass tourism. Only once many people knew what they should see would sufficient quantities go to any one place to attract the attention of hoteliers and tour operators. Tour operators added to the momentum by publishing their own guidebooks. In the 1850s, Henry Gaze, Thomas Cook's great rival, published a book for his package tourists called *Switzerland and How to See It for Ten Guineas*. Then, as now, such publishing efforts attracted scorn from people who doubted one could travel the world cheaply; *Punch* soon published an article titled "A Week in the Moon for a Pound."

The next major influence on guidebooks was the invention of the automobile. In 1900, French tire manufacturers André and Edouard Michelin began producing free travel guides for motorists, enumerating not only where they could get gas and batteries for their newfangled machines, but also where they could find a meal and a bed for the night.

By 1914, Michelin was printing more than eighty thousand guides annually, to destinations that included the Benelux countries, Switzerland, Spain, Portugal and Britain. The First World War disrupted the business somewhat, although French soldiers did find the guides — with their maps and directions — useful in the field.

For the first two decades, the free Michelin guides were rather rudimentary, although basic rankings for hotel quality were introduced in 1908. After the war, however, the guides evolved rapidly. In 1920, the company began charging for them. Then, three years later, it added a separate restaurant section. By 1933, the company had developed its famous culinary rating system of one to three stars. Michelin's word on restaurant quality has now become so highly valued in France that a restaurant that recently lost one of its three stars saw its business drop by 50 percent. Even the rumour that he might lose one of his three stars seems to have played a role in the suicide of celebrated French chef Bernard Loiseau in 2003.

Just as the rise of the middle class spawned Murray and Baedeker guides and the invention of the automobile gave rise to Michelin, the increasing affordability of transatlantic travel would generate a new generation of guidebooks, focused originally on Europe and most aimed squarely at the North American market. The trend began just before the Second World War, when a peripatetic Hungarian travel writer named Eugene Fodor published *On the Continent: The Entertaining Travel Annual*. The guide provided somewhat more detailed information on national cultures and etiquette than many of its competitors, but its main innovation was to promise annual updates.

During the Second World War, guidebook publishing largely ceased, but guidebooks still had a role to play — if not the one for which they were intended. On March 28, 1942, a Royal Air Force raid on the historic German city of Lübeck ignited a firestorm that killed a thousand people. Hitler ordered retaliatory attacks on British cities known for their heritage buildings. The first took place on April 23, 1942, when the Luftwaffe bombed Exeter, killing seventy. The next day, Nazi propagandist Baron Gustav Braun von Sturm announced, "We shall go out and bomb every building in Britain marked with three stars in the Baedeker Guide." Whether or not the Luftwaffe actually used the famous little books to plan its raids, the attacks over the next seven weeks damaged or destroyed thousands of buildings in numerous historic English cities — including Exeter, Bath, Norwich, York and Canterbury — among them the Bath Assembly Rooms and the medieval guildhall in York.

After the war, Fodor founded a guidebook company in Paris to publish a wide range of guidebooks to various countries; by 2006 the imprint, now owned by Random House, would have 440 guidebooks in print divided into fourteen series, ranging from the best-selling Gold Guides to niche publications such as the Around the City with Kids series.

Fodor pretty much ruled the American guidebook market until 1957, when a US Army lawyer named Arthur Frommer published *Europe on $5 a Day*. The genius of his book, which began as a handbook for American GIs abroad, was its focus on budget travel and the author's original conviction that everyone should — and could — travel.

As everywhere, inflation has hit the dollars-a-day concept — the 2004 edition of the company's flagship book was titled *Europe from $85 a Day*. But Frommer's dedication to the idea of affordable travel continues: in 1998, he launched *Arthur Frommer's Budget Travel* magazine. As I'll discuss later, however, Frommer is one of several travel experts whose convictions about what constitutes "authentic" travel have changed over the years, as travel has become a more mass-market phenomenon.

Budget travel would take an even more radical swing in the 1960s, when student backpackers began to travel to the Continent and beyond in increasing numbers. First out of the block with an English-language guide to serve this emerging market were some students at Harvard, who in 1960 produced a free mimeographed guide called *Let's Go Europe*; within two years, the guide had expanded considerably and cost a dollar a copy. Today, Harvard Student Agencies publishes forty-eight titles in the popular series, which has become known for its appeal to budget-conscious travellers with an appetite for adventure, taking people off the beaten pack and offering unconventional advice, all with a dash of irreverent wit.

Since then, the range of guides aimed at usually young and increasingly adventurous travellers has burgeoned. Moon Publications and Lonely Planet Guides were launched within six months of each other in 1973 by young, footloose travellers exploring Asia. In 1982, the *Rough Guide to Greece* was the first of hundreds of cheeky titles that would grow to encompass music, history and other cultural topics as well as travel.

While Fodor and Frommer were focusing on the middle-class (and often middle-aged) traveller, and Moon and Lonely Planet were targeting backpackers, a young German named Hans Hofer was developing the first in a third kind of guidebook: the inspirational series that combines detailed historical and cultural information with stunning photography. After travelling through southeast Asia in a VW bus, Hofer self-published *Insight Bali* in 1970. That book and subsequent Insight Guides owe at least as much to the educational aspects of Grand Tour guidebooks as to the *Let's Go* franchise: costlier than some of the budget guides, they aim to immerse readers in the history and culture of each destination. Other visually appealing travel guides, such as the Dorling Kindersley Eyewitness Guides with their cutaway drawings of famous buildings and eye-popping food photos, have built on the Insight Guides foundation.

...PASSPORT

Even in these days of linked computer databases, fingerprinting and iris scans, it can be difficult to determine with certainty that a stranger is who he says he is. Centuries ago, it was even more difficult. Travellers were forced to rely on one of the most basic measures of trustworthiness: a personal letter of reference.

Those letters could come from anyone, of course, but they held more weight if they were written by a powerful figure whose name would be recognized far outside the traveller's borders, such as a monarch or religious leader — someone who had the power to protect the traveller with military retaliation, if necessary. If they were personally addressed to a powerful person in the destination country, even better.

Some sort of travel identification may have been required in Egypt as far back as 1500 BC, but none has survived. One of the earliest such letters on record — we know about it because it is mentioned in the Old Testament — was written by King Artaxerxes of ancient Persia for a government official named Nehemiah around 450 BC Nehemiah wished to travel from Shushan in what is now Iran to Jerusalem. The king gave his official a letter written "to the governors beyond the river," asking people in Judah to keep Nehemiah safe from harm. The implication, of course, was that if any harm befell the man, Artaxerxes would take action against those who caused it.

That, in a nutshell, is the philosophy that still underlies the modern passport. Open any of the small booklets carried by international travellers the world over and you're likely to come across a statement such as the request in each US passport that the bearer be allowed to "pass without delay or hindrance and in case of need, to give all lawful aid and protection."

But for how many years have people been required by law to carry official passports? Surprisingly few, as it turns out.

Letters of introduction: Until the advent of mass-market travel, some of the most important items in a traveller's luggage were letters of introduction. These letters were not official documents. Instead, they were merely written evidence that the bearer was a person of good character (and, usually, someone with good connections). In our more cynical age, it is tempting to think that such letters would be easy to forge, but it appears that in times past these documents were largely genuine and accepted as such. Perhaps it was too difficult to replicate a famous person's letterhead, or perhaps people were better at recognizing the handwriting of their friends, relatives and colleagues than we are today. Perhaps it was simply that the potential embarrassment of being caught in a forgery served as a deterrent.

If it weren't for letters of introduction, it might be facetiously argued, England might never have been Christianized. In the late sixth century, Pope Gregory I (later St. Gregory the Great) decided it was high time someone visited pagan Anglo-Saxons and brought them into the Roman Catholic fold. Although the Romans had once colonized the far-off island, by Gregory's time Britain was considered as remote and unknowable as the moon. Almost no one had been there or knew much about it. In fact, few people in Rome travelled far afield, and those who did usually headed for the Holy Land. A trip to Britain would have been inconceivable to most.

Nevertheless, Gregory picked Augustine, a promising monk from his monastery of St. Andrew, to lead a small band of missionaries on the journey. The apprehensive group set off from Rome in June 596, with letters of introduction from the pope to various bishops and Christian princes whose domains lay between Rome and England. Despite this reassurance, the missionaries appear to have developed cold feet. Just a month into their journey, while staying in Provence, they were spooked by stories of the barbarity of the Anglo-Saxons and decided it might be wise to call off the mission. They promptly sent Augustine back to Rome to voice their concerns to the pontiff, then settled down in Aix-en-Provence to await Gregory's decision.

On July 23, Gregory wrote a letter for Augustine to carry back to his followers, basically instructing them to buck up and soldier on. He also made Augustine an abbot and their official leader. Finally, the pope provided at least half a dozen additional letters of introduction to ease their fears. This combination of letters seems to have restored the party's morale, because it continued on to England, where Augustine eventually became the first archbishop of Canterbury.

Letters of introduction were not just a Western custom. Three decades after Augustine headed to England, a Chinese Buddhist pilgrim named Hsuan-tsang set off on a sixteen-year trip from China to India and back, to acquire some Buddhist texts. (And you thought your interlibrary lending service was slow.) In the city of Turfan in northwestern China, he made friends with the king, who was impressed by his scholarship. When Hsuan-tsang left to continue his travels, the king gave him letters of introduction to the rulers of oases along the Silk Road.

And such letters remained a vital item for travellers for at least the next millennium. In the 1500s, Spanish writer Miguel de Cervantes found similar protection in some simple letters of introduction from fellow writers. After fighting in a war against the Turks in the eastern Mediterranean, he was sailing back to Spain when Barbary pirates captured his ship. The letters convinced his captors that he was a rich man, so instead of killing him outright, they held him prisoner in Algiers for five years, seeking a ransom.

Letters of introduction were often crucial items in the luggage of any ambitious Grand Tourist, as they granted him instant entrée into local society. With a few such letters, he would find himself invited to social events from small dinners to glittering soirees. Introductions could be arranged to prominent people: scholars, politicians, even royalty. The traveller also might be able to finesse an invitation to stay with the letter's addressee, which was particularly handy in destinations not well equipped with hotels and rental apartments. In fact, these letters were useful in so many ways that they are part of the reason aristocrats dominated the tourist scene in some countries well into the 1700s: people without lofty connections could often find it hard to put a roof over their heads.

Letters were designed to serve as proof of the bearer's good breeding and character. As British tourist Thomas Pelham wrote of travel to Paris in the 1770s:

> I find that it is necessary to be furnished with the most particular recommendations to gain admission into the society of the people of fashion, and that without a residence of some time your acquaintance with people of merit and distinction will be much confined; for the generality, not to say all the English, who have been at Paris lately have conducted themselves in such a manner as to be shunned universally and consequently obliged to live at publick places and in such *company* as may be found more or less in every town.[74]

His contemporary, one Mr. Dalrymple, was desperate to secure a good letter of introduction before he went to Strasbourg in 1789 to contradict a "report of my being a person of extreme low birth, who ought not to be taken notice of by anybody of rank and consequence in the town."[75]

I had thought such genteel concerns had gone out the window with calling cards and lace handkerchiefs, but it appears that the letter of introduction is alive and well, albeit in somewhat altered form. An international organization called Servas, whose members offer short-term accommodation in their homes for travellers, interviews each potential traveller and checks references before issuing a letter of introduction, which the traveller must present to his or her host upon arrival.

AND HOLLYWOOD CREATED GIDGET

While not technically designed solely as travel clothing, the bikini as often as not comes out only on vacations. For many people — male and female — its skimpiness and hedonism are the essence of the tropical vacation in a few scraps of string and cloth. Women who wouldn't dare wear one when swimming with their kids or neighbours at the local Y might throw one into the suitcase for that Caribbean getaway. After all, who will know?

The bikini has a longer heritage than most people realize. Mosaics from the fourth century at the Villa Romana del Casale in Sicily show women exercising in the Roman version of a two-piece bathing suit. But with the fall of the empire, the sexy ensemble disappeared from Western memory for about sixteen hundred years or so.

The modern bikini hit the world with the metaphorical bang of its namesake — the atomic bomb tests on Bikini Atoll in the Pacific — when it debuted in Paris on July 5, 1946. Lingerie manufacturer Louis Réard designed and christened the skimpy suit but couldn't find a model willing to don it for the cameras. Eventually, he had to hire a nude dancer for the task. Not surprisingly, few women dared wear it in public, until an eighteen-year-old Brigitte Bardot set off a European craze for the suit with one of her first movies, *Manina, la fille sans voile* (later marketed in the

US as *The Girl in the Bikini*). Interestingly, the 1952 flick's plot (such as it is) revolves around two guys who show up on a sunny island for a summer vacation. For about a decade, the bikini was associated mainly with Europe; as the American magazine *Modern Girl* declared in 1957, "It is hardly necessary to waste words over the so-called bikini, since it is inconceivable that any girl with tact and decency would ever wear such a thing."[76]

The link between bikinis and exotic locales continued through the early 1960s, with Ursula Andress's famous emergence from the ocean onto a Jamaican beach in the James Bond movie *Dr. No* in 1962 and the first *Sports Illustrated* swimsuit issue, published in 1964, whose cover featured model Babette March in a white bikini in the surf of Cozumel.

Not all foreign folks were thrilled with the itsy-bitsy bathing suit — at first, bikini-wearing tourists in Catholic countries such as Italy and Spain were hustled off beaches by officials enforcing countrywide bans on the swimwear. Despite hand-wringing moral authorities, however, the bikini soon made its way to more sedate beaches. By the time the Annette Funicello/Frankie Avalon movie *How to Stuff a Wild Bikini* appeared in 1965, it was acceptable swimwear for former Mouseketeers learning to surf during their California summers.

In a somewhat different vein, academics sometimes travel with a
letter of introduction from their home institution, stamped with the
university's seal, to prove they are genuine researchers if they request
access to research facilities at another institution.

Letters of safe conduct: For centuries, "letters of safe conduct" were
the main form of government-issued travel documentation. There
was no standard format — someone, usually the monarch, wrote
them if and when needed, usually for nobles and other powerful
people, and usually for a specific trip. By outlining the exact reason
why the bearer (and, often, his entourage of servants and soldiers)
was crossing foreign territory, the letter was designed to inspire
trust.

As well as protecting people while they were travelling abroad,
these letters also made it easier for the bearer to return home. This
was particularly important in the Roman Empire, where Roman citizens had an array of rights and privileges that foreigners did not. Any
stranger claiming to be a Roman was wise to have proof of his status
whenever he travelled away from home, as most people — even the
vast majority who could not read — were sufficiently impressed by a
document bearing the emperor's seal.

When the Roman Empire fell, so did the frequency of travel. As
Europe descended into the Dark Ages, most people were quite justifiably afraid to venture far from home — and had little reason to. But
the concept of the letter of safe conduct never really disappeared.

Kings and emperors didn't write letters of safe conduct just for
their own subjects. They also gave them to foreigners entering their
territories, often for peace negotiations. In negotiation situations, the
king often threw in a few of his own subjects as hostages, whom the
negotiator's side would keep until the envoy returned safely from
the peace talks. In one curious case, Richard II issued a letter of safe
conduct in 1390 to a Scottish knight named Sir David de Lindesay,
so that de Lindesay could safely cross England with an entourage,
horses, weapons and armour. His destination was London Bridge,
where he would duel with an English noble named John Welles to

settle a matter of honour. (For the record, de Lindesay won the duel and was later made an earl.)

Rulers soon realized the advantages not just of giving certain contentious travellers promises of safe passage, but also of regulating the arrival and departure of everyone coming in and out of the country. In the days before today's modern security systems and highly regulated harbours, ports and border crossings, this might have been difficult. And, indeed, more than a few travellers circumvented the rules simply by landing their ships in isolated coves under cover of night. But if someone wanted to arrive at an official border, it became more likely as the Middle Ages progressed that he would need some sort of documentation.

As early as 1078, William I of England had set up such a system. After building a ring of coastal castles, he required anyone landing on England's shores to present a document known as a king's licence, obtained in advance. Unlike the letter of safe conduct, which a traveller wrangled for his own protection, this was something the country of destination required for *its* own protection. By the middle of the twelfth century, this concept had been extended to English citizens wishing to leave as well, since rulers learned that disgruntled subjects could leave England, raise a force of sympathizers elsewhere and come back to make trouble. Much better, rulers thought, to keep potential rabble-rousers in the country, where it was easier to keep an eye on them. This provision remained in force until King John signed the Magna Carta in 1215, which technically abolished the requirement. By then, ambitious merchants were chafing at the red tape required whenever they needed to go abroad to get merchandise. After all, at this point the king himself was still signing every licence.

Despite its impracticality, later rulers periodically revived the king's licence system. In the late 1300s, for instance, Richard II required all ship's captains carrying pilgrims from England to the Continent to get a king's licence as well.

In any case, all of these rules were probably honoured as much in the breach as in the observance. If a king really wanted to keep a traveller in the country, he could probably manage to do it. And if a traveller really wanted to sneak in, he probably could.

These early travel documents — the letter of safe conduct and the king's licence — are the forerunners of our modern passports and visas.

Security from schemers, pirates and highwaymen: Until the Industrial Revolution made long-distance travel at least somewhat practical, few people travelled far from home and few countries had iron-clad rules requiring travellers to carry precise forms of identification. Most tried to acquire letters of safe conduct strictly for their own protection, rather than to avoid breaking any laws. When Martin Luther travelled to Augsburg in 1518 to defend his Protestant teachings to Cardinal Cajetan, he stayed in hiding for three days until he received the letter of safe conduct he'd requested from the emperor. Without such proof of the emperor's backing, Luther was quite reasonably afraid that the cardinal would throw him in jail, or worse.

Merchants were particularly susceptible to theft and capture because they often travelled with a large quantity of valuable goods. In exchange for remaining loyal to the sovereign, cities and towns were often granted permission to issue letters of safe conduct for merchants. This was a key economic advantage, as it gave them an edge in attracting trade to their town. The Irish city of Galway received just such a privilege from Queen Elizabeth I in July 1579.

The term "passport" is rooted in the French *passe port*, which literally means "enter a seaport" or "pass through a gate." The term entered English around 1500, first appearing in legislation in 1548. At first, it was defined as a paper giving a soldier leave from service. Until the late nineteenth century, these passports — like the documents that had preceded them — looked nothing like the little booklets with which we're now familiar. Rather, they were usually a single sheet, often quite a large one, bearing a coat of arms and declaring in Latin or some other suitably impressive language that the bearer was basically a good guy and should be allowed to go where he wished.

Interestingly, it took another half-century or so before an official government service — the Clerks of the Passage — was set up in

England to actually *check* travellers' passports. Before then, passports were checked ad hoc, if anyone thought it might be a good idea to see who was coming and going. In the 1580s, for instance, Elizabeth I's royal secretary, Francis Walsingham, sent out his own intelligence agents to do the deed.

One of the earliest surviving passports was signed by Charles I in 1641. After Charles was executed and Oliver Cromwell became Lord Protector, English passports required bearers to swear that, in their travels, they would not "act, be aiding, assisting, advising or counselling against the Commonwealth." After all, chances were high in those days that any Englishman travelling abroad would be trying to rally with royalists abroad to restore the English monarchy. Speaking of royalists, passports went through a bit of a vogue across the English Channel in France during the reign of Louis XIV, when bearers used them as proof that they were favourites of the king.

Requirements for people requesting a passport varied significantly from jurisdiction to jurisdiction. In the colony of Virginia in the 1600s, for instance, the governor seems to have modified the old custom whereby engaged couples had their banns — their intent to be married — read out or posted at church. He ordered that anyone wanting a passport to leave the colony had to post a notice of their planned itinerary on the church door for two Sundays. More pragmatically, would-be travellers had to settle all their debts before receiving permission to leave town.

By the early eighteenth century, several European countries required their citizens to have the equivalent of a passport even for domestic travel. These usually included a detailed physical description of the bearer. Interestingly, British passports — possibly because Britons greatly resented the idea that anyone would think to limit their liberty or question their honesty — didn't include any sort of physical description until 1915.

As people began to travel abroad in somewhat greater numbers, more countries set up rudimentary systems to issue passports. (The first permanent embassies in the modern world were established by several of the Italian city-states in the mid-fifteenth century.) But the volume was not large — between 1772 and 1858, the British foreign secretary individually printed and signed each British passport, and did so only for those he knew personally and for friends of friends. Intriguingly, those friends didn't have to be British — until 1858, people from any country were allowed to obtain a British passport. Rather than proof of nationality, the document was simply proof of the bearer's identity and good character. It also showed the person was educated, as all British passports were then written in French, the international language of diplomacy.

These passports were prized but expensive. Fortunately, travellers had many other options. They could also get a local passport from a governor, prince or other authority in each place they travelled through, or from an English ambassador or consul abroad. In fact, many people carried multiple passports to cover a range of destinations and situations.

Passports could make one's life infinitely smoother but were rarely mandatory except in times of civil unrest. During the French Revolution, for instance, foreigners in France often had to show identification to every local official they encountered. "I really begin to dread being searched at every village," English traveller Mary Berry wrote to a friend during a rather daring trip to France in 1790.

A passport by any other name: One source of confusion in the history of passports is that the term was used interchangeably for the documents we now know as passports and visas. For instance, historians have been able to trace the rise in British tourism to Italy between 1763 and 1796 by noting that Roman authorities issued five times more "passports" to British tourists during that time than to visitors from all other nations combined. But those passports simply gave visitors permission to enter a geographic area, like modern visas (a word that wouldn't come into English until about 1825).

The chummy nature of the passport system changed in the mid-1800s, when expanding rail systems spurred the rise of mass tourism. Overwhelmed government officials decided that the whole passport process was more trouble than it was worth. France stopped issuing both passports and visas in 1861, and by the early twentieth century most countries had abandoned the process. Even in countries that did continue to issue them, few people bothered to apply — in 1878, Canada issued just fifty passports all year.

But just as the French Revolution had increased fears about security, the First World War made nations more aware of the dangers of letting undocumented people cross their borders. Countries in Europe and elsewhere quickly started or revived their passport programs, in most cases believing they were just a temporary wartime measure. The United States passed its first mandatory passport law in December 1915.

Until a 1920 conference recommended the small booklet shape we know today, passports came in all shapes and sizes, from small cards to large certificates. Photographs weren't even standard in many countries until the early 1900s. Instead, some jurisdictions required a detailed written description of the bearer. (Not all of those descriptions were particularly flattering, either — if you were heavy or had bad skin, for instance, that information would be duly recorded for the border officer's perusal.)

Into the digital age: Until quite recently, the passport application process was an almost shockingly casual affair. Before 1970, for instance, Canadians applied for their passports by mail and didn't have to provide proof of citizenship — a process that ended shortly after assassin James Earl Ray fled the US with a Canadian passport he'd obtained directly from the Canadian government, using a false name.

Over the past four decades, however, passports have become some of the most high-tech documents on earth. The first step, which many countries took in the 1970s and 1980s, was to laminate the photograph and personal information, in an effort to foil people who stole passports and simply pasted their photos over the existing ones. Passports at this time also began to incorporate watermarks, holographic images, security thread and special inks, all in an effort to deter fraud artists. More recently, many countries have embedded the bearer's digital photograph into the paper itself. And most passports are now machine readable, which makes it easier to process visitors at the border.

Other innovations are just over the horizon. Under new international standards, all new passports must leave space for fingerprints. The United States takes digital face scans of all foreign visitors, to be compared with scans of known undesirables, and the UK is poised to introduce a passport with an embedded microchip. These features are not without controversy, as privacy groups have raised the spectre of "Big Brother" governments tracking the movements of millions of people around the globe.

In these days when passports are harder to counterfeit than currency, it seems amazing that less than a century ago, people moved freely throughout the world with no identification papers whatsoever.

...SOUVENIRS

As long as people have travelled, they've brought back physical mementoes of their journey, both to remind themselves of the adventure and to prove to the folks back home that they were not making the story up. Part of the thrill of travel has always been the opportunity to impress the neighbours. As the author of a fifteenth-century supplement to the *Canterbury Tales* explained the souvenir-buying tendencies of pilgrims:

> Then, as manere and custom is, signes there they
>   boughte,
> Ffor men of contre shulde know whom they hadde
>   [s]oughte.[77]

Or, in modern English, "Like everyone else, they bought a few mementoes to prove to the folks back home that they really did travel to the holy shrine and didn't just spend those months sitting in a pub knocking back pints."

The Romans and Greeks who roamed the Mediterranean basin sat for portraits by street artists in Athens and snapped up fake spell books in Egypt. They carted home glass bottles and other items adorned with painted images of the lighthouse at Alexandria — souvenirs so popular they've been unearthed some 3,500 kilometres away in Afghanistan. They shelled out for miniature statues of Apollo from Delphi and representations of Artemis from Ephesus. Artisans did such a roaring trade in the latter that St. Paul was inspired to speak out against their greed and idolatry when he lived in the city; a mob of irate Ephesians chased him out of the local stadium for his pains.

A millennium and a half later, souvenir medallions from major Christian pilgrimage sites were big business. Usually made of pewter or lead and known as *brochis* or *sygnys,* they were designed so that a pilgrim could sew them onto his cap or tunic, much like the souvenir pins so beloved of modern service club members (or, in a slightly different form, the bumper stickers that paper the backs of RVs). Some of the most prized were the scallop shell medallions from Santiago and the two crossed palm fronds from Jerusalem, which fought for space on the well-travelled pilgrim's hat with Virgin Mary medals from Rocamadour, miniature flasks filled with holy water from Canterbury, the small wheel that signified a visit to St. Catherine's tomb on Mount Sinai and images of the head of St. John the Baptist from Amiens.

Pilgrims who made too big a show of their collection of medals were ripe targets for ridicule. In a Renaissance-era satire, Erasmus has a character remark on the clutter of medals adorning a friend recently returned from a pilgrimage to Santiago: "I pray you, what array is this that you be in; me thynke that you be clothyd with cockle schelles, and be laden on every side with bruches of lead and tynne."[78]

In many places, a convent or a family had the exclusive right to produce these lucrative souvenirs, often through an arrangement that saw them split the profits with local church officials. It wasn't long, though, before everyone wanted a piece of the action. Like the counterfeiters who line the streets of Asia with ersatz Swatch watches and Prada purses, medieval medal fakers in Rocamadour brought down the wrath of the local authorities by churning out unauthorized medallions. Every so often, officials would pass laws to clamp down on the practice, but, then as now, counterfeiters proved remarkably ingenious and resilient.

In the days of the Grand Tour, some of the most popular souvenirs were a bit more unwieldy, leading to some serious cases of non-buyer's remorse. Travelling in Lorraine in August 1728, an English tourist named Robert Trevor dithered for some time over buying some Callot engravings. He eventually decided that their heavy frames would make them impractical to transport back home, but, he added, "it was a great mortification to me to leave them."[79]

Wish you were here: One of the most ubiquitous souvenirs of modern times, the postcard, didn't start as a souvenir at all. Instead, it was a utilitarian item without pictures designed to give senders a cheap way to communicate. Correspondents wrote the address on one side of a plain card and a brief message on the blank back. Printers and post offices in a number of countries introduced various types of postcards throughout the 1860s, but the first to enjoy widespread use were developed by Dr. Emanuel Hermann and introduced in the Austro-Hungarian Empire on October 1, 1869. The inexpensive cards were an immediate success, with eager correspondents buying almost three million by the end of that year. The US first permitted postcards in May 1873, and sixty million flew off the shelves within the first six months. Those printed by the US Postal Service required only a penny in postage, while those produced by private printers cost twice as much to mail, which effectively dampened demand for private postcards for several decades, particularly since most postcards from any source were still plain.

But in the late 1880s, things slowly began to change. French postcards with small illustrations of the Eiffel Tower in one corner of the "message" side of the postcard appeared around 1889. Around the same time, postcards in German-speaking countries began to sport small pictures of churches and castles on the message side, along with the slogan *Gruss aus* (greetings from).

The first postcards designed specifically as souvenirs were produced for the Columbian Exposition in Chicago in 1893. The souvenir postcard wouldn't really take off for another decade or so, however, because such cards either skimped on the size of the image or the size of the space available for the correspondent's message. Those with a large picture often had a small border where the correspondent could write a brief sentence and sign his or her name.

The souvenir postcard truly took off in the early 1900s, spurred by the British Post Office's decision in January 1902 to permit postcards with divided backs. The space on the left was reserved for the correspondent's message, while the right-hand side was reserved for the address. That meant that the entire front of the card could be devoted to a photo or illustration. The US Postal Service followed the UK's lead in October 1907, again with immediate success. The following year, Americans mailed more than 677 *million* postcards — more than seven postcards for every man, woman and child in the country.

Postcard sending and collecting soon became something of a mania. Not all postcards commemorated travels; people also sent greeting postcards to mark birthdays, anniversaries and holidays, and some postcards featured jokes, caricatures, artistic illustrations or historical scenes. Every family with any pretensions to sophistication soon had a bulging postcard album in the parlour. Not only did such an album attest to the family's travel experiences and wide circle of acquaintances; in the days before inexpensive cameras, it provided a portrait of the world — or at least the world a middle-class person might be likely to visit — in pictures.

And not all of those pictures were of what we might consider today to be standard tourist sights. Civic boosters with Babbit-esque dreams produced cards commemorating local institutions such as hospitals, courthouses and schools — anything that would let the recipient know that Zenith (or wherever) was a happening town and a great place to live. Hoteliers and tourist attraction operators realized the potential of postcards early on. By producing beautiful cards highlighting their properties, they could co-opt customers as advertising agents, even convincing them to pay for the privilege! Not surprisingly, countless millions of such postcards were produced.

Many postcard collectors (or *deltiologists*, for you trivia buffs) consider the era between 1907 and 1915 to be the golden age of postcards. German printers quickly developed a reputation for their excellent lithography, and postcard manufacturers from around the world were soon getting their wares printed there. Like so much else, this short golden age came to an end with the inconvenient interruption of the First World War. After the war, printers in the devastated Weimar Republic couldn't regain their pre-war status, and printers in other countries scrambled to fulfill local demand. Many resorted to printing illustrations with white borders, to save on ink costs, and the quality of these cards was widely acknowledged to be not quite up to snuff, in comparison to the pre-war German cards.

Finally, around 1930, American printers developed a linen-style postcard stock with a high rag content that allowed them to print inexpensive, brightly coloured cards with a luxurious, textured surface. The Depression put a serious dent in leisure travel, but by 1939, photochrome cards — the glossy photographic cards we know and love (or hate) today — were introduced. By the end of the Second World War, they had largely supplanted the linen cards.

. . . TRAVELLERS' CHEQUES

Travellers, quite naturally, have always been loath to take large sums of cash with them on the road. Anything could happen to that bundle of bills or bag of coins: a highwayman might steal it, a careless servant might leave it behind, it might fall out of a carriage or trunk. Tourists often hid what cash they carried in hatbands or hidden carriage compartments. Even if one managed to keep one's hands on the cash, it would likely prove worthless within a few miles of travel. In the days of the Grand Tour, the mighty British pound was not accepted as legal tender much beyond Calais and Rotterdam. It would be several centuries before American greenbacks would become the second official currency — or the grease of the underground economy — in developing nations around the world.

In the days before credit cards and bank machines, how did people finance their travels? As with so much else, it wasn't particularly easy.

To get money abroad, aristocratic Grand Tourists relied on their connections. Many negotiated letters of credit with their British bankers, which the traveller could present to a "corresponding banker" abroad to draw local currency. Working with such a banker had benefits beyond money, since many also offered their clients an entrée into society in a foreign city. Some provided introductions to local luminaries, helped clients find a place to stay or served as translators.

The letters of credit system worked fairly well for travellers who stuck to the usual tourist trail — Paris, Rome, Naples and so forth — and who had had the foresight to use a British banker with a wide foreign network. For instance, in 1728, the wonderfully named Sir Carnaby Haggerston of Northumberland was able to get fifty pounds in Marseilles, one hundred pounds in Leghorn and two hundred pounds in Rome, all by relying on the correspondents of Nicholas Fenwick, his banker in Newcastle.

For travellers who ventured beyond their banker's usual contacts, however, things got a little trickier. Sometimes they could parlay one contact into several — for instance, if their British banker had a corresponding banker in Paris but nowhere else, and the tourist wished to go to Rome, he might ask the Parisian banker for a letter of credit for a bank in Rome. Once in Rome, he could ask the Roman banker for a letter of credit for a bank in Naples, and so on. It was a complex system, but in most cases it served its purpose adequately. One drawback, however, was that it severely limited spontaneity. If the tourist only had a letter of credit for a banker in Rome, for instance, it was tricky to alter plans and head to Florence instead. Given the slowness and difficulty of travel, however, that wasn't as big a problem then as it might be now. Many travellers were also greatly rankled by the commissions bankers charged to honour these letters. Charges of 2 to 5 percent of the value of the transaction were common.

In an effort to overcome such obstacles, some London bankers began issuing bills of exchange in the mid-1700s. In theory, these bills served the function of modern travellers' cheques, as they could be cashed at any foreign bank. Even merchants could cash them. In

CAMERAS AND CLAUDE GLASSES

On our honeymoon in San Francisco, my husband and I went to a fair bit of effort to get to two particular spots, solely because we had seen them in famous photographs and wanted to recapture the image for ourselves. Steep little Lombard Street, in the Russian Hill neighbourhood, is called the crookedest street in America. Its sharp switchbacks, lined with stately mansions and pretty gardens, have made it a popular spot for postcard photographers. Arguably even more popular is Alamo Square, where San Francisco's famous hills make it possible to photograph a row of colourful townhouses with the Transamerica Pyramid and other downtown skyscrapers in the background. So many amateur and professional photographers have made this pilgrimage that the grass under the best vantage point has been worn to dirt by countless feet.

Why, I wonder, do people (myself included) feel compelled to see exact famous views "in the flesh," as it were? Perhaps its our innate cynicism and suspicion of technology. Surely, we think, such attractive juxtapositions are merely photographers' tricks. Whether we seek to prove such cynical thoughts right, or merely to enjoy the view if we are wrong, there's no doubt that we love to see "the" view, so much so theme parks used to have Kodak Photo Spots, marking the perfect place to stand while taking your vacation snaps.

But we are far from the first people to attempt to capture famous views for ourselves. Experts pointed the Grand Tourists toward the officially approved beautiful sights. Cameras had not yet been invented, of course; instead, a good Grand Tourist would never think of going abroad without his Claude glass. This small device, also known as a landscape mirror, was named for seventeenth-century artist Claude Gellée (also known as Claude Lorrain, for his birth place). Like modern tourists who almost unconsciously frame every famous sight through a viewfinder, a Grand Tourist would use this device to frame a famous landscape until it looked almost exactly like the famous painting that had brought him to the site in the first place. In a supreme bit of irony, the tourist first had to turn his back on the world-famous lake or mountain. Next, he would hold up his Claude glass so that the scene was reflected in the device's small convex mirror. (For added authenticity, the mirror was often tinted, so that the natural scene would be washed with the same sort of golden tones as Claude's varnished paintings of the countryside outside Rome.) Then the tourist would shift about until the scene in the mirror looked as close as possible to that in the famous picture, which he might well have brought along for reference. Only then would he feel he had properly "seen" the famous view.

Many contemporary commentators decried this way of experiencing the landscape. Not surprisingly, that staunch defender of nature, Wordsworth, was one of the leading critics. In "The Prelude," he lamented that many tourists were so focused on seeing a scene in a particular way that they failed to adequately enjoy the actual attributes of the landscape at the time they visited:

Although a strong infection of the age,
Was never much my habit, giving way
To a comparison of scene with scene,
Bent over much on superficial things,
Pampering myself with meagre novelties
Of colour and proportion, to the moods
Of time and season, to the moral power
The affections, and the spirit of the place,
Less sensible.[80]

practice, however, the story was somewhat different. Then as now, bankers and merchants were a cautious lot. Accustomed as they were to requiring letters of credit that vouched for the reliability of the bearer, they were skittish about giving some stranger money based on nothing more than an odd-looking certificate. One group of British tourists in Bruges in 1721 found this out to their frustration when they asked some Irish merchants to honour a bill of exchange. "[T]hey were so little acquainted with things of that nature that they told us they should not know one if they saw it," they reported.[81]

If a traveller found himself in dire straits — his letter of credit lost in the post, his bills of exchange dismissed by local merchants and his funds running low — all was not lost. Many an aristocratic British tourist found a sympathetic ear and a discreet loan at the local British embassy or consulate. Others prevailed on friends and acquaintances to spot them a few sous in a pinch. There are even records of tourists' borrowing money from complete strangers.

Even when they could get money, travellers faced one additional frustration: every small principality (and, in the case of Switzerland, every canton) had its own currency, and exchanging bills and coins between them could be difficult and expensive.

Even within the same country, financial turmoil still could pose serious complications. In 1716, a Scotsman named John Law convinced the French regent to allow him to establish a bank and issue paper currency as part of an effort to resolve the French national debt. To make a long story short, Law's bank issued too much paper currency, inflation ran rampant and people started hoarding coins and treating paper money with extreme suspicion. In February 1720, it became a crime to possess more than five hundred livres in coin.

In the midst of the ensuing chaos, a British tourist named Joseph Burnet decided to travel from Paris to southern France. His timing couldn't have been worse. He got as far as Orléans before he ran out of coins, and rural Frenchmen (with some justification) didn't think his bank notes were worth the paper they were printed on. Burnet was forced to turn back to Paris.

Clearly, modern tourism couldn't thrive in such conditions. But it would be another 150 years before the enterprising Thomas Cook solved the problem. By the 1870s, Cook had access to such a wide variety of hotels in the UK and abroad that he was ideally placed to launch an innovation that would prove to be a boon to middle-class travellers for a century or more to come: the traveller's cheque.

Cook called the five-pound and ten-pound certificates "circular notes," and issued the first ones in New York in 1873. A tourist could cash them only with hotels, bankers and agents with which Cook already did business, but there were already about two hundred hotels in the Cook system. By 1876 there were some four hundred, and by 1880 there were almost a thousand. Travellers loved this safe new way of carrying money, and hotels loved attracting travellers with cash to spend. It was, as later generations might say, a win-win situation.

Cook's circular notes were practical for short-term travellers, but they didn't work as well for long-term expatriates. Such nomads continued to present letters of credit to banks abroad affiliated with their bank at home, with all the risk that doing so could entail. In *Letters of Travel (1892–1913)*, Rudyard Kipling recalled the sudden failure of the New Oriental Banking Corporation in Yokohama around the turn of the last century. Ex-pats drank in the devastating news at the Overseas Club; some had lost a thousand dollars or more in the failure. In the midst of their own panic, they thought about their compatriots in transit to Japan, expecting a smooth arrival on the basis of now-worthless documents:

> "Gad, think of the chaps at sea with letters of credit. Eh? They'll land and get the best rooms at the hotels and find they're penniless," said another.

CANADIANS CONQUER THE WORLD...WITH HATS

If you've ever found yourself shuffling through the cathedrals of Europe behind a large bus tour of people wearing identical beige brimmed hats and multi-pocketed vests, blame a Canadian entrepreneur and avid sailor named Alex Tilley. In 1980 Tilley couldn't find a decent sunhat that both fit well and could float, so he invented one. The success of the eponymous Tilley hat, with its hidden pocket that both helped the hat float and provided a handy place to stash money and ID, launched a Canadian company that now outfits countless sensible, well-heeled travellers wherever they may find themselves. Today the line includes skirts with secret money pockets, fast-drying socks and underwear, trousers with mid-thigh zippers that convert the garment to shorts, purses designed to foil pickpockets and garments designed to repel stains and wrinkles. Tilley products are sold through 2,600 retailers around the world.

The Business of Travel

*When preparing to travel, lay out all your clothes
and all your money. Then take half the clothes and
twice the money.*

— Susan Heller, New York
Times *journalist*

In 112 BC, in what is one of the earliest surviving records of the use
of a travel middleman, a Roman VIP heading to Egypt asked one
of his minions to write a letter to an official in the city of Arsinoe.
"Lucius Memmius, a Roman Senator in a position of considerable
importance and honour is sailing [up the Nile] from Alexandria to
the district of which Arsinoe is capital to see the sights," the minion
wrote. The unnamed scribe asked his Egyptian correspondent to receive Lucius "in the grand style," find him a place to stay, make sure
that people were standing by with particular gifts at specific docking
places and that he got to see the region's two main tourist attractions: a labyrinth and some crocodiles associated with a crocodile
god named Petesouchos. The official in Arsinoe was even asked to
provide Lucius with some crocodile food. "In general, remember to
do everything possible to please him; put forth all your efforts," the
minion urged his correspondent.

Aside from booking a rental car and arranging for a basket of fruit
in Lucius's room, the servant had carried out most of the functions
of a modern-day travel agent.

Other elements of what we now call tourism existed before
modern times. By the days of the Roman Empire, tourists were already visiting a standard circuit of famous temples throughout the
Mediterranean. Not surprisingly, locals claiming unique knowledge

of the revered sights pestered the incoming visitors, and tourists were already jaded about the usefulness of these people's services. As one weary traveller prayed, "Jupiter, protect me from your guides at Olympia!"

Similarly, some travellers in the Middle Ages made their living as professional pilgrims, regaling people near and far with tales of their adventures and asking for alms in return for providing amusement — much like a modern travel writer. And the monastic orders that provided their accommodations, with their shared standards and management, could be seen as the very early predecessors of modern hotel chains.

But the true roots of the modern travel agency lie much later, with our old friends the Grand Tourists.

THE BRITISH ARE COMING! AND THEY'RE BRINGING MONEY!

Among the earliest forerunners of the modern bus tour operator were the *vetturini*, who plied their trade in Italy and Switzerland in the heyday of the Grand Tour. These enterprising guides hung out at major tourist destinations, keeping their eyes and ears open to find out who was heading where. After painstakingly assembling a group of six to twelve travellers who wanted to travel to the same destination, the *vetturino* would offer them a package deal: transportation, meals and accommodation along the route, all for one negotiated price. This system appealed to eighteenth-century travellers for the same reason bus tours and cruises appeal to their twenty-first-century descendants: it offered a reasonably priced way to travel and relieved them of the stress of arranging for food and lodging in an unfamiliar language.

Of course, like the modern package tour, there were drawbacks to travelling with a group of strangers and keeping to someone else's schedule. To cover a decent distance in the small, cheap wagons *vetturini* usually hired, travellers often had to get up at the crack of dawn and spend long days on the road.

Those with a bit more money to spend had the option of hiring a personal guide to shuttle them around Europe. Families usually sent a tutor along with their Grand Tourist sons, but older travellers often hired multilingual guides to help them hire local painters, arrange transportation and hotels, buy classical artworks or better understand historic sites.

By the 1740s, enterprising Britons abroad could make a comfortable living by introducing their countrymen to their adopted home. In 1741, one Lady Pomfret wrote home from Rome to extol the virtues of a guide named Mr. Parker, "who goes about with the English to show them what is most remarkable assisting them also in buying what picture paintings and other curiosities that they fancy most."[82] Not to cast aspersions on the late Mr. Parker, but some guides and retailers were not completely on the up and up. Particularly in Italy, there was a good market for fake paintings, medals and statues, and forgers often made alliances with malleable guides, who would encourage their unwitting charges to buy the fakes and then share the profits with the forgers.

Expatriate Englishmen were not the only ones to try to make a little money from the rich tourists flocking to Italy. Naturally enough, local residents hoped to carve a piece of the pie for themselves, but their more aggressive approach sometimes annoyed rather than enticed their quarry. Granted, permanently dyspeptic traveller Tobias Smollett might not be the best judge of the charm of the *servitori de piazza* (guides) who clamoured to serve tourists arriving in Rome — Smollett famously hated almost everything about everywhere he travelled, even finding French food abysmally lacking compared to a good English roast with boiled veg. But it's hard not to sympathize with him as he is besieged upon entering Rome through the Porta del Popolo in 1765:

> Having given our names at the gate, we repaired to the dogana, or custom-house, where our trunks and carriage were searched; and here we were surrounded by a number of *servitori de piazza*, offering their services with the most disagreeable importunity. Though I told them several times I had no occasion for any, three of them took possession of the coach, one mounting before

and two of them behind; and thus we proceeded to the
Piazza d'Espagna, where the person lived to whose house
I was directed.[83]

As European and North American tourists ventured further afield,
guides, all too eager to help them, emerged wherever they went. In
the 1860s, while touring the Middle East, Swedish tourist Frederika
Bremer met a man already used to showing Europeans the sights:
"Hameth, who was accustomed to conduct Christian pilgrims on
this road, knew what was interesting to them by the way, and told
me the names of various remarkable places as we went along,"[84] she
reported. Hameth also already had the savvy to recommend she stay
with friends of his in Tiberias.

By the time Bremer was making her largely independent way
around the eastern Mediterranean, though, the nature of tourism was
already changing. The days when anyone who wanted help abroad
had no choice but to rely on informal networks of guides and *vetturini* were coming to an end. The invention of the steam engine had
made it possible to move large numbers of people to an increasing
number of places all at the same time. Once that happened, never
again would travel be solely small scale and personal.

FROM TEMPERANCE TO TOURISM

On Monday, July 5, 1841, about six hundred excited teetotallers
— well, as excited as any group of teetotallers can be — set off on a
twelve-mile chartered train trip through the English Midlands from
Leicester to Loughborough, their journey would change the nature
of tourism forever. They had each paid between one shilling and one
shilling and sixpence for a day trip to a temperance meeting in the
dry town of Loughborough, which had been widely publicized with
posters and handbills pasted all over the Midlands.

The day started gaily, with a brass band playing as the train
steamed out of Leicester station. After arriving in Paget's Park in
Loughborough, the day trippers munched on ham loaves, drank tea,
played games like kiss-in-the-ring and cricket and listened to speeches

about the evils of the demon drink and the joys of temperance. By contemporary accounts, it appears that most people had a lovely, sedate, Victorian day.

That evening, a thirty-two-year-old printer and cabinetmaker named Thomas Cook likely breathed an enormous sigh of relief. For the past month, he had expended all of his energies on convincing temperance campaigners and the Midland Counties Railway that such a trip could benefit them all. He'd printed posters and walked for miles to post them, sometimes in the dead of night. He'd overcome the railway's skepticism that he could fill an entire train. And, in so doing, he'd changed his life.

At first glance, Cook would seem an unlikely candidate for what would be his historical legacy: the founder of mass-market tourism. As secretary of the Leicester Temperance Society, he organized the 1841 excursion to Loughborough in the hopes of providing a wholesome, affordable amusement for the working class — and bolstering the funds of the Temperance Society, which paid him a salary for his secretarial duties. He ran that trip, and a number of others for Sunday schools and temperance societies over the next three summers, on a non-profit basis. The only fees he earned directly from the trips were small sums for printing handbills and posters.

In 1845, four years after he had organized his first train trip, Cook — perpetually short of money — decided to give up cabinet making, printing, market gardening and the other odd jobs he'd pursued over the years and try to earn his living in a totally new type of business: commercial tour organizer. It was a calculated risk — until then, he'd relied on his network of temperance societies to fill his non-profit train trips. Now, he'd be flying without a net.

He started by organizing his first excursion to the seaside, which took travellers from Leicester to New Brighton and Liverpool. Cook worked hard to make sure there would be no surprises for his customers. He travelled to Liverpool and personally checked out each hotel and restaurant; he wrote and printed a sixty-page guidebook for his passengers; he arranged side trips with English-speaking Welsh guides. His success was immediate: all 350 tickets sold out. Interest was so high that some tickets even traded hands on the black market.

Within a year, Cook had expanded his sights to a multi-day trip to Scotland, which required him to be a bit more creative. There was no train line across the border, and the main steamship line between Newcastle and Edinburgh saw him as competition and shut the door in his face. So Cook took travellers as far through England as he could by train, then hired his own steamer for a trip up the coast. The steamer deposited his 350 travellers at Ardrossan, from where they would take a series of trains to Glasgow and Edinburgh. The logistics of such a trip so impressed the people of Glasgow that they greeted the Cook travellers with a brass band.

In 1851, all the talk in Britain was of the Great Exhibition in London. After speaking with two of the exhibition's organizers — who, by happy coincidence, were also involved with both the temperance movement and the Midland Railway — Cook recognized an excellent opportunity to shuttle large numbers of people to an indisputably educational event.

To whip up enthusiasm, he launched a newspaper called *The Excursionist and Exhibition Advertiser*, which he distributed every way he could think of: on city streets, outside factories and through temperance societies. Since few of his readers had ever been to London or even contemplated such a journey, he ran articles extolling the attractions of the capital in general and the benefits of the exhibition in particular. He ran ads for approved boarding houses and detailed train schedules to allay readers' concerns. At least one article noted with approval that there would also be a large international temperance demonstration in London in August, which would provide a worthy diversion once the amusements of the exhibition had been exhausted.

Cook also had to use his talents of persuasion to overcome the doubts of factory owners who weren't at all sure that giving their workers time off to travel to London was a wise idea. He tailored messages to specific industries, such as this plea aimed at the owners of cotton factories:

> The particular advantage to be derived from visiting the
> Exhibition by all those employed in preparing and manu-

facturing cotton goods will be that Bolton, Manchester, Glasgow, Carlisle and Dundalk each and all will be [there] in friendly competition in workmanship, raw material and variety of patterns, and will also be found in rivalship with the foreign producer of such goods.[85]

He originally priced his rail tickets at fifteen shillings, until he realized that the railroad companies themselves were getting into the bulk travel business and were poised to undercut him. He renegotiated his deal with the Midland Railway and was able to drop his price to five shillings to match the Great Northern Line's discount rate. The only hitch was that Cook's new railway deal required him to put even more bums on seats.

To ensure that substantial numbers of workingmen could afford the trip, Cook set up Exhibition Clubs throughout the Midlands to help people save a small amount each week toward the journey. In London, he cut aggressive deals with hotels, such as the thousand-bed Ranelagh Club lodging house, which he renamed the "Mechanics Home" for the duration of the exhibition. For a shilling or two a night, his working-class customers got a roof over their head and breakfast. In the end, Cook's railway partners had little cause for complaint. By the time the exhibition closed, Cook had arranged for more than 140,000 customers to visit the event.

As the popularity of Cook's excursions grew, there was an inevitable backlash. Cook himself attributed such feelings to envy, believing that wealthier people travelling alone or in small groups looked longingly at the lively Cook groups. And Cook's own customers felt no shame at all in joining these massive tours. As one return customer exclaimed in an article published in *The Excursionist* in 1856:

Hurrah for the Excursion Trains, say I! They are a fine invention for men like myself, of small means and not much leisure... He who can travel first-class express, with a valet to take his ticket and look after his carpet-bag, can afford to despise the humble mode of locomotion whose praises I sing: but these are the days of the million; and

for my part, I am heartily thankful that the wants of the
million are cared for, and that Bobson, Dickson, and
Tomson (of course with Mistresses Bobson, Dickson, and
Tomson), can o'erleap the bounds of their own narrow
circle, rub off rust and prejudice by contact with others,
and expand their souls and invigorate their bodies by an
exploration of some of Nature's finest scenes.[86]

KEEPING IT SIMPLE

In the early days of his Temperance Society journeys, Cook personally escorted all of his excursions. By the time of the Great Exhibition
trips, however, this had clearly become unfeasible. While continuing
to escort some trips, which attracted up to five hundred travellers at
a time, Cook searched for a way to serve greater numbers of customers. And he found he could still play a valuable role for those who
didn't mind travelling unescorted.

In most countries at this time, including Britain, railways were
owned and operated by a huge range of companies, each of which
might control only a few miles of track. And railways didn't reach
all destinations, so it was often necessary to make part of the journey
by road, river or sea. If you wanted to do a trip of any distance, you
often needed to buy tickets from multiple providers and spend hours
determining the most efficient way to get from point A to point B.

Cook took the hassle out of this experience by devising what he
called a Circular Ticket. He would plan an itinerary between two
popular destinations, then sell travellers the tickets they needed for
railways, steamships and coaches. The customers would travel in-
dependently, and since the tickets were usually good for two weeks,
they could maintain some flexibility in their schedule. They could
even exchange tickets *en route* or cash in unused tickets with Cook
after their trip.

THE GRASS IS ALWAYS GREENER
ON THE OTHER SIDE OF THE CHANNEL

With the experience he'd gained bringing travellers to the Great Expedition, Cook began looking farther afield and in 1855 he arranged excursions to an international exhibition in Paris. His confidence bolstered, he started taking his increasingly middle-class customers along the popular Grand Tour routes. It wasn't always easy. Some railway companies saw him as a threat and wouldn't let him use their ports and lines, leading Cook to develop some rather creative routings. For example, instead of ferrying his groups across the English Channel to Calais, the most common port of entry, he was forced for a while to start his European tours in Antwerp.

Undaunted, he soldiered on. In 1863 he led his first tour to Geneva. Three years later, a huge group of his customers picnicked on chicken, sandwiches, cakes and fruit in the amphitheatre of Pompeii. The menu for that meal shows that Cook had moved beyond his original client base. Teetotallers could still sip on essence of lemon, but other guests could quietly imbibe wine or cognac.

Whenever he could, Cook tried to prepare his neophyte travellers for life abroad, often through the pages of *The Excursionist*. In 1863, for instance, he warned them that food in France would seem unfamiliar to Britons used to dining on roast beef and Yorkshire pudding: "A little charity and allowance for taste and custom must be exercised at a French table d'hôte, or the best French dinners would be by some disesteemed."[87]

The infiltration of the middle class into places once the private preserve of their social "superiors" didn't go unnoticed by the Victorian chattering classes. In *Blackwood's Magazine*, Charles Lever — an Irish novelist serving as a British diplomat in Italy — fumed that the "enterprizing [sic] and unscrupulous" Thomas Cook had had the gall to conceive and promote a package tour to Naples for forty-odd people that included food, transportation and activities for a set fee. Lever continued:

When I first read the scheme...I caught at the hope that
the speculation would break down. I imagined that the
characteristic independence of Englishmen would revolt
against a plan that reduces the traveler to the level of
his trunk and obliterates every trace and trait of the
individual. I was all wrong. As I write, the cities of Italy
are deluged with droves of these creatures.[88]

OTHERS GET IN ON THE ACT

While Cook's was one of the biggest and best-known early
tour packagers, it was far from the only company making
things easier for the rising numbers of people who wanted
to travel but had no idea how to begin. In Britain, Cook's
was locked in heated competition with a firm run by Henry
Gaze, who beat Cook to both Paris and the Middle East.
By the end of the century, a range of travel agencies had
opened up in the UK, Germany, the US and elsewhere.

Independent travel agencies weren't the only companies
organizing trips for eager travellers. Railroads and shipping
companies also advertised widely. Canadian Pacific, for example, worked hard to entice tourists to its trains and ships;
by 1883, it was already using a relatively new medium,
full colour posters, to promote its fares from Toronto to
destinations both humble and exotic. For $24.50, the trav-
eller could get a return trip ticket to the White Mountains
of New Hampshire; eight dollars more would see him all
the way to Bar Harbour, Maine. Duluth and Saint John,
Honolulu and China, San Francisco and Japan — all of
these and more were dangled as bait in front of people who
likely had never dreamed of long-distance leisure travel
before. There was even a round-the-world fare.

It had taken Cook's middle-class passengers a century to follow in the footsteps of the aristocratic Grand Tourists, but Cook would soon make sure they wouldn't have to wait that long to enjoy the new destinations of the rich and famous; by 1869, when the opening of the Suez Canal inspired the Prince and Princess of Wales to visit Egypt, Cook and his customers weren't far behind.

The Middle East required even more ingenuity from Cook than his earlier forays into Europe, but by this point he was more than

The First World War disrupted travel, particularly in Europe, where harbours and rail lines lay in ruins for several years after 1918. But a burst of post-war prosperity soon opened up opportunities. By 1924, Canadian Pacific was running annual around-the-world cruises, which it promoted with the simultaneously memorable and boastful slogan: "See This World Before the Next by the World's Greatest Travel System, Canadian Pacific."

In Switzerland, a man named Antonio Mantegazza had less grandiose plans that eventually developed into another leading twentieth-century travel company. In the late 1920s, he realized there was money to be made in transporting tourists around the shores of Lake Lugano, so he launched a company called Globus Viaggi with a fleet of twelve motorcoaches. For its first two decades, the company concentrated on short trips in Switzerland, Italy and southern France, but by 1950 it had begun offering multi-day, multi-country trips. Later in the decade, it started selling luxury bus tours in the American market, and in 1961 it launched Cosmos, a budget-priced bus tour company aimed at the British market. In later years, it branched out into package air holidays and escorted tours on six continents.

up to the task. Faced with a lack of hotels in Palestine, he brought tents; when he couldn't find suitable boats to ship his passengers down the Nile to Luxor, he had steamers built in Scotland and sent them to Egypt. And no matter where his customers went, he ensured they had the comforts of home, from Bibles and English-language guidebooks to the Union Jack (which fluttered from the top of those tents in Palestine).

As the first large-scale travel packager, Cook enjoyed a unique advantage: he could be all things to all classes simply because he was often the first — or the best — to offer organized trips to a particular destination. His (and, later, his son's) continuing to help factory workers and their families take short trips to the English seaside didn't discourage middle-class doctors and lawyers from signing on for a Cook's tour of Switzerland. And even though Cook was taking the petit bourgeoisie to Europe — and curmudgeons such as Charles Lever had long been complaining about it — VIPs such as the Duke of York, Cecil Rhodes and the Empress Eugenie had no problem contracting with Cook's for a more exotic tour. By the beginning of the twentieth century, it was a badge of honour among all social classes to have travelled with Cook's.

Of course, classlessness never lasts long in the Western world. By the time the 1920s roared round, however, even middle-class people who had never travelled widely were showing signs of skepticism about the authenticity of packaged travel. Returning to our friends Sam and Fran Dodsworth, just as they decide to set out on their travels, we see that Fran is having a bit of a mid-life crisis and isn't sure a packaged trip is at all the way to solve it. "I only have five or ten more years to continue being young in….Can't you understand?" she wails to Sam. "I'm begging for life — no, I'm not! — I'm demanding it! And that means something more than a polite little Cook's trip to Europe!"[89]

Cook's responded to such sentiments by continuing to innovate. Already experts in the package tour by train and ship, Cook's was one of the first companies to realize the package potential of air travel. In 1939, it offered an around-the-world tour that began with a *Yankee Clipper* flight from Southampton to New York. On a series of Imperial Airways and Pan Am planes, travellers would cross the United States, traverse the Pacific, touch down in Hong Kong and then return to Britain. The price for this audacious itinerary: a cool £475. Clearly, this wasn't mass tourism. The rise of the mass-market airline vacation would have to wait until after the Second World War and the invention of the jet plane.

BABY BOOMERS ROCK THE BUS MARKET

In the affluent post-war years, a subspecies of traveller suddenly emerged in greater numbers than had ever been seen before: young adults keen to see Europe.

People in their twenties weren't a new species of traveller by any means. They had been the backbone of the Grand Tour, but in those days they were usually rich and intent, at least in theory, on broadening their education. Less moneyed young Victorians were quick to see the appeal of Cook's tours; a group of seven young Britons, including lively diarist Jemima Morrell, joined Cook's first trip to Geneva and then spent two weeks on their own racing through Switzerland. They rose at the crack of dawn each day to cram in as many mountains, waterfalls, spas and cathedrals as they could muster, and they specifically sought out hotels off the beaten track — both to save money and to try to get a more "Swiss" experience.

But in the early 1960s, for the first time in history, large numbers of young adults from North America, Europe, Australia and New Zealand had both the time and money to travel. And for most of them, Europe was the promised land.

New Zealander John Anderson was part of this early wave. He arrived in London in 1961, determined to see the Continent on a limited budget. After meeting other travellers in the same situation, Anderson suggested they travel together and split the costs. He put down a deposit on a minibus and they set off for twelve weeks in Europe. At the end of the summer, Anderson tried to sell the minibus but could find no buyer. To recoup his costs, he advertised his trip again the following year and managed to fill two back-to-back minibus loads, all with people ages nineteen to twenty-nine. Spotting a business opportunity, Anderson launched Contiki Holidays, still going strong with bus tours aimed at travellers eighteen to thirty-five.

Just like earlier travellers who decried noisy passengers on *diligences* and trains, not all modern travellers are exactly fond of bus travel.

Irish novelist Marian Keyes describes a week-long bus trip she and her husband took a few years ago through some unnamed country. When someone produced a guitar and an extended, middle-of-the-night singalong erupted, Keyes began fantasizing about jumping out of the speeding vehicle. Realizing escape was impossible, she jammed in her earplugs, to no avail:

> When we'd exhausted all the Irish songs, we had a Beatles medley; then the "Rock Around the Clock" type ones; then something about a red rooster, where everyone had to flap their arms and make "bokabokabok" roostery-type noises; for reasons that escaped me, "Take Me Home, Country Roads" reappeared on a loop, every ten songs; then finally we had a Rolling Stones tribute where one of the "most hilarious" of all the (extremely hilarious) passengers took it upon himself to strut up and down the aisle, with his arse stuck out in an approximation of Mick Jagger's, while everyone else yelled, "Go on, you good thing!"...It was a living hell.[90]

COME SEE OUR TOWN!

The idea of marketing a whole town, region or country as a travel destination arose slowly. Individual hotels and railroads advertised widely, but governments as a rule largely left them to their own devices. In England, the resort town of Blackpool was the first local government in Britain to assess taxes for tourism promotion.

Around the world, countless places have undergone a transformation so consistent that it almost seems as though people were unconsciously following steps from some secret manual.

First, an intriguing local culture springs up. It might be known for its haunting music or its tortured painters, its embroidered clothing or energetic dancing, its melancholy literature or colourful houses. Or, instead of culture, a place might be known for a breathtaking natural attraction: a mountain, a cave or a waterfall, for instance. Whatever its claim to fame, it is unique.

Next, someone from afar "discovers" this culture or natural attraction and tells someone about it. Before the days of mass media, this didn't usually make much of a difference, unless the person doing the discovering told the tale to someone influential or became famous in his own right. If he happened to have the tale-telling capabilities of Marco Polo, he might spur some interest in arduous international travel. But most early travellers did not.

Once printing presses, newspapers, the telegraph, magazines, movies, radio, television and the Internet came on the scene, however, it was a whole new ball game. Our traveller who has discovered an intriguing new place now records his (or, increasingly, her) observations in a book, an article or a broadcast piece with a potential audience of say, a million. If even 1 percent of those people think, "Wow, I'd like to go there," that's ten thousand intrigued people. If "there" is a tiny village of two hundred souls, life on the ground suddenly begins to change. The curious start to arrive by steam train and paddle wheeler, Model T and bicycle, bus and RV.

Locals scramble to greet the newcomers. They establish a tourist board, build an inn, set up a few rudimentary tours. The dancers embroider a few new outfits. The folk singers record a CD. Someone builds a cable car or scenic lookout. Money pours in. A big-name Hollywood director sets a movie there. Travel magazines extol the virtues of the place. More tourists come.

The inn expands, adds a conference centre and spa. It interferes with the mountain view a bit, but that's progress. A theme restaurant hires the dancers to perform in a floorshow. A few of the colourful houses are knocked down to provide space for an interpretive centre. The village becomes one of its region's top ten tourist attractions.

Someone builds a wax museum. The local melancholy poet gets busted for drug possession. The mountaintop is speckled with rubbish discarded by day hikers. Hotel room prices soar. The media turns on the overgrown village, claiming it has become too tacky, too busy, too commercialized. Droves of tourists continue to visit, even as the cognoscenti begin sniffing out less unsullied pastures.

Finally, someone — a writer for *Wall*Paper*, a Hollywood star trying to escape the paparazzi, an indie rock band looking for a secluded place to work on their new CD — stumbles on some formerly unsung corner of the globe where a cup of really good coffee costs only fifty cents and no one has ever heard of Botox. It's unspoiled. It's authentic. And it's the next hot thing. Come here before it's gone, the siren song begins.

And we do.

Until, of course, the original little village undergoes a renaissance, and the cycle of tourism life begins again.

Don't believe me? Ask the Amish.

IS IT WONDERFUL GOOD?

For the sleepy farms of Lancaster County, attention came early. Even in an era when most of Americans still lived in rural areas, it was clear that this corner of southeastern Pennsylvania had something different. Mainly, it had the Amish.

Perhaps it was the upheaval of the Civil War that made people long for quiet and simplicity, because the 1860s and the 1870s saw a spate of magazine articles about the "simple" folk of what soon came to be called Pennsylvania Dutch Country. (They weren't Dutch at all, by the way — "Dutch" was a corruption of the German word *Deutsch*, meaning "German.")

Even though passenger trains served the area, it took the invention of the Model T to make Lancaster County a mass-market tourism destination, in conjunction with continuing attention from prestigious publications such as *National Geographic*. In the late 1930s, an ongoing news story, rather than a travel feature brought intense media scrutiny to the area, when several Amish men were jailed for refusing to send their children to consolidated state schools.

Like everything else, tourism slowed during the Second World War. But by 1946, a Lancaster hotel had begun running weekend bus

WHEN ROADSIDE ATTRACTIONS GO ARTISTIC

Sometimes, private labours of love become tourist attractions by design or accident. There's Carhenge, a replica of Stonehenge built of vehicles in Alliance, Nevada, and its thematic cousin, the Cadillac Ranch, a collection of ten Caddies planted nose down in the ground by a group of artists in Amarillo, Texas. In Los Angeles, road trippers can visit Watts Towers, seventeen sculptures of steel, wire mesh, mortar, glass, porcelain, seashells and tile that took Italian immigrant Simon Rodia more than thirty years to build as an odd but heartfelt ode to his adopted country.

And, of course, there's the world's most famous labour of love, the Taj Mahal in Agra, India. Built in the mid-1600s, the structure is actually a mausoleum for the favourite wife of the Shah Jahan. Her name was Arjumand Bano Begum, but she was better known as Mumtaz Mahal, which means "beloved ornament of the palace" in Persian.

As the story goes, Shah Jahan planned to build a companion structure, in black instead of white, as his own tomb. Instead, he was deposed by his own son and imprisoned, but in a cell where he had a view of his greatest legacy.

tours to Mennonite and Amish locations. Six years later, when a *New York Times* writer quoted a local farmer as saying that he thought his life was "wonderful good," the region even gained its own catch phrase.

Tourist attractions with names like "Dutch Wonderland" and "Amish Homestead" began popping up along the Lincoln Highway to serve the growing numbers of visitors, who in 1954 totalled 25,000. One farmer joked that the rise in the region's popularity was linked to the two-hundredth anniversary celebrations of the village of Intercourse that year: "Mix together the word Intercourse and some Amish buggies and you're bound to attract some tourists."

Tourist numbers skyrocketed after a musical about the Amish, *Plain and Simple*, debuted on Broadway in 1955 and later opened in Los Angeles and London. Enthralled playgoers beat a path to Lancaster County, and the locals formed a tourist bureau in 1958. They were just in the nick of time, as it turned out: a million tourists descended on the county in 1961 alone.

Tourism in Pennsylvania Dutch country was battered by a series of shocks in the 1970s, starting with the oil crisis, moving through the outbreak of Legionnaire's disease in Philadelphia (which made many travellers think twice about the entire state of Pennsylvania) and culminating in 1979 with the nuclear accident at Three Mile Island. Tourism started to rebound in the early 1980s, and then got two powerful shots in the arm. First, *National Geographic* ran an evocative photo essay about Lancaster County in April 1984. Not long afterward, Harrison Ford did the previously inconceivable — he made the Amish *sexy* in the movie *Witness*.

There's nothing like having Han Solo show up in your town to attract the tourists. Visitor numbers soared once again, and tourism promoters scrambled to diversify, reasoning that if millions of people started chasing every Amish buggy, something of the local charm would be lost. The tourism bureau started working harder to attract conventions and to promote non-Amish attractions such as a steam train.

These days, Pennsylvania Dutch country is somewhat more diverse. But there are steam trains and fudge shops across America. For the foreseeable future, I think tourism promotion in this corner of Pennsylvania is likely to continue to feature lots of buggies and quaint hats.

As for other places, if they don't happen to have a ready supply of colourful pacifists, they'll just have to build a big Easter egg or two.

OUR GIANT LOBSTER COULD WHUP YOUR JUMBO GOOSE

In the mid-1990s, the people of Davidson, Saskatchewan, had a dream. They wanted to build a big roadside attraction — something that would truly symbolize the town and, coincidentally, persuade drivers to stop for at least a minute to snap a picture and perhaps buy a coffee or meal or postcard. Since Davidson is halfway between Regina and Saskatoon, it often hosts meetings of people from each city. Drawing on this theme of hospitality, the town commissioned a nearby agricultural manufacturing company to design and build a 7.3-metre-high sheet metal coffee pot. Festooned with murals and theoretically capable of holding 150,000 cups of coffee, the Davidson Coffee Pot was unveiled in 1996.

It joined a wide range of oversize dinnerware scattered across North America, including another coffee pot in Winston-Salem, North Carolina; a big fork behind an ad agency in Springfield, Missouri; a large purple spoon in East Glacier Park, Montana; and a giant knife in Moose Pass, Alaska. Some are standalone structures, while many others were built to promote related businesses.

So desperate are people to drive tourist traffic to their towns or their businesses that the range of roadside sculptures seems as vast as the human imagination. On one stretch of northern Ontario highway alone you'll pass a huge nickel, ironically made of stainless steel (in Sudbury), a giant goose (Wawa) and Maximilian Moose (Dryden). Other notable Canadian roadside art includes a giant pysanka (Ukrainian Easter egg) in Vegreville, Alberta; the world's largest lobster in Shediac, New Brunswick (not to be confused with the world's largest lobster *trap*, in Cheticamp, Nova Scotia); a giant mosquito in Komarno, Manitoba (that doesn't say "Come visit" to me, but what do I know?); and the world's largest hockey stick and puck in Duncan, British Columbia. Meanwhile, in the US you can find everything from the world's largest catsup bottle (Collinsville, Illinois) to a forty-foot otter (Fergus Falls, Minnesota).

This isn't a strictly North American phenomenon by the way; among many other roadside delights, Australia is home to the Big Prawn (a giant illuminated shellfish that sits atop a building full of

gift shops and restaurants in Ballina, New South Wales) and the Big
Banana (which promotes a banana plantation tour in Coffs Harbour,
New South Wales).

The competition for "world's biggest" bragging rights can become
more than slightly surreal, as detailed on the highly entertaining
Web site RoadsideAmerica.com. The good folk of Paris, Tennessee
— proud owners of a sixty-foot replica of the Eiffel Tower — were
fighting mad when their counterparts in Paris, Texas, unveiled a *sixty-
five-foot* model. The Tennesseans then tore down their now-puny
tower and replaced it with a *seventy-foot* one. Mighty miffed, the
Texans retaliated by topping their sculpture with a big red tilted
cowboy hat. The rivalry might have continued indefinitely, but — in
one of the few things we can legitimately be grateful to Vegas for
— the Paris Las Vegas hotel built a 540-foot Eiffel Tower in 1999.
Even in Texas, where everything is bigger, they conceded defeat. (A
similar competition for bragging rights to the world's largest chair
went on for seventy-six years before a furniture store in Anniston,
Alabama, topped all contenders in 1981 with a thirty-one-foot-high,
ten-ton behemoth.)

But perhaps the most outrageous roadside statue ever proposed
was never actually built. In probably my favourite episode of the
sitcom *Corner Gas*, a small group of civic-minded souls in fictitious
Dog River, Saskatchewan, are sitting in the local diner brainstorming
ideas for a new roadside attraction that will inspire drivers to stop in
the little town. What's unique about Dog River? they ask each other.
Well, it's a rural community, so they decide their "world's biggest
thing" should be a farm implement. They discuss various options and
finally settle on a hoe. But it shouldn't be a shiny, new-looking hoe,
someone says. Dog River is a hardworking town, after all. It should
have clumps of earth on it and look as though it's been well used.

What the town needs, the mayor's grandmother concludes, is "a
big dirty cracked hoe."

After a moment of stunned silence, the rest of the group decides
that she's right. There's nothing like a big dirty cracked hoe on the
edge of town for attracting the tourist trade.

A MUSEUM FOR EVERY INTEREST

If you've ever hankered to know about your favourite consumer product, movie star, fetish or outlaw, somewhere in the world there's likely a museum devoted to your enthusiasm. The product ones are often (but not always) run by the makers of said product; the rest by people just like you, although slightly more obsessive.

The modern museum evolved from the "cabinets of curiosities" once kept by wealthy eccentrics. As time went on, some of these collections were incorporated into august, public, sober museums, such as the British Museum and the Smithsonian Institution.

But the impulse to run one's own private museum never really died, and the roadsides of the world are lined with the evidence. Ventriloquists talk shop at the Vent Haven Museum in Fort Mitchell, Kentucky, while LaCrosse, Kansas, has a Barbed Wire Museum. The Museum of Bad Art (MOBA) is in Boston, and nearby Salem has a wax museum dedicated to the witch trials. There is a Museum of Questionable Medical Devices in Minneapolis. At the American Sanitary Plumbing Museum in Worcester, Massachusetts — founded by a local plumber in 1979 and now run by his daughter-in-law — you can see a wooden toilet from the 1800s and a 1920s' dishwasher called an electric sink. Sadly, the Madison Museum of Bathroom Tissue in Madison, Wisconsin, closed its doors in 2000.

The list goes on in mind-boggling profusion. Small-town New York state seems to be a particular hotbed, with attractions ranging from the Lucille Ball-Desi Arnaz Center in Jamestown (where you can buy pyjama pants speckled with images of Lucy, Ricky, Fred and Ethel) to the Jell-O Museum in LeRoy (where, among other fascinating facts, you can learn that a jiggling bowl of Jell-O has the same EEG "brainwave" pattern as an adult human brain).

Again, oddball museums are not a uniquely American phenomenon. Canada is home to the Gopher Hole Museum in Torrington, Alberta (stuffed gophers dressed up like preachers, Mounties, hairdressers and more, which has earned it the wrath of ever-humourless PETA) and the Prince Edward Island Potato Museum — although Canada did lose the History of Contraception Museum in 2004,

DROP BY MY HOUSE SOMETIME …
ADMISSION IS VERY CHEAP

 If you've ever sat through a dinner party where the entire conversation revolved around mortgage rates, kitchen renovations and landscaping, you'll understand that real estate is one of the true obsessions of our times. And so, not surprisingly, huge, architecturally significant or just plain weird houses are some of the most enduring road trip tourist attractions.

In San Jose, California, the Winchester Mystery House is testament to Sarah Winchester's belief that if she didn't keep building twenty-four hours a day, seven days a week, the people killed by the guns her late husband's family invented would come back to haunt her. And so, in one of the world's longest home reno projects, Winchester kept contractors working around the clock for thirty-eight years. Even the 1906 earthquake, which knocked three storeys off the house, didn't deter her. By the time she died in 1922,

when its owner transferred it from Toronto to Case Western Reserve University in Cleveland. Across the pond in London's Hunterian Museum, founded by an eighteenth-century surgeon, you can view endless jars of biological bits and pieces, from nipples to digestive tracts, preserved in alcohol. In Japan, Tokyo alone is home to museums devoted to parasites, buttons, kites, tobacco and salt (both in the same museum, oddly) and laundry.

Top marks for creativity in my book, though, go to the Vulcan Tourism and Trek Station in Vulcan, Alberta, which opened in 1998 and includes such don't-miss attractions as a reconstructed bridge from the *Enterprise*, complete with life-sized cardboard cutouts of various *Star Trek* characters.

the house had expanded to include forty-seven fireplaces, two ballrooms, at least five kitchens and forty staircases (including one leading directly to a ceiling).

Just as odd, but in a totally different way, is the Coral Castle in Homestead, Florida. Built by a slight Latvian immigrant named Ed Leedskalin over a period of twenty-eight years, it's meant as a tribute to the love of his life, Agnes Scuffs, who broke off their engagement a day before they were to be married in 1913. So many things about this place are unusual that it's hard to know where to begin. There's the fact that he built the entire structure, made out of 1,100 tons of coral rock, by hand — even though each block weighed about 125 pounds and Ed himself weighed only 100. There's the fact that no one saw him do it. And then there's the fact that he once moved the partially completed castle sixteen kilometres (ten miles), piece by piece, on an old truck chassis pulled by a tractor. The house's Web site claims, "He has baffled engineers and scientists! People have compared Ed's secret method of construction to Stonehenge and the Great Pyramids [sic]."

THERE IS SUCH A THING AS BAD PR! WHO KNEW?

Sometimes, however, a destination gets more than it bargained for when a TV or movie crew arrives. The blizzard of reality shows that has overtaken much of the Western world over the past few years has given an increasing number of places their fifteen minutes of fame — and millions of dollars worth of free advertising.

Take the MTV show *The Real World*. When its camera crews came to Denver in 2006 to shoot the show's eighteenth season, a spokesman for the local tourist bureau raved to a *New York Times* reporter, "They're in our hip historic district... To have them on national TV showing that side of Denver is fantastic for us."

The problem with reality shows, from a tourism promotion point of view, is that their version of "reality" and yours might not jibe.

Take *Tuesday Night Book Club*, for example, a CBS show from the summer of 2006. Before dying after just two episodes, it exposed viewers to seven whiny rich women from the Phoenix suburb of Scottsdale. They didn't talk much about the books they were supposedly reading, but they made up for it with endless discussions of their disastrous-sounding marriages and their predilection for shopping. Even TV critics, many of whom hate all reality shows on principle, were particularly scathing about this one. The *Pittsburgh Post-Gazette* called the show's stars "a bunch of ill-behaved exhibitionist women," while *Variety* concluded that "you can't say 'so long' to this neighborhood soon enough."

Back at the Scottsdale Area Chamber of Commerce, chamber president Rick Kidder was distinctly displeased by the way *Tuesday Night Book Club* and other reality shows that had recently touched down in his burg had portrayed his town. Not surprisingly, he likes to tout the upscale city as a great place to do business and golf under the Arizona sun. "These types of shows do nothing to polish that brand," he complained to the *New York Times*.

Places, in the world of tourism promotion, are no longer *places*, full of the highs and lows that make destinations — and life — interesting. They have become "brands," known for one or two salient qualities that a committee has decided will make them stand out from the pack.

The funny thing is that the trash-talking socialites of *Tuesday Night Book Club* didn't tell the whole story of Scottsdale, either. The folly of modern tourism promotion is thinking that it's even possible to tell just one story of any one place — even though it seems, more and more, choice-addled travellers want to hear just that.

AND NOW, A KIND WORD ABOUT THOSE FOLKS WHO HELP YOU CHOOSE

There are those who say that the day of the travel agent is done, that they're due to go the way of the milkman and the blacksmith. I'm not so certain, and I'll tell you why: Emma Nunn and Raoul Sebastian.

In the summer of 2002, the pair of nineteen-year-olds from England went online and booked the trip of a lifetime: three weeks in sunny Australia. They paid £740 each for their airline tickets for the globe-spanning journey, and congratulated themselves on their savvy Internet shopping skills.

They weren't puzzled by the fact that the trip would take only nine hours, nor did it seem odd that it would be routed through Halifax, Nova Scotia. That they were flying from the UK to Australia on Air Canada also didn't raise any alarm bells. The first minor note of worry appeared after they arrived in Halifax, when they were transferred to a twenty-five-seat prop plane. "I'm not the best flyer in the world, and I said I really couldn't see a small plane like that going all the way to Sydney," Nunn later told a reporter.

Well, she was wrong in one respect. The plane did indeed make it to Sydney. The only problem was, it was the wrong Sydney.

As the couple's friends waited for them at an airport Down Under, Nunn and Sebastian disembarked in Sydney, Nova Scotia. They had paid the equivalent of $1,850 each for the privilege of flying to a small, depressed industrial city on the edge of North America.

It's cruel but infinitely fun to laugh at the hapless couple, who actually came out all right in the end — they got a warm welcome from the folks in Cape Breton and an Australian board of trade offered them free airline tickets to Oz for a future trip. But they are far from alone in their aviation confusion; a few years ago, a British woman reportedly ended up in Dakar, Senegal, when she meant to go to Dhaka, Bangladesh. And more than a few people have wound up in Saint John, New Brunswick, instead of St. John's, Newfoundland, and vice versa.

Until everyone becomes geographically literate — which, frankly, I don't see happening anytime soon, if the average contestant on *Who Wants To Be A Millionaire* is any indication — travel agents will always have a job.

WHO KNOWS?
IT MIGHT BE THE NEXT STONEHENGE

Sometimes locals don't properly appreciate the economic opportunity sitting right on their doorstep. Such is the case with The Abode of Chaos, a house-*cum*-artwork in the village of St-Romain-au-Mont-D'Or, France. After making a dot-com fortune, artist Thierry Ehrmann started transforming his seventeenth-century stone farmhouse into a political-religious statement. Seven years and $5 million later, with the help of other artists, the property has been adorned with everything from a sculpture of a wrecked helicopter to giant portraits of George W. Bush, Osama bin Laden, Kofi Annan and various popes. The walls are crawling with steel salamander sculptures, which reflect Ehrmann's belief in alchemy. And, oh yes, there's a model of an oil platform on the roof.

You can see where the neighbours might be a little bit annoyed. "It's humanly intolerable, ugly, dramatic, with its images of destruction," local mayor Pierre Dumont told a reporter. "Whatever you think, for me it's not art, it's a provocation." Not surprisingly, Ehrmann begs to differ. Already, he claims, a Japanese tourist has told him, "I have seen the church of the twenty-first century."

Some neighbours are fed up with the crowds of tourists that arrive every weekend to gawk at the house, but not all the neighbours hate it. One, Marc Allardon, has already begun to decorate his own house in an affectionate parody of The Abode of Chaos.

"It's like the Eiffel Tower," Allardon told the reporter. "At first, people were against it. Here it will be like that. Some day the Japanese tour buses will come."[91]

If they're not already on their way to the Paris Las Vegas, that is.

The Future of Travel

Spacewalk is the ultimate experience that we've managed to invent as humans.
— *Space Adventures advisor and former astronaut Tom Jones*

The $25,000 Orteig Prize presented to Charles Lindbergh for his transatlantic flight was just one of hundreds of prizes offered between 1905 and 1935 that spurred early aviators and aircraft designers to fly faster and further — and to raise the money they needed to do so. Several pilots before Lindbergh had tried and failed to claim Orteig's jackpot. Together with Lindbergh, they spent about $400,000 — sixteen times the value of the prize — on the attempts.

In 1995, a group of space-travel visionaries decided to tear a page from the history of aviation's earliest days. People had been talking about commercial space travel almost from the moment Yuri Gagarin parachuted out of *Vostok 1* on April 12, 1961. More than thirty years later, it was still little more than the pipe dream of a few people who had spent too many of their formative years watching *Star Trek*. Perhaps what was needed to light a fire under entrepreneurs, inventors and daredevils was some cold, hard cash. The four founders of the X PRIZE Foundation, led by International Space University co-founder Peter Diamandas, set out to raise some. Their goal: a $10 million reward for the first person to build a suborbital private spacecraft and successfully fly it twice.

They soon attracted the attention of a group of movers and shakers in St. Louis, who offered to help the X PRIZE Foundation raise the prize money if they would move the foundation from Rockville,

Maryland, to St. Louis. Within a few months, the Foundation had set up shop in Missouri.

Almost seventy years earlier, nine St. Louis investors called the Spirit of St. Louis Organization had pooled their funds to bankroll Lindbergh's $25,000 flight. By March 1996, a group called the New Spirit of St. Louis Organization had convinced some thirty local investors — including Enterprise Rent-a-Car CEO Andrew Taylor and McDonnell Douglas Foundation chair John McDonnell — to kick in $25,000 apiece to fund the X Prize.

From the beginning, the fledgling foundation had a genius for marketing. As well as borrowing the name of Lindbergh's backers, they cashed in on the mystique by holding their first dinner at the same club in which Lindbergh had inked his final financing deal. They even had the latest investors sit at the same table Lindbergh had used.

Momentum started to build. Tech-loving author Tom Clancy donated $100,000 to the pot. Science fiction writer Arthur C. Clarke lent his endorsement to the effort, as did twenty astronauts and two of Lindbergh's grandsons. BankOne offered an affinity credit card that gave cardholders the chance to win a space flight. In 2004, venture capitalist Amir Ansari and his sister-in-law, tech entrepreneur Anousheh Ansari, gave the foundation several million dollars and the $10 million reward was renamed the Ansari X Prize.

In fall 2004, twenty teams from seven countries competed to win the juicy jackpot. Despite the $10 million on the table, some of the competitors didn't really need the cash — the eventual winner was bankrolled by Microsoft co-founder Paul Allen, who probably has $10 million in small bills stashed in a cookie jar to pay the pizza delivery guy. The craft Allen financed, *SpaceShipOne*, flew two suborbital flights within five days of each other in September and October 2004.

And this time, instead of watching for signs mounted above Paris newspaper offices, as was the case in Lindbergh's day, we all got to follow on the Web. By spring 2006, no fewer than a dozen companies were vying with each other in the race to be the first to shoot non-astronauts into suborbital space in a private craft.

By this time, a company called Space Adventures had already stolen a bit of the thunder by arranging for US businessman Dennis Tito to spend a week on the International Space Station in 2001. Several other wealthy tourists have since followed in Tito's space footsteps, each forking out an estimated US$20 million for the privilege. Even pop singer Lance Bass gave it a shot, before the money ran dry. Suborbital space travel, by contrast, will be a comparative bargain, with initial ticket prices estimated in the $100,000 to $250,000 range. Just to put that in context, the $400 Abram Pheil spent on his twenty-minute flight across Tampa Bay is roughly equivalent to $7,800 today. Not chump change, but not the price of a modest house, either.

One of the most prominent of the new space travel entrepreneurs is — who else? — Richard Branson, who hopes that his Virgin Galactic "space line" will have rich tourists staring down at earth from *SpaceShipTwo* by 2009. So far, hundreds of people have plunked down $20,000 deposits on the $200,000 tickets.

To read the breathless promotional materials from Virgin Galactic is to be swept up into a science fiction world that sounds as unlikely to many of us as Juan Trippe's dreams of glamorous, affordable air travel probably sounded to a lot of skeptics in the 1920s. Virgin has already signed a deal to build a $200 million spaceport on a twenty-seven-square-mile parcel of land in southern New Mexico. The company has collected deposit cheques from celebrities of various stripes, including ex-*Dallas* star Victoria Principal — again mirroring the early history of aviation. Branson even hired international man of design Philippe Starck to design Virgin Galactic's logo, which meshes a big blue eyeball with a sleek silver typeface that recalls a science fiction movie poster.

On the Virgin Galactic Web site, the company admits with uncharacteristic restraint that it hasn't ironed out the fine details of the trip yet. (There's still the matter of a few zillion layers of government approvals, for instance.) But the Web site does dangle promises that recall the glory days of white-gloved stewardesses.

The trip it asks prospective customers to imagine begins with a flight — possibly on an executive jet — to the "Virgin Galactic space resort." After six days of training and medical testing, travellers will board the VSS *Enterprise* (there is apparently some intergalactic law that requires the first of every type of spacecraft to be named after Captain Kirk's vessel).

After a mother ship carries the *Enterprise* to almost sixteen kilometres (ten miles) above sea level and releases it, rocket engines will blast it into space. "All the time, the ergonomic design of the seats will keep you comfortable," Virgin tells its prospective passengers, much as Thomas Cook once reassured early air travellers that its pilots wouldn't try any fancy aerobatics. Once the ship has entered suborbital space and the rocket motor cuts out, Virgin explains, "[Y]ou can look for the first time back at the planet you have just come from. The view will be over a thousand miles [sixteen hundred kilometres] in any direction...It will be humbling. It will be spiritual."

After the humble, spiritual millionaires return to Earth, the grand finale of the trip may be a gala dinner back at the spaceport, where each passenger will receive astronaut wings.

And now, for the kicker:

> Video and photographic images of your moment of making space history will be yours to show your kids and grandkids. Remember, of course, in their lifetime Virgin Galactic might have made it possible so that space travel is as common and as fun as flying with Virgin Atlantic. You can tell them you helped make it happen.[92]

Two salient facts don't get a great deal of play in Virgin's promotional materials, though. First, the flights will pass only through suborbital space — one hundred kilometres above the Earth — rather than deep space. Second, they'll be shorter than the average Hollywood blockbuster; most promoters expect the average trip to last about two hours (during which passengers will experience only five weightless minutes.)

Then again, the Wright brothers' first flight would barely clear a tennis court and was over in less than the time it takes the average modern passenger to open a package of airline peanuts.

KINDER, GENTLER TRAVEL?

At the same time that Branson and his brethren are trying to fire intrepid travellers into space, another group of advocates is trying to focus our attention back on earth. And at least one of them, far from encouraging us to head for the stars, is begging us to keep our feet on the ground.

British newspaper columnist George Monbiot, author of *Heat: How to Stop the Planet from Burning*, is convinced that we need to eliminate all but the most essential air travel if we hope to put a dent in the carbon emissions responsible for climate change. As Monbiot put it in a 2006 column in *The Guardian*, "if we want to stop the planet from cooking, we will simply have to stop travelling at the kind of speeds that planes permit."

His compatriot Richard Chartres, the bishop of London, added his voice to the growing howl of concern about the environmental impact of travel. "Making selfish choices such as flying on holiday or buying a large car are a symptom of sin," Chartres said. "Sin is not just a restricted list of moral mistakes. It is living a life turned in on itself where people ignore the consequences of their actions."[93]

Ouch.

With everyone from Anglican bishops to Al Gore talking about the perils of global warming, it's impossible not to think about the pounds of greenhouse gases each and every airline passenger spews into the atmosphere with each and every kilometre they travel. According to *Lonely Planet*, a round-trip flight for two people between North America and Europe will have as much of an impact on climate change as the average household's annual electricity and gas use.

Just think of that — all that money we spend to caulk our drafty windows and improve the efficiency of our furnaces, all seemingly gone for naught in the contrails of an airplane passing over our house.

So should we fly at all? It's tempting to just say no, as Monbiot does. Alternatively, those with the time, money and inclination could follow the example of Barbara Haddrill, a twenty-eight-year-old environmental activist from Wales. In the fall of 2006, she spent six

weeks journeying from the UK to Australia by bus, train and ship,
then another six weeks getting home. In the process, she spent three
and a half times more than she would have to take a twenty-two-hour
flight each way, but generated only a quarter of the carbon emissions
the air travel would have produced.

But where does that leave the rest of us, who want to see the
world without cooking it in the process? Gazing into my crystal ball,
I predict that this question is going to worry more and more travellers
in the decades ahead, and that long-distance travel styles are going
to change as a result.

If the societal pressure to avoid short leisure trips eventually builds
to the levels that discourage people from drinking and driving — and
there's no guarantee that they will, I admit — we may start flying less
often but staying in our destinations longer, an approach that would
simultaneously consume less jet fuel and give us more time to really
understand the places that we visit. If we could visit a far-off place
for a month or two instead of a week, it would be more feasible to
rent a furnished apartment (rather than stay in a chain hotel), take
language lessons or contribute to a volunteer project. There would
be more opportunities to meet local people, and a greater chance
that we could spend at least part of the time doing something besides
rushing from one famous sight to another.

The notion of longer vacations seems like a pipe dream in these
days of shrinking holidays, when "productivity" is the mantra of
every business guru and workaholism is the Western world's last per-
missible addiction. But a small movement to advocate for more time
off is slowly gathering steam. The Work to Live Vacation Campaign is
lobbying valiantly for a minimum three-week guaranteed vacation for
all Americans. And countless "balance" consultants around the world
are urging companies to take steps to avoid employee burnout.

Will these efforts pay off? The pessimist in me wonders, but the
optimist looks at past labour efforts, such as campaigns to establish
minimum wages and workweeks, and thinks there might just be a
chance.

There's also a growing focus on the effects of our travel activities
on the places we visit, from the effluents emitted by some cruise ships

to the rainforests chopped down to build tropical resorts. Ecotravel is a young and still evolving industry — groups such as Ecotourism Australia and Canada's Green Tourism Association only took shape in the 1990s — and as such it has its share of both passionate defenders and committed skeptics. But, again, I predict (and hope) its time has come.

HAS ALL THIS EFFORT BEEN WORTH IT?

Travel may seem at first a lightweight topic for investigation. It's about days at the seashore and nights at the casino, stays in nondescript motels and encounters with giant Mickey Mice.

But the human urge to explore this planet — to see great sights, to meet strangers, to eat unfamiliar food and experience exotic customs and just generally shake ourselves out of the lethargy that can envelop us when we spend day after week after month after year in overly familiar surroundings — has shaped the modern world in many ways.

Without travel, it might have been decades before businesses reaped the benefits of standard time.

Without travel, there would have been little incentive to preserve ancient Roman ruins or medieval castles or Victorian mansions from the wrecking ball.

And without travel, everyone on earth would still be living within a very short distance of humanity's birthplace in Africa.

In short, without travel, the world would be a very different place than the one we inhabit today. Think about that the next time you pack your bags.

Endnotes

1   J.J. Jusserand, *English Wayfaring Life in the Middle Ages* (1889; repr. Chatham, UK: W. & J. Mackay, 1950), p. 215.
2   Ibid., p. 223.
3   Ibid., p. 195.
4   Ibid., p. 217.
5   Ibid., p. 206.
6   Ibid.
7   Jeremy Black, *The British and the Grand Tour* (London: Croom Helm, 1985), p. 232.
8   http://en.wikipedia.org/wiki/Grand_Tour.
9   Lynne Withey, *Grand Tours and Cook's Tours: A History of Leisure Travel, 1750 to 1915* (New York: William Morrow, 1997), p. 16.
10 Quoted in Leo Hamalian, ed., *Ladies on the Loose: Women Travellers of the 18th and 19th Centuries* (New York: Dodd, Mead, 1981), p. 4.
11 Lionel Casson, *Travel in the Ancient World* (Toronto: Hakkert, 1974), p. 37.
12 Quoted in Richard Trench, *Travellers in Britain: Three Centuries of Discovery* (London: Aurum Press, 1990), p. 71.
13 Quoted in Black, *The British and the Grand Tour*, p. 19.
14 Ibid., p. 60.
15 Quoted in Hamalian, ed., *Ladies on the Loose*, p. 18.
16 Charles Dickens, *American Notes* (1842; repr. Harmondsworth, UK: Penguin Books, 1972), p. 184.
17 http://www.ehma.com/index.php?option=com_content&task=view&id=138&Itemid=55.
18 Joan E. Rankin, *Meet Me at the Chateau: A Legacy of Memory* (Toronto: Natural Heritage Books, 1990), p. 90.
19 Quoted in Casson, *Travel in the Ancient World*, pp. 158-59.
20 Ibid., p. 195.
21 Quoted in Black, *The British and the Grand Tour*, pp. 17-18.

22   "Days of the Old Packet," *New York Daily Times*, December 13, 1891, p. 17.

23   Sinclair Lewis, *Dodsworth* (1929; repr. New York: The Modern Library, 1947), p. 35.

24   Ibid., pp. 37-38.

25   Paul Fussell, *Abroad: British Literary Traveling Between the Wars* (New York: Oxford University Press, 1980), p. 37.

26   Gordon Lightfoot, "Canadian Railroad Trilogy" (New York: Witmark Music, 1967).

27   Quoted in Hamalian, ed., *Ladies on the Loose*, p. 53.

28   Frank Rowbottom, "The Rowbottom Diaries," *Saskatchewan History* 21, no. 1 (1968), pp. 57-58, 61.

29   Toni Ross, *Oh! The Coal Branch: A Chronicle of the Alberta Coal Branch* (Edmonton: T. Ross, 1974), p. 263.

30   *Car Window Glimpses En Route to Quebec, by Daylight, via Quebec Central Railway* (1881?; repr. Quebec: Page-Sangster, 1952), p. 15.

31   D.B. Hanna, as told to Arthur Hawkes, *Trains of Recollection* (Toronto: Macmillan of Canada, 1924), pp. 190-91.

32   Ibid., p. 193.

33   Quoted in Hugh A. Dempsey, ed., *The CPR West: The Iron Road and the Making of a Nation* (Vancouver: Douglas & McIntyre, 1984), p. 153.

34   Ibid., p. 151.

35   Quoted in Condé Nast Publications, *Travel in Vogue* (London: Macdonald Futura, 1981), p. 24.

36   Ibid.

37   Donald Mackay, *The People's Railway: A History of Canadian National* (Toronto: Douglas & McIntyre, 1992), p. 134.

38   Hamalian, ed., *Ladies on the Loose*, pp. 74-75.

39   Marguerite Woodworth, *History of the Dominion Atlantic Railway* (Kentville, NS: Kentville Publishing, 1936), p. 88.

40   Quoted in Black, *The British and the Grand Tour*, pp. 52-53.

41   Ibid., p. 52.

42   Quoted in Withey, *Grand Tours and Cook's Tours*, p. 13.

43   Quoted in Hamalian, ed., *Ladies on the Loose*, p. 45.

44   Ibid., p. 214.

45   Richard F. Weingroff, "From Names to Numbers: The Origins of the U.S. Numbered Highway System." United States, Department of Transportation, Federal Highway Administration, http://wwwcf.fhwa. dot.gov/infrastructure/numbers.htm (accessed July 8, 2006).

46 Ibid.

47 Ibid.

48 http://www.wbcci-denco.org/Wally/Wally.html.

49 David Schwartz, "RVs at Wal-Mart," *Time*, June 4, 2001, p. 6.

50 Mitch Teich, "RV campers take advantage of Wal-Mart parking lots for free camping," National Public Radio, *All Things Considered*, May 30, 2001.

51 Dahleen Glanton, "Wealthy baby boomers increasingly drawn to luxury RV lifestyle," *Seattle Times*, April 24, 2006.

52 Andrew Martin, *New Statesman*, July 17, 2000; http://www.newstatesman.com/200007170009.

53 Quoted in Douglas Martin, "Ralph Lee, a king of the road, is dead at 99," *New York Times*, October 6, 2002, sec. 1, p. 45.

54 Quoted in Alastair Gordon, *Naked Airport: A Cultural History of the World's Most Revolutionary Structure* (New York: Metropolitan Books, Henry Holt, 2004), p. 75.

55 Patricia D'Souza, "A wing and a prayer: Will the $3.4b upgrade at Pearson make traveling through it any more enjoyable?" *Canadian Business*, October 9, 1998, p. 24.

56 Ibid.

57 Quoted in United Airlines, "Flight Attendant History," http://www.united.com/page/article/0,6722,3211,00.html.

58 Quoted in Industry Canada, "Canada's Digital Collections," http://collections.ic.gc.ca/high_flyers/steward.htm.

59 Nina Morrison, "Married women need not apply," CBC-TV, November 27, 1995, http://archives.cbc.ca/IDC-1-73-1125-6187/politics_economy/air_canada/clip4.

60 http://www.2wice.org/issues/uniform/stew.html.

61 Annie Wu, "The History of Airport Security," *The Savvy Traveler*, September 15, 2000.

62 David Lodge, *Paradise News* (London: Secker & Warburg, 1991), pp. 3-4.

63 Lisa Fitterman, "The suitcase send-off," *Globe and Mail*, July 15, 2006, p. T2.

64 Quoted in Cindy S. Aron, *Working at Play: A History of Vacations in the United States* (New York: Oxford University Press, 1999), p. 86.

65 Quoted in Hamalian, ed., *Ladies on the Loose*, p. 62.

66 Ibid., pp. 66-68.

67 Quoted in Aron, *Working at Play*, p. 120.

68 Quoted in Fred Inglis, *The Delicious History of the Holiday* (London: Routledge, 2000), p. 52.

69 Ibid., p. 108.

70 Quoted in Dave Smith and Steven Clark, *Disney: The First 100 Years* (New York: Hyperion, 1999), pp. 78-79.

71 Wayne Ellwood, "Inside the Disney dream machine," *New Internationalist*, December 1998.

72 Quoted in Tralee Pearce, "The new kids on the block," *Globe and Mail*, July 15, 2006, p. L1.

73 Peter Bicknell, ed., *The Illustrated Wordsworth's Guide to the Lakes* (Exeter, UK: Webb & Bower, 1984), p. 34.

74 Quoted in Black, *The British and the Grand Tour*, p. 168.

75 Ibid.

76 http://www.americanheritage.com/articles/web/20060705-bikini-swimming-suit-louis-reard-micheline-bernardini-paris-brigitte-bardot.shtml.

77 Quoted in Jusserand, *English Wayfaring Life in the Middle Ages*, p. 210.

78 Ibid.

79 Quoted in Black, *The British and the Grand Tour*, p. 216.

80 Bicknell, ed., *The Illustrated Wordsworth's Guide to the Lakes*, p. 16.

81 Black, *The British and the Grand Tour*, p. 138.

82 Ibid., p. 215.

83 Quoted in Paul Fussell, ed., *The Norton Book of Travel* (New York: W.W. Norton, 1987), p. 221.

84 Quoted in Hamalian, ed., *Ladies on the Loose*, p. 117.

85 Quoted in Edmund Swinglehurst, *Cook's Tours: The Story of Popular Travel* (Poole, Dorset, UK: Blandford Press, 1982), pp. 21-22.

86 Quoted in Withey, *Grand Tours and Cook's Tours*, p. 145.

87 Ibid., p. 153.

88 Charles Lever, *Blackwood's Magazine* 97, February 1865.

89 Lewis, *Dodsworth*, p. 31.

90 Marian Keyes, *Cracks in My Foundation* (New York: Avon Trade/HarperCollins, 2005), pp. 170-71.

91 John Tagliabue, "It's his house. But, village traditionalists ask, is it art?" *New York Times*, July 19, 2006.

92 http://www.virgingalactic.com/en/like.asp.

93 Quoted in Jonathan Leake, "Be good to the Earth, church says." *Ottawa Citizen*, July 25, 2006, p. A3.

Bibliography

GENERAL REFERENCES

Aron, Cindy S. *Working at Play: A History of Vacations in the United States*. New York: Oxford University Press, 1999.

Casson, Lionel. *Travel in the Ancient World*. Toronto: Hakkert, 1974.

Cocks, Catherine. *Doing the Town: The Rise of Urban Tourism in the United States, 1850–1915*. Berkeley: University of California Press, 2001.

Condé Nast Publications. *Travel in Vogue*. London: Macdonald Futura, 1981.

Franklin, Adrian. *Tourism: An Introduction*. London: Sage, 2003.

Frommer, Arthur. *Arthur Frommer's New World of Travel*, 5th ed. New York: Macmillan, 1996.

Fussell, Paul. *Abroad: British Literary Traveling Between the Wars*. New York: Oxford University Press, 1980.

———, ed. *The Norton Book of Travel*. New York: W.W. Norton, 1987.

Hamalian, Leo, ed. *Ladies on the Loose: Women Travellers of the 18th and 19th Centuries*. New York: Dodd, Mead, 1981.

Harrison, Julia. *Being a Tourist: Finding Meaning in Pleasure Travel*. Vancouver: University of British Columbia Press, 2003.

Howard, Claire. *English Travellers of the Renaissance*. London: John Lane, The Bodley Head, 1914.

Inglis, Fred. *The Delicious History of the Holiday*. London: Routledge, 2000.

Jusserand, J.J. *English Wayfaring Life in the Middle Ages*. 1889. Reprinted, Chatham, UK: W. & J. Mackay, 1950.

Lewis, Sinclair. *Dodsworth*. 1929. Reprinted, New York: The Modern Library, 1947.

Lodge, David. *Paradise News*. London: Secker & Warburg, 1991.

MacCannell, Dean. *The Tourist: A New Theory of the Leisure Class.* Berkeley: University of California Press, 1999.

Morris, Mary, with Larry O'Connor, eds. *The Illustrated Virago Book of Women Travellers.* London: Virago Press, 1994.

National Geographic Society. *Great Journeys of the World.* Washington, DC: National Geographic Society, 1996.

Nickerson, Norma Polovitz, and Paula Kerr. *Snapshots: An Introduction to Tourism,* 2nd Canadian ed. Toronto: Prentice Hall, 2001.

O'Brien, Patrick K., general ed. *The Oxford Atlas of World History.* New York: Oxford University Press, 2002.

Parkes, Joan. *Travel in England in the Seventeenth Century.* 1925. Reprinted, Oxford: Clarendon Press, 1968.

Perrottet, Tony. *Pagan Holiday: On the Trail of Ancient Roman Tourists.* New York: Random House, 2002.

Swinglehurst, Edmund. *Cook's Tours: The Story of Popular Travel.* Poole, UK: Blandford Press, 1982.

Towner, John. *An Historical Geography of Recreation and Tourism in the Western World 1540–1940.* Chichester, UK: John Wiley, 1996.

Trench, Richard. *Travellers in Britain: Three Centuries of Discovery.* London: Aurum Press, 1990.

Urry, John. *The Tourist Gaze,* 2nd ed. London: Sage, 2002.

Withey, Lynne. *Grand Tours and Cook's Tours: A History of Leisure Travel, 1750 to 1915.* New York: William Morrow, 1997.

PILGRIM'S PROGRESS

Cousineau, Phil. *The Art of Pilgrimage: The Seeker's Guide to Making Travel Sacred.* Berkeley, CA: Conari Press, 1998.

THE GRAND TOUR:
Where Modern Leisure Travel Began

Black, Jeremy. *The British and the Grand Tour.* London: Croom Helm, 1985.

Dolan, Brian. *Ladies of the Grand Tour: British Women in Pursuit of Enlightenment and Adventure in Eighteenth-Century Europe.* New York: HarperCollins, 2001.

Norwich, John Julius. *Paradise of Cities: Venice and Its Nineteenth-Century Visitors.* London: Viking, 2003.

PUTTING ON THE RITZ:
Hotels and Other Homes Away from Home

Denby, Elaine. *Grand Hotels: Reality and Illusion*. London: Reaktion Books, 1998.
Dickens, Charles. *American Notes*. 1842. Reprinted, Harmondsworth, UK: Penguin, 1972.
Pregarz, Roberto. *Memories of Raffles: 22 Years With a Grand Old Hotel*. N.p.: Treasury Publishing, 1990.
Rankin, Joan E. *Meet Me at the Chateau: A Legacy of Memory*. Toronto: Natural Heritage Books, 1990.

GOING DOWN TO THE SEA IN SHIPS

Garin, Kristoffer A. *Devils on the Deep Blue Sea: The Dreams, Schemes and Showdowns That Built America's Cruise-Ship Empires*. New York: Viking, 2005.
Howard, Judith A. *Ford's Freighter Travel Guide...and Waterways of the World*. Winter 2000-2001, 96th rev. ed. Northridge, CA: Ford's Travel Guides, 2000.
Klein, Ross A. *Cruise Ship Blues: The Underside of the Cruise Industry*. Gabriola Island, BC: New Society Publishers, 2002.

ALL ABOARD:
Our Enduring Love Affair with Trains

Car Window Glimpses En Route to Quebec, by Daylight, via Quebec Central Railway. 1881? Reprinted, Quebec: Page-Sangster, 1952.
Choco, Marc H., and David L. Jones. *Canadian Pacific Posters 1883-1963*. Montreal: Meridian Press, 1988.
Cohen, Norm. *Long Steel Rail: The Railroad in American Folksong*. Urbana: University of Illinois Press, 1981.
Cookridge, E.H. *Orient Express: The Life and Times of the World's Most Famous Train*. New York: Harper Colophon, 1980.
Dempsey, Hugh A., ed. *The CPR West: The Iron Road and the Making of a Nation*. Vancouver: Douglas & McIntyre, 1984.

Ellis, Hamilton. *British Railway History 1830-1876*. London: George
    Allen and Unwin, 1954.

Hanna, D.B., as told to Arthur Hawkes. *Trains of Recollection*. Toronto:
    Macmillan Company of Canada, 1924.

Mackay, Donald. *The People's Railway: A History of Canadian National*.
    Toronto: Douglas & McIntyre, 1992.

Ross, Toni. *Oh! The Coal Branch: A Chronicle of the Alberta Coal Branch*.
    Edmonton: T. Ross, 1974.

Rowbottom, Frank. "The Rowbottom Diaries." *Saskatchewan History* 21,
    no. 1 (1968).

Sherwood, Shirley. *Venice Simplon Orient-Express: The Return of the
    World's Most Celebrated Train*. London: Weidenfeld & Nicolson,
    1983.

Woodworth, Marguerite. *History of the Dominion Atlantic Railway*.
    Kentville, NS: Kentville Publishing, 1936.

ON THE ROAD

Hall, Jaimie, and Alice Zyetz. *RV Traveling Tales: Women's Journeys on
    the Open Road*. Livingston, TX: Pine Country Publishing, 2002.

Hofmeister, Ron, and Barb Hofmeister. *Movin' On: Living and
    Traveling Full Time in a Recreational Vehicle*. Livingston, TX: R&B
    Publications, 1999.

Miller, Joseph M., Daan Joubert, and Marion Butler. "Fall of the French
    Monarchy." Grand Super Cycle National Bankruptcies, Part VI.
    http://www.freebuck.com/articles/elliott/030312bankruptcies1.htm.

Paumgarten, Nick. "Getting There: The Science of Driving Directions,"
    The New Yorker, April 24, 2006.

Weingroff, Richard F. "From Names to Numbers: The Origins of the
    U.S. Numbered Highway System." Washington, DC: United States,
    Department of Transportation, Federal Highway Administration.
    http://wwwcf.fhwa.dot.gov/infrastructure/numbers.htm.

FLIGHT PATTERNS: A Century of Air Travel

Gordon, Alastair. *Naked Airport: A Cultural History of the World's Most Revolutionary Structure*. New York: Metropolitan Books, Henry Holt, 2004.

Hudson, Kenneth, and Julian Pettifer. *Diamonds in the Sky: A Social History of Air Travel*. London: The Bodley Head/British Broadcasting Corporation, 1979.

McGrath, T.M. *History of Canadian Airports*. N.p.: Lugus Publications, 1992.

TO YOUR HEALTH: Spas and Other Cures

Brue, Alexia. *Cathedrals of the Flesh: My Search for the Perfect Bath*. New York: Bloomsbury, 2003.

IF YOU BUILD IT, THEY WILL COME: Resorts and Theme Parks

Alspaugh, Emmanuelle, ed. *Fodor's Walt Disney World, Universal Orlando, and Central Florida 2006*. New York: Fodor's Travel Publications, 2006.

Koenig, David. *More Mouse Tales: A Closer Peek Backstage at Disneyland*. Irvine, CA: Bonaventure Press, 1999.

Majendie, Paul. "British seaside holiday camps dump tacky traditions for slick '90s revival." *National Post*, January 22, 1999, p. A15.

Smith, Dave, and Steven Clark. *Disney: The First 100 Years*. New York: Hyperion, 1999.

THE WELL-PACKED BAG

Bicknell, Peter, ed. *The Illustrated Wordsworth's Guide to the Lakes*. Exeter, UK: Webb & Bower, 1984.

Lloyd, Martin. *The Passport: The History of Man's Most Travelled Document*. Stroud, UK: Sutton Publishing, 2003.

Westcott, Kathryn. "The bikini: Not a brief affair." BBC News, July 5, 2006. http://news.bbc.co.uk/go/pr/fr/-/2/hi/in_depth/5130460.stm.

Index

A

Aachen Germany 191
Abbey of St. Albans 125
Acapulco Mexico 174
accommodations 39-67
    caravanserai 43-45, 46
    caupona 42
    hospitium 42
    khans. See caravanserai
    mansio 42
    mutatio 42
    pandokeion 40, 41
    taberna 42
    villas 41
    See also hostels; hotel chains; hotels;
        inns; motels
Adelaide Australia 121
Afghanistan 43, 128, 235
Agra India 261
airlines 79, 144
    Air Canada 184, 186, 269
    Air France 158, 169, 186
    American 143, 176, 177, 178
    American Export 169
    Boeing Air Transport 175, 176
    Braniff International Airways 170,
        177, 178
    British Aircraft Transport and Travel
        158
    British Airways 158
    Continental 177, 179
    DELAG 157
    Eastern 143
    Hooters Air 179
    Imperial Airways 158, 160, 167,
        168, 257
    JetBlue 186
    KLM 158, 169, 186

Lufthansa 158
Northwest Orient 180
Pacific Western 178
Pan Am 153, 158-161, 163, 167,
    168, 169, 172, 257
Ryanair 144
Sabena 158, 169, 186
SAS 169
SCADTA 160
Southwest 186
St. Petersburg-Tampa Airboat Line
    155-156
Swissair 169
Tango 186
Ted 186
Thomas Cook 171
Trans-Canada 176, 177, 184
TWA 169, 178
United 175, 177, 179, 186
Varig 186
Virgin Atlantic 274
WestJet 186
airplane hijackings 179
airplane movies
    Air Force One 181
    Airplane! 181
    Airport 178, 181
    Pursuit of D.B. Cooper, The 179
    Snakes on a Plane 180
    Terminal, The 182
    United 93 181
    View From The Top 175
airplanes 9, 11, 13, 86, 89, 95, 98,
    153-186
    B-314 flying boats 168
    Benoist seaplane 155, 156
    Boeing 707 161
    Boeing 727 180

Boeing 747 161
clippers 168
Concorde 80
DC-4 169
de Havilland 4A bomber 158
F-16 fighter 185
jumbo jets 168
Lockheed Constellation 169
Pan American Clipper flying boats
    145
Spirit of St. Louis 156
Super Constellation 169
Wright Flyer 154
Yankee Clipper 1687, 256
airport
  security 178
  terminals 173, 175, 182
airports 9, 10, 87, 119, 162-165,
    166-169, 170
  Calgary 175
  Changi 174
  Dallas-Fort Worth 170
  Dallas Love Field 170, 178
  Fairfax 162
  Gander 169
  Gatwick 173, 179
  Greater Pittsburgh 173
  Hartsfield-Jackson 181
  Heathrow 173, 179, 182
  John F. Kennedy 181
  LaGuardia 163, 167, 168
  Le Bourget Aerodrome 156, 157,
    163
  Lester B. Pearson 173
  Los Angeles 153, 163
  Newark 181
  Pierre Elliott Trudeau 183
  Roosevelt Airfield 156
  San Francisco 175, 178, 181
  Schiphol 174
  Seattle-Tacoma 180
  Shannon 169
  St. Louis 181
  Swan Island 162
  Tempelhof 163
  Vancouver 174
airships 157

Airstream 146
air travel
  and bombings 180-181
  discount 186
  and lost luggage 182-185
  and passengers 170-172
  and radio frequency identification
    (RFID) microchips 185
Aix-en-Provence France 224
Aix-les-Bains France 189
Ajmer India 34
al-Umari 30
Albany NY 81, 82, 198
Albert, Prince 100
Aldrich, Chester 163
Alexandra, Queen 255
Alexandria Egypt 72, 160, 235, 245
Algiers Algeria 224
Allahabad India 155
Allardon, Marc 270
Allen, Paul 272
Alliance NV 261
Alps 12, 34, 42, 131
Amarillo TX 261
American Automobile Association 137
Amiens France 235
Amish 260-262
Amsterdam Holland 158, 174
Anaheim CA 13, 208, 212
Anatolia 43
Anderson, John 257
Andress, Ursula 227
Andrews, John 133
Andrews, Julie 206
Annan, Kofi 270
Anne, Queen 190
Anniston AB 264
Ansari, Amir 272
Ansari, Anousheh 272
Ansari X Prize 272
Antalya Turkey 187
Antioch Turkey 126
Antipodes Island New Zealand 114
Antwerp Belgium 253
Appian Way 42
Aral Sea 126
Ardrossan Scotland 250

Aristides, Aelius 189
Arsinoe Egypt 245
Artaxerxes, King 222
Arthur, King 10
Arundel, Thomas 29
Astor, John Jacob 85
Athens Greece 44, 72, 160, 234
Atlanta GA 143, 163, 179, 181
Atlantic Ocean 50, 70, 78, 82, 83, 89, 136, 157
Auchinleck, Lord 33, 34
Augsburg Germany 230
Augustine 223, 224
Australia 74, 99, 121, 130, 137, 149, 157, 160, 257, 263, 269, 276
Austro-Hungarian Empire 236
automobile rental 141-144
automobile rental companies
    Avis Airline Rent-a-Car System 143
    Budget Rent-a-Car 143
    Enterprise Rent-a-Car 272
    Hertz Rent A Car 142-143
    National Rent-a-Car 143
    Rent-a-Ford 142
automobiles 118, 136-138, 141-144
    Chevrolet Corvette 150
    Lotus 150
    Model T 138, 141, 142, 259, 260
    Nissan Sunny 150
    Porsche 911 150
Avalon, Frankie 227
Avignon France 78
Avis, Warren 143
Azores 168

B

Bactria 128
Baedeker, Karl 218, 219, 220
Baghdad Iraq 44, 158, 160, 172
Bahamas 90, 211
Bahrain 158
Bain, Donald 178
Bali 208
Ballina Australia 264
Baltimore MD 168
Bamiyam Afghanistan 128
Banff AB 196

Banff National Park 196
Banff Springs AB 115
Bardot, Brigitte 226
barges 73, 78
Bar Harbor ME 254
Barrymore, Lionel 58
Barrymore, John 58
Bass, Lance 273
Batavia Indonesia. See Jakarta Indonesia
Bath UK 189, 190, 191, 220
Baum, Vicki 58
Beatles 258
Becket, St. Thomas 22, 28, 30
Beery, Wallace 58
Begum, Arjumand Bano 261
Bel-Air CA 32
Belgium 149, 186
Benz, Karl 136
Berg, Larry 173
Bergama Turkey 188
Bergen, Candice 175
Berlin Germany 58, 108, 163
Bermuda 79, 90, 168
Bernhagen, Paul 147
Berry, Mary 232
Bethlehem Israel 20
Beverly Hills CA 32
bicycles 21, 134-136, 137, 259
    boneshaker 135
    Draisienne 134
    hobbyhorse 135
    velocipede 135
bikini 226, 227
Bikini Atoll 226
bin Laden, Osama 270
Birmingham UK 201
Black Sea 109, 110
Blair, Tony 92
Blitz, Gérard 207
Blowitz, Henri Opperde 110
boats
    canal 76, 78
    mail 78
    paddle wheeler 259
    river 76, 78
    rowboat 75
    steam 154

Bocca, Geoffrey 69
Bohun, Humphrey de, Earl of Hereford
     and Essex 24
Bologna Italy 131
Bolton UK 251
books
   Abroad 95
   Airport 178
   Art of Pilgrimage, The 15
   Bible 19, 73
   Book of Roger, or the Delight of whoso
     loves to make the Circuit of the
     World, The 216
   Britannia 129
   Canterbury Tales, The 29, 234
   Chronica majora 125
   Codex Calixtinus 21
   Coffee, Tea or Me? 178
   Coryat's Crudities 34
   Delicious History of the Holiday, The
     215
   Dodsworth 87-88, 97
   Dorling Kindersley Eyewitness Guides
     222
   England Made Me 163
   Europe from $85 a Day 221
   Europe on $5 a Day 216, 221
   Grand Tour containing an exact
     description of most of the cities,
     towns and remarkable places of
     Europe 35, 216
   Hand-Book for Travellers 218
   Hand-Book for Travellers on the
     Continent 218
   Heat: How to Stop the Planet from
     Burning 275
   Heidi 39
   Insight Bali 222
   Insight Guides 222
   Last Tycoon, The 171
   Let's Go 216
   Let's Go Europe 221
   Letters of Travel (1892-1913) 243
   Letters to a Young Gentleman on His
     Setting Out for France 133
   Lonely Planet guides 221, 275
   Lord of the Rings, The 15

   Michelin travel guides 219, 220
   Moon Publications 221
   Murder on the Orient Express 110
   On the Continent: The Entertaining
     Travel Annual 220
   On the Road 11
   Paradise News 182
   Peregrinationes 216
   Photo-Auto Guide 138
   Pilgrim's Progress 10
   Post Chaise Companion 129
   Precepts 187
   Pride and Prejudice 48
   Qur'an 10
   Ramayana 10
   River Duddon, a Series of Sonnets:
     and other Poems 217
   road 129
   Rough Guide to Greece 221
   Select Views in Cumberland,
     Westmoreland, and Lancashire 216
   Ship of Fools 77
   Some Observations Made in Travelling
     Through France and Italy & in the
     years 1720, 1721 and 1722 216
   Stamboul Train 110
   Sun Also Rises, The 10
   Switzerland and How to See It for Ten
     Guineas 219
   Tom Jones 10
   Tour through the Whole Island of
     Great Britain 191
   Under the Tuscan Sun 215
   Year in Provence, A 215
   See also guidebooks
boondocking 147
Booth, John Wilkes 105
Bosch, Hieronymus 77
Boston MA 50, 51, 52, 111, 112, 159,
     265
Boswell, James 12, 33-34, 37
Botwood Harbour NL 167
Bournemouth UK 169
Bradford, Norman 205
Branson, Richard 157, 273, 275
Brazil 186
Bremer, Frederika 248

Brindisi Italy 73, 108
Brisbane Australia 158, 172
Bristol UK 82
broadcasting companies
    American Broadcasting Company
        (ABC) 91, 208, 209
    British Broadcasting Corporation
        (BBC) 206, 207
    Canadian Broadcasting Corporation
        (CBC) 101, 177, 178, 184
    Columbia Broadcasting System (CBS)
        268
    Music Television (MTV) 267
    National Public Radio 148
Brooklyn NY 95
Brougham, Lord Chancellor Henry 202
Bruges Belgium 242
Brunel, Isambard Kingdom 82, 83, 100
Brussels Belgium 158
Bubastis Egypt 16
Buddhism 16, 128
Bulgaria 109
Bunyan, John 10
Burbank CA 208
Burnet, Joseph 242
buses 32, 98, 151, 255, 259
Bush, George W. 92, 270
bus tour companies
    Cosmos 255
bus tours 244, 246, 255, 258, 261
Butlin, Billy 203-207
Byam, Wally 144-146

C
cabs 9, 13
Caesar, Julius 71
Caesarea Palaestina Israel 19
Cairo Egypt 30, 145, 158
Cajetan, Cardinal Thomas 230
Calais France 35, 75, 130, 132, 133,
    238, 253
Calixtus II, Pope 21
Callot, Jacques 236
Camelot 10
cameras 97, 226, 237, 240
Cana Israel 20

Canada 101, 137, 138, 141, 145, 184,
    185, 203, 204, 233
Cannes France 202, 203
Canterbury UK 16, 22, 28-31, 220, 235
Cape Town South Africa 145, 158
Caravan Club 150
Carême, Marie-Antoine 55
Caribbean Sea 69, 90
Carlisle UK 251
Carmichael, James 111
Carrère, John Merven 116
carriages 50, 76, 129, 130-131, 133
Carteret, Edward 36
Castaway Cay 211
Catherine, St. 235
Catskill Mountains 13
Cervantes, Miguel de 10, 224
Chalon-sur-Saône France 76
Charles, King of Hohenzollern 110
Charles I, King 231
Chartres, Richard 275
Chaucer, Geoffrey 16, 28, 29, 30
Chautauqua 200
Cherbourg France 156
Cheticamp NS 263
Chicago IL 52, 104, 105, 118, 119,
    138, 140, 141, 142, 172, 175,
    177, 179, 237
Chichester UK 23
China 31, 71, 113, 126-128, 224, 254
Chirac, Jacques 92
Christianity 10, 128
Christians 16, 18-31, 30, 71, 77
Christie, Agatha 110
Chunnel 75
Church, Ellen 175
Church of England 30
Cicero 36, 41
Cisco TX 61
Civil War 104, 108, 193, 260
Clacton-on-Sea UK 205
Clancy, Tom 272
Clarke, Arthur C. 272
Clarksdale MS 141
Clarkson, Jeremy 150
Claude glass 240, 241
Claudius, Emperor 71

Clearwater FL 31
Clerkenwell UK 45
Clermont France 19
Cleveland OH 266
Co-operative Holidays Association 204
coaches 252
    Dutch 130
    Turkish 130
Coffs Harbour Australia 264
Coke, Lady Mary 75
Collinsville IL 263
Colmar France 125
Cologne France 23
Columbus OH 155
companies
    21st Century Airships 166
    Airstream 145
    BAA 173
    BankOne 272
    Body Shop 173
    Boeing 168
    Coca-Cola 159
    Compagnie Internationale des
        Wagons-Lits 109, 110
    Dunlop 135
    Eaton's 203
    General Electric 210
    General Motors 146
    Globus Viaggi 255
    Harrods 173
    International Fiberglass 141
    Liberty Coach 148
    McDonald's 123, 140, 212
    Michelin 135
    Microsoft 159, 272
    New Oriental Banking Corporation
        243
    Nike 212
    PB Cafe 141
    Railway Extension Inc. 142
    Rand McNally & Company 138
    Random House 220
    Reebok 212
    Reo Motorcar Company 137
    SITA 183
    Standard Oil 116
    United Fruit Company 160

Victoria's Secret 173
    Wal-Mart 147, 148
    WED Enterprises 208
    Yellow Cab and Yellow Truck
        and Coach Manufacturing
        Company 142
    Zeppelin 166
    See also automobile rental companies;
        broadcasting companies; bus tour
        companies; travel companies
Compiègne France 110
Confucius 9
Congo 158
Constantinople Turkey. See Istanbul
    Turkey
Continent, The 33-37, 75, 76, 133,
    221, 257
convents 45
Cook, Thomas 145, 200, 203, 219,
    242, 243, 249-257, 274
Cooper, Dan 180
Corinth Greece 41
Cork Ireland 124
Coryat, Thomas 34
Costa Brava Spain 207
Côte d'Azur. See Riviera
Cousineau, Phil 15
Coventry Guild 25
Coward, Noël 60
Cowell, Simon 150
Cozumel Mexico 227
Craigellachie BC 101
Craven, Lady 50
Crawford, Ellis 176
Crawford, Joan 58
Crete Greece 16, 40
Crimea 50
Croesus, King 17, 18
Cromwell, Oliver 231
Crosby, Bing 11, 61
Cumberland MD 137
Cummings, Bob 209
Curtiz, Michael 163
Cuzco Peru 16
cycling clubs 135
Cyclists' Touring Club 135

D

Daimler, Gottlieb 136
Dakar Senegal 269
Dallas TX 178
Dalrymple, Mr. 225
Damascus Syria 44
Danube River 109
Dark Ages 19, 74, 190, 228
Darwin Australia 121
Dashew, Steve 141
Davidson SK 263
da Vinci, Leonardo 36, 134
Dayton OH 155
Defoe, Daniel 191
de Gama, Vasco 128
Delano, William Adams 163
Delos Greece 16
Delphi Greece 16, 18, 235
Dempsey, Jack 172
Denmark 129
Denver CO 118, 267
Depression 11, 58, 59, 141, 142, 146,
    151, 157, 159, 166
Detroit MI 143
Dhaka Bangladesh 269
Diamandas, Peter 271
di Caprio, Leonardo 70
Dickens, Charles 51
Dieppe France 75
diligences 132, 133, 134, 258
dirigibles 161, 165-166
    Goodyear blimp 166
    Graf Zeppelin 165, 166
    Hindenburg 162, 166
Disney, Walt 208, 209, 210, 212
Disney-MGM Studios 210
Disneyland 208-212, 213
    Adventureland 209
    Euro 211
    Fantasyland 209
    Frontierland 209
    Paris 211
    Tokyo 210
    Tomorrowland 209
Doors, The 77
Doty, Thomas 179
Dover UK 28, 35, 75

D'Oyly Carte, Richard 55, 56
Drais, Baron Karl von 134
Dryden ON 263
Dubai 62
Dublin Ireland 32
Duchesnay QC 63
Duluth MN 141, 254
Dumont, Pierre 270
Duncan BC 263
Dundalk Ireland 251
Duvall, Robert 180
Dylan, Bob 141
Dysart, Lord 36

E

Earhart, Amelia 157
East Glacier Park MT XE 263
Ecotourism Australia 277
ecotravel 277
Edgar, King 22
Edinburgh Scotland 250
Edson AB 103
Edward I, King 28, 45
Edward II, King 25
Edward III, King 24
Edward VII, King 55, 57, 58, 100,
    202, 255
Edward VIII, King 203
Egan, Mabel 65
Egypt 10, 17, 31, 43, 71, 222, 235,
    245, 256
Ehrmann, Thierry 270
Eiffel Tower 236, 264, 270
Elizabeth I, Queen 230, 231
Elizabeth II, Queen 150
Ellwood, Wayne 212
Empire State Building 92, 164, 165
England. See Great Britain
English Channel 75, 76, 130, 150,
    231, 253
Ephesus Greece 16, 189, 235
Erasmus, Desiderious 235
Escoffier, Auguste 55, 56
Etzlaub, Ehrhard 129
Eugenie, Empress 256
European Hotel Managers Association 65
Exeter UK 220

F

Fairbanks, Douglas 162
Fenwick, Nicholas 239
Fergus Falls MN 263
ferries 75, 109, 131,
Fictional people
   Baggins, Bilbo 15
   Baggins, Frodo 15
   Baker, Trudy 178
   Bennet, Elizabeth 48
   Bond, James 110, 149, 170, 227
   Bunyan, Paul 141
   Buzz 140
   Christian 10
   Darcy, Fitzwilliam 48
   Dodsworth, Fran 87, 256
   Dodsworth, Sam 87, 256
   Finn, Huckleberry 10
   Flaemmchen, Miss 58, 59
   Gailhard, Jean 37
   Geigern, Baron Felix von 58
   Granger, Farley 98
   Grusinskaya, Madame 58
   Holmes, Sherlock 110
   Jim 10
   Jones, Rachel 177
   Kendall, Eve 120
   Kirk, Captain James T. 274
   Kringelein, Otto 58, 59
   Otternschlag, Dr. 58
   Pearson, Leslie 182
   Poirot, Hercule 110
   Pomeroy, Susanna 91
   Preysing, Mr. 58, 59
   Quixote, Don 10
   Solo, Han 262
   Thornhill, Roger 119, 120
   Tod 140
Field, Kate 102
Fielding, Henry 10
Finland 194, 195, 196
First World War 10, 86, 103, 110, 141,
   157, 219, 233, 238, 255
Fitterman, Lisa 183
Fitzgerald, F. Scott 171
Flagler, Henry Morrison 116-118
Flagler, Ida 116

Flagler, Mary 116
Flagstaff AZ 141, 147
Fleming, Ian 110
Fleming, Sandford 112-113
flight attendants 175-179
Florence Italy 35, 36, 131, 239
Flushing Meadows NY 167
Fodor, Eugene 218, 220, 221
Ford, Harrison 180, 262
Ford, Henry 136, 138, 162
Fort Mitchell KY 265
Fowler, Joe 209
Foynes Ireland 168
France 10, 21, 31, 33, 49, 76, 106, 108,
   125, 129, 130, 131, 132, 135,
   202, 220, 231, 232, 253, 255
French Revolution 35
Fresh Air Fund 204
Frommer, Arthur 145, 221
Fuller, Margaret 134
Fulton, Robert 81, 82, 154
Funicello, Annette 227
Fussell, Paul 86, 95

G

Gagarin, Yuri 153, 271
Galway Ireland 230
Gander NL 169
Garbo, Greta 58
Gaul 124, 189
Gaze, Henry 219, 254
Gellée, Claude. *See* Lorrain, Claude
Geneva Switzerland 35, 39, 40, 253,
   257
Genoa Italy 44, 76, 216
George V, King 256
Germany 48, 62, 77, 129, 131, 133,
   165, 166, 254
Ghana 31
Girardi, Teresa 103
Giurgi Romania 109
Gladstone, William Ewart 100, 102
Glasgow Scotland 250, 251
Glenn, John 153
global warming 275
Goldsmith, Oliver 78
Goliath 20

Gore, Al 275
Graceland 15, 18
Grand Canyon 140
Grand Tour 33-37, 48, 75, 104, 132,
    215, 216, 218, 222, 236, 238,
    246, 253, 257
Grant, Cary 61, 70, 86, 119
Grateful Dead 77
Great Britain 17, 19, 21, 22, 34, 45-48,
    75, 79, 108, 109, 112, 124, 125,
    129, 133, 135, 149, 150, 157,
    161, 167, 168, 173, 206, 219,
    223, 224, 228, 229, 231, 234,
    250, 252, 254, 257
Greater Toronto Airports Authority 174
Great Exhibition 250, 252
Greece 16, 40, 41, 43
Greene, Graham 110, 163
Greenland 168
Green Tourism Association 277
Gregory I, Pope 223, 224
Gretzky, Wayne 17
Guadeloupe 207
Guam 160
Guggenheim, Benjamin 85
guidebooks 13, 21, 35, 51, 90,
    215-222, 256
guides 246, 247, 248
Gunther, Bishop of Bamberg 19

H

Haddrill, Barbara 275
Haggerston, Sir Carnaby 239
Hailey, Arthur 179
hajj 30
Halifax NS 79, 132, 137, 269
Hamptons, The, NY 41, 159
Haney, Jack 137, 138
Hanna, D.B. 106, 107
Han Wu-ti 127
Harvard Student Agencies 221
Harvard University 221
Hastings, Thomas 116
Havana Cuba 159
Hefner, Hugh 177
Hemingway, Ernest 10
Henderson, Shirley 206

Hendrix, Steve 199
Henry, Prince of Wales 34
Henry II, King 28
Henry VIII, King 30, 46
Hereford Cathedral 22
Hermann, Dr. Emanuel 236
Herodotus 125
Hertz, John 142-143
highways 61, 137, 140-141
    Lincoln 140
    Route 66 140, 141
    Theodore Roosevelt International
        Highway 139
    US Highway 49 141
    US Highway 61 141
Hill, Dan 12
Hillsborough River 155
Hilton, Conrad 60, 61
Hinduism 16, 128
Hippocrates 187
Hirst, Arthur R. 139
Hitchcock, Alfred 98, 110, 119, 120
Hitler, Adolf 110, 204, 220
Hockey Hall of Fame 32
Hoevenberg, Rudolf von 63
Hofer, Hans 221
Holidays with Pay Act 206
Holland 33
Holy Grail 10
Holy Land 18, 19, 20, 22, 24, 125, 223
Homestead FL 267
Honduras 160
Hong Kong 257
Honolulu HI 254
Hoover, J. Edgar 61
Hoover Dam 151
Hope, Bob 11
Horace 73, 74
hostels 25, 40, 62, 64
hotel chains 60-62, 63
hotel movies
    Grand Hotel 58-59
hotels 10, 39, 40, 42, 50, 52, 60,
        63, 64, 65-67, 79, 246
    Algonquin 116
    American 198
    Art Deco Grand 58

Astor House 52
Banff Springs 115, 196
Berghotel Obersteinberg 39
Beverly Hilton 61
boutique 63, 65
Breakers, The 117
Burj al-Arab 62
Carlton 57, 65
Chateau Frontenac 116
Chateau Lake Louise 66, 116
Chateau Laurier 65, 66
Chateau Montebello 116
Choice 61
Desert Inn 196
Exchange Coffee House 50
Farm on the Hill 63
Faubourg Saint-Honoré 55
grand 50-54 , 57, 83
Grand Union 53
Holiday Inn 61
honeymoon 63
Hôtel de Glâce 63
Hydropolis 62
Ice 62
Metropolitan 54
Mobley 61
Montezuma 196
Palace 53
Palm Beach Inn. *See* Breakers, The
Paris Las Vegas 264
Ponce de Léon 117
Raffles 60, 66
railway 115
Rigi-Kulm 55
Ritz 57
Royal Poinciana 117
Savoy 56, 57
Tremont House 51, 52
underwater 62
United States 53
Vancouver 115
Waldorf-Astoria 53
Westin 61, 63
Houston TX 183
Hsuan-tsang 224
Hudson, Henry 154
Hudson River 87, 95, 154

Huffman Prairie OH 154
Hugh of Leven, Abbot 25
Huie, Nancy 94
Huskisson, William 100

I

Imperial Bath House 198
India 16, 17, 33, 34, 43, 74, 113,
      124, 128, 136, 224
Industrial Revolution 99, 217, 230
Inglis, Fred 206, 215
inns 25, 39, 40, 41, 42, 45, 46-48, 49,
      64
  White Hart 47
Intercourse PA 262
International Spa Association 197
International Space Station 273
International Space University 271
Iraq 43
Ireland 86, 112, 123, 156, 161, 167,
      169
Islam 19, 21
Istanbul Turkey 20, 50, 109, 110
Italy 12, 33, 76, 131, 132, 218, 227,
      232, 246, 247, 253, 254, 255
Izmir Greece 189

J

Jackson, Samuel L. 181
Jacobs, Walter 142
Jagger, Mick 258
Jahan, Shah 261
Jakarta Indonesia 158
James, Henry 117
James I, King 46
James of Galicia, St. 24
James the Greater, St. 20, 21
Jamestown NY 265
Jannus, Tony 155
Japan 31, 66, 89, 243, 254, 266
Jerome, St. 19
Jerusalem Israel 10, 16, 19, 125, 222,
      235
Jesus Christ 10, 20, 26, 71
Jews 16, 19
John, King 28, 229
John Chrysostom, St. 20

John F. Kennedy Space Center 32
Johnson, Amy 157, 204
Johnson, Robert 141
John the Baptist, St. 235
Jones, Tom 271
Jones, Will 209
Joseph, Archduke of Austria 108
Joyce, James 32
Jukkasjarvi Sweden 62

K

Kansas City KS 162, 179
Karachi Pakistan 158, 160
Kazakhstan 126, 127
Kelowna BC 197
Kemble, Fanny 99
Kerouac, Jack 11
Kerr, Deborah 70
Keyes, Marian 258
Key West FL 118, 159
Khan, Genghis 128
Kicking Horse Pass BC 115
Kidder, Rick 268
King, Martin Luther 141
Kingston ON 62
Kipling, Rudyard 243
Kiribati 114
Kitchin, Thomas 129
Kitty Hawk NC 154
Knights Hospitallers 25, 45, 64
Knock Ireland 31
Knossos Greece 40
Koblenz Germany 218
Komarno MB 263
Kraft durch Freude 204
Krakow Poland 50
Kuala Lumpur Malaysia 212
Kuwait 158
Kyrgyzstan 62

L

LaCrosse KS 265
Lake Chautauqua 199
Lakehurst NJ 164, 166
Lake Lugano 255
Lake Superior 137
Lakeville PA 63

Lamour, Dorothy 11
Lancaster, Earl of 25
Land's End UK 47
Langtry, Lillie 106
Lapointe, Frank 119
Las Vegas NM 196
Lauterbrunnen Switzerland 39
Law, John 242
Leach, Archie. *See* Grant, Cary
Leach, David 180
Lee, Muriel 149
Lee, Ralph 149, 150
Lee, Spike 12
Leedskalin, Ed 267
Leghorn Italy 239
Le Havre France 87
Leicester Temperance Society 249
Leicester UK 248, 249
Leipzig Germany 163
Leland, John 190
Leland family 54
Leningrad Russia 163
Leopold II, King 108
LeRoy NY 265
Lethbridge AB 184
Lever, Charles 253, 256
Lewis, Sinclair 87, 97
Lexington MA 111
Leysin Switzerland 207
Lightfoot, Gordon 101, 102
Lille France 132
Lincoln, Abraham 104, 105
Lincoln UK 24
Lindbergh, Charles 156, 157, 162, 165, 167, 271, 272
Lindesay, Sir David de 228
Linkletter, Art 209
Lisbon Portugal 167
litters 131
Liverpool UK 79, 80, 81, 100, 249
Lloyd, Harold 172
Lockerbie Scotland 180
Lodge, David 182
Loire Valley France 115
Loiseau, Bernard 220
London UK 28, 35, 36, 56, 57, 75, 100, 123, 158, 160, 163, 167, 169,

171, 172, 190, 202, 205, 212,
250, 251, 257, 262, 266
Long Island NY 156, 164, 167
Lorrain, Claude 36, 241
Lorraine France 236
Los Angeles CA 140, 163, 171, 172,
208, 261, 262
Loughborough UK 248, 249
Louis-Philippe, King 108
Louisbourg NS 32
Louis VII, King 28
Louis XIV, King 231
Lourdes France 31, 32
Lübeck Germany 220
Lucian 72
Luther, Martin 230
Luxor Egypt 256
Luzon 160
Lyceum Movement 199
Lydia 17, 18
Lyons France 42, 76, 78, 131, 132, 133
Lytton BC 144

M
Madison WI 265
Madras India 136
Madrid Spain 102
magazines
    Architectural Digest 92
    Arthur Frommer's Budget Travel 221
    Blackwood's Magazine 253
    Canadian Business 172, 173
    Condé Nast Traveler 92
    Cruise Industry News Quarterly 94
    Departures 92
    Economist, The 149
    Excursionist, The 253
    Good Housekeeping 40
    Gourmet 92
    Modern Girl 227
    New Internationalist 212
    New Statesman 150
    New Yorker, The 92
    Playboy 177
    Spa Finder 198
    Sports Illustrated 227
    Time 147, 153

    Variety 268
    Vogue 117
    Wall*Paper 260
    Western Highways Builder 140
mail 125-126
    air 153
    Persian system 125, 126
    Roman system 126
Majorca Spain 207
Malaysia 120, 207
Mali Empire 30
Malta 73
Mammoth Cave 151
Manchester UK 99, 201, 251
Manhattan NY 32, 53, 78, 81, 82, 86,
95, 116, 164, 165
Mann, Colonel William d'Alton 109
Mantegazza, Antonio 255
maps 123, 129, 135, 137, 147
    cartogram 124
    Gough 129
    Lenox Globe 74
    Peutinger Table 124, 125, 126
    road 138-139
    sheet 129
March, Babette 227
Marquez, Elsa 209
Marseilles France 76, 168, 202, 239
Marshall SK 103
Martin, Andrew 150
Martin, Bradley 53
Martin, Mrs. Bradley 53
Maugham, Somerset 60, 66
Maybach, Wilhelm 136
Mayle, Peter 215
McAdam, John 137
McDonnell, John 272
McDonnell Douglas Foundation 272
McNally II, Anthony 138
Mecca Saudi Arabia 10, 16, 30
Mechanics Home 251
Mediterranean Sea 16, 19, 71, 73, 74,
89, 90, 234, 245, 248
Melba, Dame Nellie 56
Memmius, Lucius 245
Memphis TN 61
Mennonites 261

Mesopotamia 40
Mexico 77, 145, 208
Miami FL 117, 118, 163, 209
Michaux, Pierre 135
Michelin, André 219
Michelin, Edouard 219
Middle Ages 20, 22, 30, 31, 45, 46,
    74, 129, 190, 229, 246
Middle East 43, 45, 128, 172, 248,
    254, 255
Midway 160
Milan Italy 97, 219
Millennium Island Kiribati 114
Miller, Lewis 199
Milwaukee WI 138, 143
Mineral King CA 210
Minneapolis MN 265
Mississippi River 10, 82, 141
Mitchell, Noel 155
Monaco 202
monasteries 45, 46
Monbiot, George 275
Mongolia 126
monorails 170
    Jetrail 170
Montagu, Lady Mary Mortley 130
Monte Carlo Monaco 55, 202
Montreal QC 16, 98, 112, 116,
    183, 184
Moose Pass AK 263
Morales, Geraldo Machado y 159
More, Thomas 30
Morrell, Jemina 257
Morrison, Nina 177, 178
Moscow Russia 50
Moses 10
motels 40, 61, 65
Mountain Park AB 103
Mount Cenis 108, 131
Mount Parnassus 16
Mount Sinai 235
Mount Vesuvius 37
movies
    Bridget Jones's Diary 206
    Casablanca 163, 168
    Cinderella 208
    Dr. No 227

How to Stuff a Wild Bikini 227
It's a Wonderful Life 13
Manina, la fille sans voile 226
Shirley Valentine 215
Speedy 172
Witness 262
See also airplane movies; hotel
    movies; road movies; ship movies;
    train movies
Muhammad 10
mule train 144
Murray, John 217, 218, 220
Musa, Mansa 30
museums 265-266
    American Sanitary Plumbing 265
    Barbed Wire 265
    British Museum 265
    Gopher Hole 265
    History of Contraception 265
    Hunterian 266
    Jell-O 265
    Lucille Ball-Desi Arnaz Center 265
    Madison Museum of Bathroom
        Tissue 265
    Museum of Bad Art 265
    Museum of Questionable Medical
        Devices 265
    Prince Edward Potato 265
    Smithsonian Institution 265
    Vent Haven 265
    Vulcan Tourism and Trek Station 266
    Witch 265
Muslims 16, 19, 128
Myrtle Beach FL 179
Mythological figures
    Actaeon 47
    Aphrodite 175
    Apollo 16, 17, 18, 189, 235
    Artemis 16, 189, 235
    Diana 16, 47, 189
    Gaia 16
    Hera 41
    Jason and the Argonauts 10
    Jupiter 246
    Petesouchos 245
    Zeus 16

N

Nagelmackers, Georges 108, 109, 110
Naples Italy 12, 35, 37, 239, 253
Napoleonic Wars 35, 99
Nashville TN 171
Nasseri, Merhan 182
National Baseball Hall of Fame 15
National Cyclists' Union 135
National Organization for Women 177
National Road Congress 139
Nehemiah 222
Nepal 113
Nether Stowey UK 47
New Brighton UK 249
Newcastle UK 239, 250
New Orleans LA 141
New Spirit of St. Louis Organization
        272
New York NY 52, 54 , 79, 80, 81, 82,
        83, 84, 87, 88, 90, 95, 112, 115,
        119, 154, 156, 159, 161, 163,
        167, 168, 169, 171, 172, 177,
        181, 182, 243, 256
New York Public Library 117
New York State Forest Preserve 151
New Zealand 114, 257
Nice Italy 55, 202, 203
Nile River 256
Nixon, Richard 179
North Bay ON 183
Norway 149
Norwich UK 220
Nugent, Thomas 35, 216
Nunn, Emma 268, 269

O

Oakland CA 174
Odcombe UK 34
Ogilby, John 129
Omaha NE 141
Oracle of Delphi 16-18
Orlando FL 182, 210, 211
Orléans France 242
Orteig, Raymond 155
Orteig Prize 271
Osaka Japan 212
Ostend Belgium 108

Ostia Italy 72
Ottawa ON 62, 65, 101, 116, 123, 197
Ottawa River 116
Overseas Club 243
Oxford University 92, 112

P

Pacific Ocean 160, 167, 257
Painted Forest 140
paintings
    Ship of Fools 77
Pakistan 113
Palestine 20, 73, 256
Palm Beach FL 117
Paltrow, Gwyneth 175
Pamplona Spain 21
Pan Am flight 103 180
Paris France 3, 34, 35, 36, 55, 57, 75,
        89, 97, 108, 109, 110, 120, 121,
        131, 132, 133, 134, 156, 158,
        160, 161, 165, 171, 202, 220,
        225, 226, 239, 242, 253, 254,
        272
Paris, Matthew 125
Paris TN 264
Paris TX 264
Parker, Mr. 247
passengers
    first-class 80, 82, 84, 85, 88
    second-class 85, 88, 90
    steerage 80
    third-class 82, 85, 88
passports 9, 222-234
    king's licence 229, 230
    letters of introduction 223-228
    letters of reference 222
    letters of safe conduct 228-230
Patti, Adelina 106
Paul, St. 20, 73, 235
Pearl Harbor 143
Pelham, Thomas 132, 225
Pelican Lake 148
Penang, Malaysia 60
Pequet, Henri 155
Persia 124, 125, 222
Persian Empire 17
Pheil, Abram C. 155, 273

Philadelphia PA 262
Phoenix AZ 196, 268
Pickford, Mary 162
pilgrimages 15-30, 31, 32
Piozzi, Hester Lynch 37
Piraeus Greece 72, 92
Pittsburgh PA 173
Plains of Abraham QC 32
Plant, Robert 77
Plataea Greece 41
plays
  Agamemnon 119
  Plain and Simple 262
  Ship of Fools 77
Plummer, Doug 198
Poconos Mountains 63
poems
  "Prelude, The" 123, 241
  "Song of the Open Road" 123
Poland 129
Polo, Marco 216, 259
Pomfret, Lady 247
Pompeii Italy 253
Pontine Marshes Italy 73
populuxe 140
Porter, Katherine Ann 77
Porter, Mackenzie 65
Porter, Sir James 50
Portland ME 139
Portland OR 139, 162, 180
Portugal 132, 219
post chaises 133, 135
Pregarz, Roberto 66, 67
Presley, Elvis 141
Price, Bruce 115
Principal, Victoria 273
Prohibition 59, 142
Provence France 224
Prussia 108
Pucci, Emilio 178
Puente la Reina Spain 21
Pullman, George Mortimer 104-105,
  108, 109
Pyrenees Mountains 21, 31

Q
Quebec City QC 16, 63, 116

R
radio programs
  Savvy Traveler, The 180
Raffles, Sir Stamford 60
railways 35, 135, 143, 154, 252
  Atchinson, Topeka and Santa Fe 196
  Burlington, Chicago and Quincy 118
  Canadian National 106, 119, 184
  Canadian Pacific 101, 112, 114-116,
    196, 254, 255
  Eastern & Oriental Express 120
  Grand Trunk Pacific 103
  Great Northern Line 251
  Great Western 82, 112
  Jacksonville, St. Augustine and
    Halifax 116
  Liverpool and Manchester 99, 101
  London and North Western 106
  Midland 250, 251
  Midland Counties 249
  Quebec Central 104
  VIA Rail 120
Rama 10
Ranelagh Club 251
Rangoon Myanmar 60
Ranipat India 136
Raskob, John J. 164, 165
Ray, James Earl 233
Reagan, Ronald 209
Réard, Louis 226
Recreation Vehicle Industry Association
  146, 148
recreational vehicles 130, 146-150, 259
  amphibious 148
  caravans 149-150
  Terra Wind 148, 149
Regina SK 263
Reid, Bill 174
Reims France 154
Renaissance 74, 235
resorts 199-213
  Alcudia 207
  Blackpool 201, 202, 203, 204, 258
  Club Méditerranée 207
  Cove Haven 63
  holiday camps 203-207
  Morecambe 201

resort towns 48
Revere, Paul 111
revival meetings 199
Rhine 218
Rhodes, Cecil 256
Richard, St. 23
Richard I, King 28
Richard II, King 26, 228, 229
Riga Latvia 163
Rio de Janeiro Brazil 165
Ritz, César 55-58, 62, 65, 67
Riviera 13, 203
road construction 151
road movies
About Schmidt 12
Badlands 12
Blue Brothers, The 12
Bonnie and Clyde 12
Drugstore Cowboy 12
Easy Rider 12
Get on the Bus 12
Grapes of Wrath, The 12
It Happened One Night 11
Motorcycle Diaries, The 12
O Brother, Where Art Thou? 12
Rain Man 12
Raising Arizona 12
Road to Hong Kong 11
Road to Singapore, The 11
South of Wawa 12
Sure Thing, The 11
Thelma & Louise 12
Thieves Like Us 12
Transamerica 12
roads 71, 131, 137, 138
Old Spanish Trail 139
RoadsideAmerica.com 141, 264
roadside attractions 261, 263-264, 266,
267, 270
Abode of Chaos, The 270
Anniston giant chair 264
Ballina big prawn 263
Cadillac Ranch 261
Carhenge 261
Cheticamp lobster trap 263
Coffs Harbour big banana 264
Collinsville catsup bottle 263

Coral Castle 267
Davidson coffee pot 263
Duncan hockey stick and puck 263
Fergus Falls otter 263
Komarno mosquito 263
Las Vegas Eiffel Tower 264
Maximilian Moose 263
Moose Pass knife 263
Muffler Men 141
Paris TN Eiffel Tower 264
Paris TX Eiffel Tower 264
Shediac lobster 263
Springfield fork 263
Sudbury nickel 263
Vegreville pysanka 263
Watts Towers 261
Wawa goose 263
Winchester Mystrey House 266
Winston-Salem coffee pot 263
Roberts, Garth 198
Robinson, Anne 150
Rocamadour France 26, 27, 235
Rochester NY 123
Rockville MD 272
Rocky Mountains 66, 97, 114, 115
Rodia, Simon 261
Roger of Sicily 216
Rogers, Will 162
Rogers Pass BC 115
Rolling Stones 258
Roma 147
Roman Catholic Church 20, 25, 31
Roman Empire 41, 71, 72, 74, 124,
188, 189, 228, 245
Romania 149
Rome (ancient) 13, 35, 71, 72, 73, 124,
190
Rome Italy 12, 20, 22, 24, 33, 34, 71,
129, 134, 186, 204, 223, 224,
239, 241, 247
Roncesvalles France 21
Roosevelt, Franklin 166
Rory Storm and the Hurricanes 206
Rotterdam, Netherlands 238
Rousseau, Jean-Jacques 34
Route 66. See highways: Route 66
Rowbottom, Frank 103

Royal Air Force 220
Royal Canadian Institute 112
RVHometown.com 147

S
Saigon Vietnam 158
Saint, Eva Marie 120
Ste-Anne-de-Beaupré QC 16
St. Augustine FL 116, 139
Saint John NB 254, 269
St. John's Hospital 190
St. John's NL 269
St. Joseph's Oratory 16
St. Lawrence River 116
St. Louis MO 141, 209, 271
St. Petersburg FL 155, 156
St-Romain-au-Mont-D'Or France 270
St. Vincent, Earl 76
Salem MA 265
San Bernardino CA 140
San Diego CA 139
San Francisco CA 33, 53, 240, 254
San Jose CA 266
San Juan Puerto Rico 161
Santander Spain 102
Santiago de Compostela Spain 21, 22,
    24, 25, 27, 32, 235
Saône River 76
Saratoga Springs NY 53
Sarkies Brothers 60
Saskatoon SK 263
Saudi Arabia 16
Saul 10
Saunders, Joe 141
Saverne France 42
Savoy Theatre 56, 57
Schirrmann, Richard 62
Scotland 62, 100, 250
Scottsboro AL 185
Scottsdale AZ 197, 268
Scuffs, Agnes 267
sculptures
    "Spirit of Haida Gwaii, The" 174
Sea of Galilee 71
Sebastian, Raoul 268, 269
Second World War 11, 63, 88, 110,
    118, 140, 145, 149, 168, 206,
    220, 238, 257, 260

sedan chair 131
Sekket's shrine 16
Selden, George Baldwin 136
Septumanus 42
Sequoia National Park 210
Servas 225
Shannon Ireland 160, 169
Shaw, George Bernard 39
Shediac NB 263
Sherwood, James 120
Shikoku Japan 16
ship movies
    Affair to Remember, An 70
    Poseidon Adventure, The 70
Ship of Fools 77
shipping lines
    American Export Lines 89
    American President 91
    Black Ball 78, 79, 80
    Carnival Cruise 69, 91, 92
    Cunard 85, 90
    French 87
    Princess Cruises 91
    Royal Caribbean 92, 93, 94
    White Star 84, 86
ships 69-94
    America 84, 95
    Bismarck. See Majestic
    Canada 80, 81
    cargo 72
    City of New York 84
    City of Paris 84
    Clermont. See ships: *North River Boat*
    cruise 69, 83, 85, 90-94
    Disney Magic 211
    Freedom of the Seas 92, 93
    grain 72
    Great Britain 83
    Great Western 82, 83
    Île de France 87, 88, 89
    Independence 95
    James Monroe 78, 79, 80, 81
    Liberté 95
    Lusitania 85, 86
    Majestic 86
    Mauretania 85, 95
    Michelangelo 95
    New Orleans 82

North River Boat 81
Oceanic 84
ocean liners 86-89, 90, 120, 164
Ocean Queen 91
packet 72, 79, 80, 81
Paradise 69, 78
passenger liners 70, 84
President Cleveland 91
Queen Elizabeth 90, 95
Queen Elizabeth 2 90
Queen Mary 72, 92, 93, 95
Queen Mary 2 70, 85, 92, 95
Rafaello 95
sailing 82
Sovereign of the Seas 92
steam 81-83, 252
Stella Polaris 90
Titanic 70, 72, 84-86, 87, 93
troop 86, 88
Ultima (fictional) 87
Voyager of the Seas 92
World, The 93
shows
    "Great Moments with Mr. Lincoln"
        210
    "It's a Small World" 210
Shushan Iran 222
Sicily 226
Siena Italy 34
Sierra Nevada Mountains 210
Silk Road 126-128, 224
Silverton CO 62
Sinatra, Frank 153, 177
Singapore 60, 66, 120, 158, 174
Sita 10
Skegness UK 203, 204, 205
Slough UK 100
Smith, Al 164, 165
Smith, Bessie 141
Smollett, Tobias 247
Smyrna Greece. *See* Izmir Greece
Sofia Bulgaria 97
Somerset UK 47
songs
    "April in Paris" 153
    "Brazil" 153
    "Canadian Railroad Trilogy, The" 101

    "Come Fly with Me" 153, 177
    "Fly Me to the Moon" 153
    "Highway 61 Revisited" 141
    "On the Road to Mandalay" 153
    "Rock Around the Clock" 258
    "Take Me Home, Country Roads"
        258
Soubirous, Bernadette 31
South Africa 121, 160, 203
Southampton UK 84, 168, 256
Southwark UK 29
souvenirs 234-238
    Christian 235
    postcards 236-238
Soviet Union 149
Space Adventures 271, 273
space lines
    Virgin Galactic 273, 274
SpacePort 174
spaceships
    Enterprise, VSS 274
    SpaceShipOne 272
    SpaceShipTwo 273
    Vostok I 271
space travel 271-274
Spain 10, 20, 21, 35, 71, 74, 102, 132,
        207, 219, 224, 227
spas 187-198
    Aix-la-Chapelle 191
    and ant-heap bath 195
    and asthma 192
    Bagnigge Wells 191
    Bath 191
    Berkeley Springs 192
    Beyond Wrapture 197
    Blackpool 193
    Camelback Mountain 197
    Canyon Ranch 188
    Club Med 205, 207
    and cures 190, 191, 192
    EuroSpa 197
    Finnish bath 194, 195
    and gout 192
    Golden Door 188
    and hot springs 189, 191, 192, 196
    Karlovy Vary 190
    and leprosy 190

Pergamum 188, 189, 197
and respiratory infections 192
and rheumatism 192, 195
Roman baths 189, 190
Sanatorium 197
Saratoga Springs 192, 193, 194
Sharon Springs 198
and smallpox 190
Spa 191, 194
and tuberculosis 192, 197
Tunbridge Wells 191
and waterfall bath 195
Spirit of St. Louis Organization 272
Springfield IL 105
Springfield MO 263
Sri Lanka 124
stagecoaches 132
Stamboul Turkey 97
Stanhope, Walter 49
Starck, Philippe 273
Starke, Mariana 218
Starr, Ringo 206
starship
Enterprise (fictional) 100, 266
Steinbeck, John 140
Stephen, St. 20
Stevens, Sacheverell 48, 76, 133
Stevenson, Robert Louis 196
stewardesses. See flight attendants
Stewart, James 13
Stimpson, Steve 175, 176
Stockholm Sweden 186
Stone, Lewis 58
Stonehenge 32, 261, 267
Storm, Gale 91
Strasbourg France 225
Sturm, Baron Gustav von 220
Sudbury ON 263
Suez Canal 255
Suffolk UK 47
Sulphur Mountain 196
Super Bowl 187
Switzerland 55, 133, 204, 219, 242,
246, 255, 256, 257
Sybils 16, 17
Sydney Australia 212, 269
Sydney NS 269

T
Taj Mahal 261
Taliban 128
Tallinn Estonia 163
Tampa Bay 153, 273
Tampa FL 153, 187
Tang dynasty 128
Taylor, Andrew 272
Taylor, John 47, 48
Tay River 100
television shows
American Idol 150
Corner Gas 264
Dallas 273
Gale Storm Show, The 91
Love Boat, The 70, 91-92
Oh! Susanna. See Gale Storm
Show, The
Price is Right, The 146
Real World, The 267
Sex and the City 32
Star Trek 146, 266, 271
Tuesday Night Book Club 268
Wheel of Fortune 146
Who Wants To Be A Millionaire 269
Thailand 120, 212
theme parks
Disney-MGM Studios 213
Hard Rock Café 212
Ripley's Believe It or Not! 212
Sega World 212
Universal Studios 212
See also Disneyland; Walt Disney
World
Thicknesse, Philip 37
Thompson, Charles 75
Thorpe, William 27, 29
Thrale, Mrs. See Piozzi, Hester Lynch
Three Mile Island PA 262
Thunder Bay ON 141
Tilley, Alex 244
time 111-114
Atlantic 113
daylight savings 113
Greenwich Mean 112
International Date Line 114
Newfoundland 113

standard 113
Tito, Dennis 273
Tokyo Japan 187, 266
Tonga 114
Toronto ON 97, 112, 173, 203, 213,
     254, 266
Torrington AB 265
tour operators 248-257
   vetturini 246, 248
trade routes 126
train movies
   From Russia With Love 110
   Lady Vanishes, The 110
   North by Northwest 119-120
   Seven Percent Solution, The 110
   Silver Streak, The 118
   Strangers on a Train 98
   Twentieth Century 119
trains 137, 97-121, 258, 260
   20th Century Limited 119, 120
   Best Friend of Charleston 101
   Blue Train 121
   Canadian, The 97, 120
   Ghan, The 121
   GrandLuxe 121
   Lalee 106
   Northumbrian 99
   Orient Express 109-110, 120
   Pioneer 104, 105
   Rocky Mountaineer 121
   steam 50, 259, 262
   Venice Simplon-Orient Express 120
   Zephyr 118
train stations 52
transatlantic flights 159, 166-170, 171
Transoxiana 127
travel agents 173, 245, 269
travel companies
   Contiki Holidays 258
travel industry 245-269
travellers' cheques 13, 238
   bills of exchange 239
   letters of credit 239, 242, 243
travel permit 26
travel trailers 145-146, 150
   Airstream Clipper 145
travel writers 246

Tree, Viola 117
Trevor, Robert 236
Trieste Italy 97
Trinity Bay 167
Trippe, Juan 153, 158-161, 162, 167,
     168, 169, 186
Troy NY 53
Trump, Donald 164
Tunney, Gene 172
Turfan China 224
Turin Italy 131
Turkey 43, 46, 126, 130, 187, 207
Turkish bath 187, 188
Turpen, Louis 174
Twain, Mark 10
Tweedie, Edith 194, 195, 196

                    U
Uluru Australia 32
Unabomber 77
Unclaimed Baggage Center 185
Union Army 109
United Kingdom 137, 254, 269, 276
   Post Office 237
United States 50, 51, 60, 64, 85, 95, 99,
     101, 106, 118, 138, 146, 158,
     162, 165, 166, 167, 170, 185,
     193, 233, 234, 254, 257
   Army 221
   Navy 163, 184
   Postal Service 236, 237
Urban II, Pope 19
Uzbekistan 126, 127

                    V
Valantia Island Ireland 167
Vancouver BC 97, 184
Vancouver International Airport
     Authority 173
Vandalia IL 137
Vanderbilt, Commodore Cornelius 108
Van Horne, William Cornelius 115
Van Nuys CA 163
Varna Bulgaria 109
Vegreville AB 263
Venice Italy 20, 34, 35, 97
Versailles France 37, 53

Victoria BC 137, 138, 184
Victoria, Queen 55, 100, 106, 108
Vienna Italy 55
Vikings 74
Villa Romana del Casale 226
Vincent, John 199, 200
Vinkovci Croatia 97
Virgil 36
Virgin Mary 26, 27, 31, 235
visas 230, 232
Voltaire 34
Vulcan AB 266

W
Wake Island 160
Wales 129, 149, 276
walking 21, 131, 135
walking tours 32
Walsingham, Francis 231
Walsingham UK 31
Walt Disney World 32, 199, 211,
    212, 213
    Animal Kingdom 211
    Celebration 211
    Disney Institute 211, 213
Washington, George 192
Washington DC 12, 61, 105, 113,
    117, 119, 140, 143, 209
Watkinson, Captain James 79
Waugh, Alec 87
Waugh, Evelyn 90
Wawa ON 263
Welles, John 228
Wellington, Arthur Wellesley, Duke
    of 99, 100
Wells, Mary 178
Western Roman Empire 19
Westinghouse, George 102
Westphalia Germany 48
White Mountains 254
Whitman, Walt 123
Wilby, Thomas 137, 138
Wilkinson, Reverend Joseph 216
William I, King 229
Williams, Tom 147
Williams, Treat 180
Wilson, Kemmons 61, 62

Wilson, Woodrow 113
Winchester, Sarah 266
Winnipeg MB 103, 184
Winslet, Kate 70
Winston-Salem NC 263
Wollstonecraft, Mary 49
Worcester MA 265
Wordsworth, William 216, 217, 241
Workman, Fanny Bullock 136
Work to Live Vacation Campaign,
    the 276
World Party 77
Wright, Edward 216
Wright, Orville 154
Wright, Wilbur 154
Wright Brothers 154, 157, 274
Wyclif, John 29

X
Xian China 126, 127, 128
Xiongnu 126, 127
X PRIZE Foundation 271

Y
Yarmouth NS 132
Yeats, William Butler 37
Yogi, Maharishi Mahesh 33
Yokohama Japan 243
Yorkshire UK 25, 201
York UK 220
Young, Arthur 133
Yueh-chih 126, 127

Z
Zagreb Croatia 97
zeppelins. *See* dirigibles
Zhang Qian 126, 127